The prince in his Dark Days

Hico Yamanaka

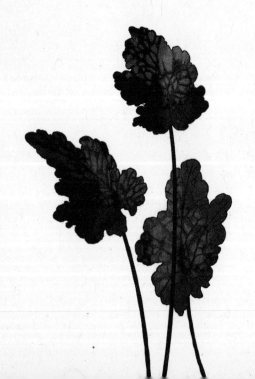

character

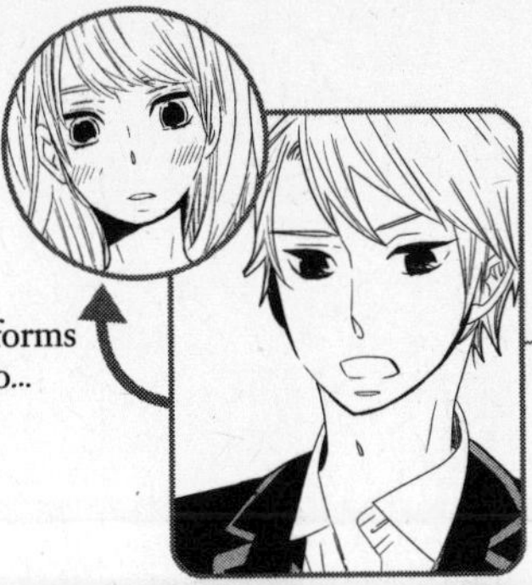

Transforms into...

The stand-in.

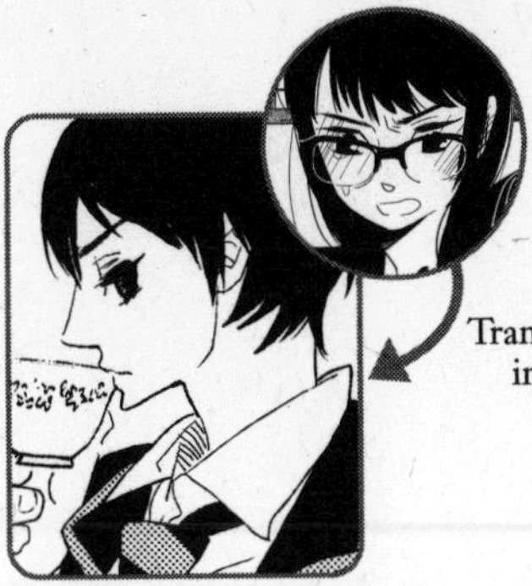

Transforms into...

Itaru Nogi

Heir to a wealthy family. His hobby of dressing in women's clothing is a dire secret. Fed up with the restraints of his princely lifestyle, he runs away.

Atsuko Ôkawa

A high school girl born into a poor household. She looks just like Itaru, so she is dressing as a man and acting as his double.

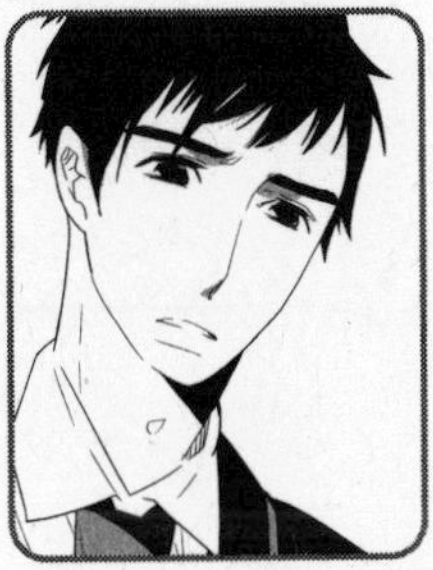

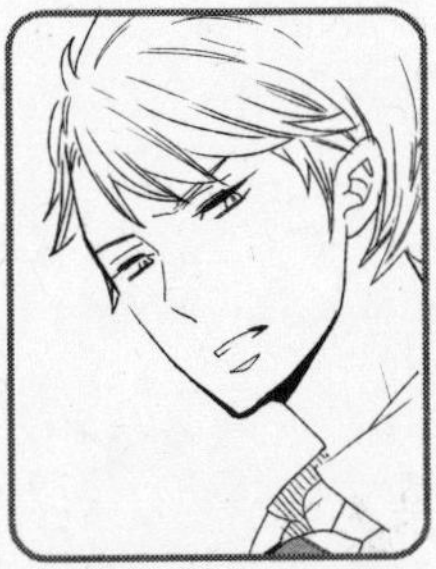

Nobunari Mukai

A longtime friend of Itaru and Ryô. Found Itaru after his disappearance.

Ryô Sekiuchi

Itaru's half-brother, who grew up with another part of the Nogi family. Has been training Atsuko since Itaru's disapearance.

story

Atsuko is a high school girl living a miserable life of poverty. One day, she meets Itaru—the heir to the Nogi Group—and his right-hand men, Ryô and Nobunari. Atsuko's fate changes when Itaru, the wealthy heir who looks just like her, suddenly disappears. She begins to dress as a man and live in a palatial estate as Itaru's double. As she earnestly takes on the role of Itaru, the distance between Atsuko and Ryô gradually begins to narrow. However, when the Anzai family holds a party and Atsuko attends as Itaru, their only son Daigo discovers her true identity. And when he demands that he be allowed to borrow her for one night, Ryô does not hesitate to comply…

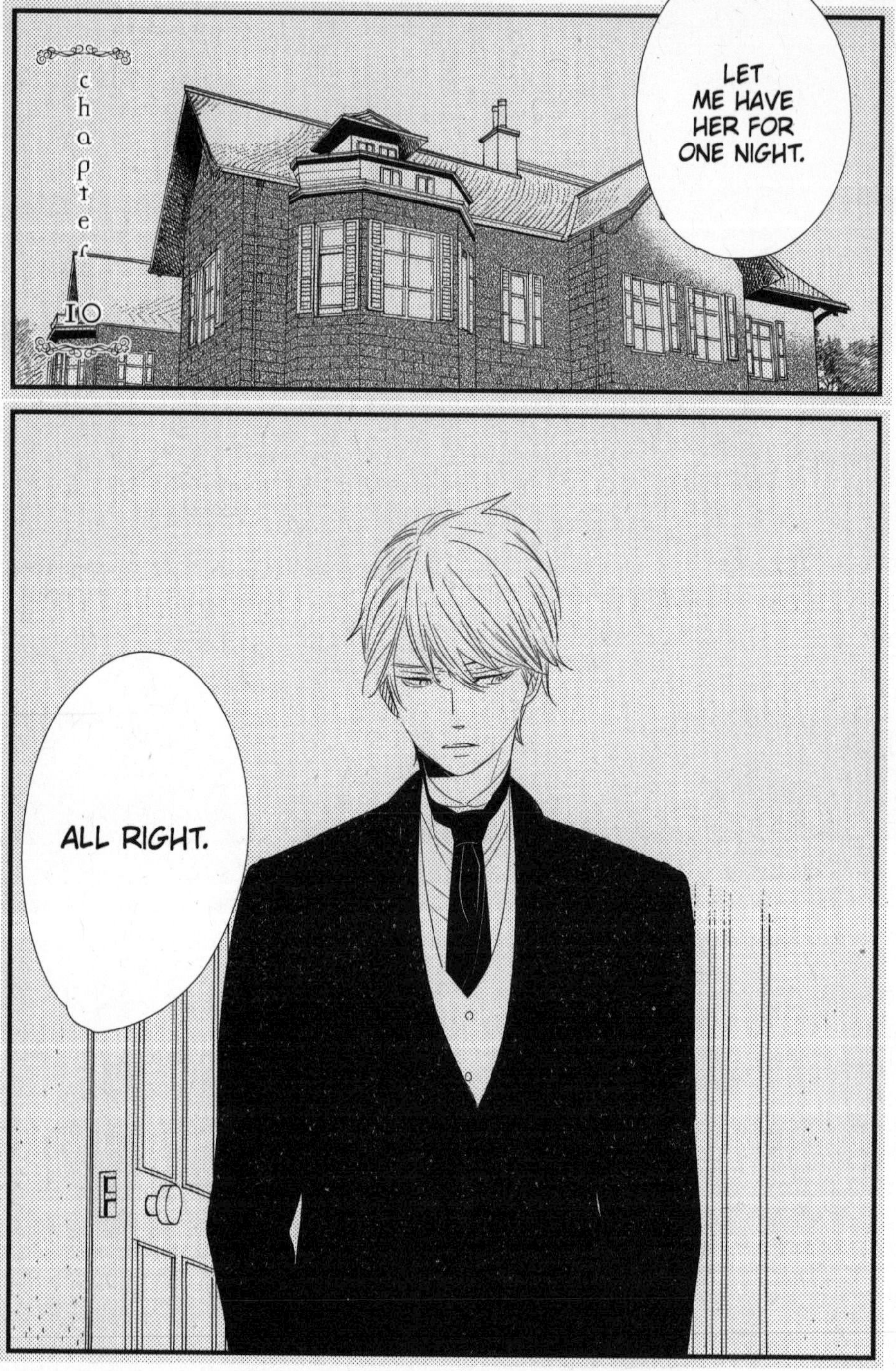
LET ME HAVE HER FOR ONE NIGHT.
chapter 10
ALL RIGHT.

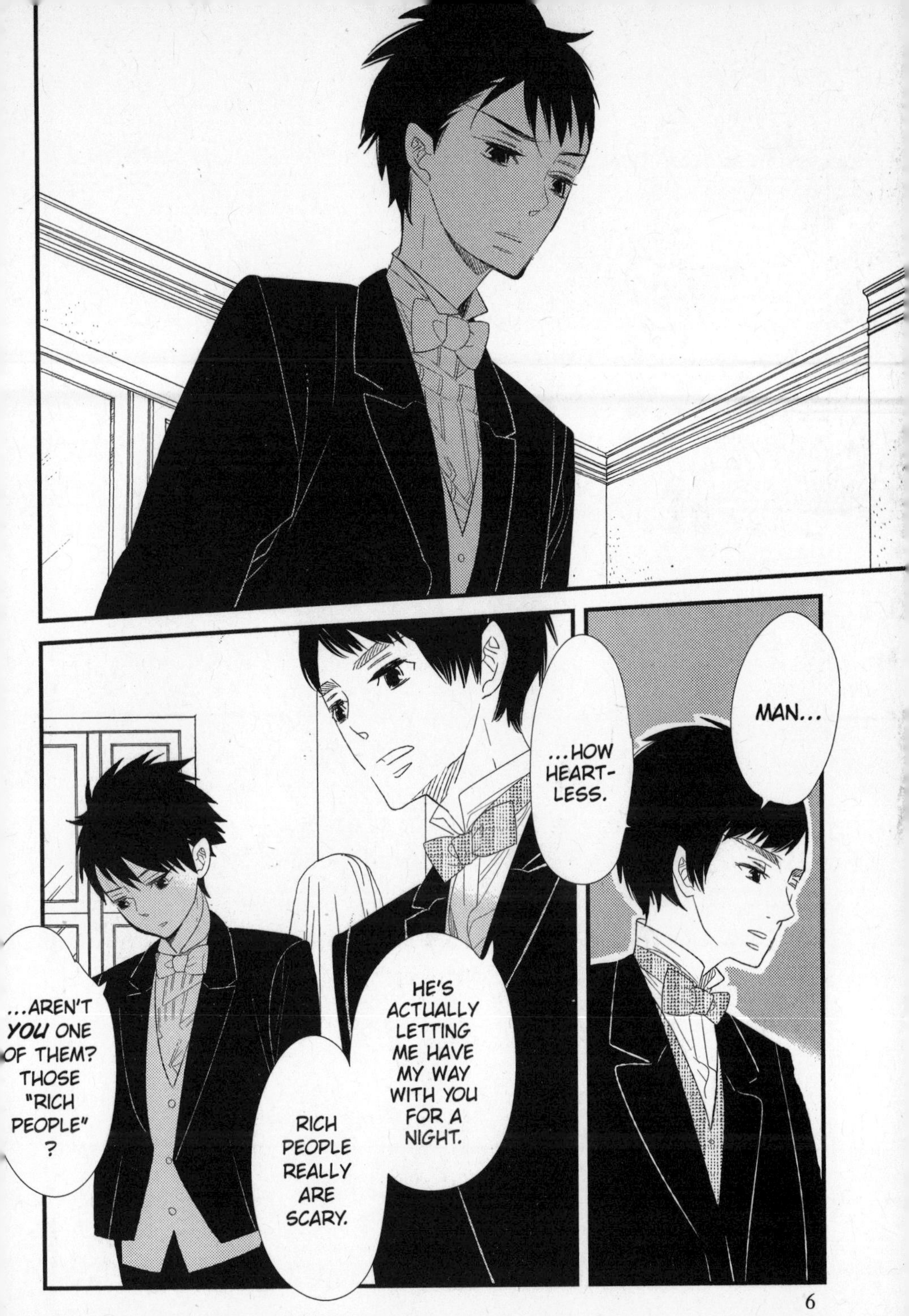
MAN...
...HOW HEART-LESS.
HE'S ACTUALLY LETTING ME HAVE MY WAY WITH YOU FOR A NIGHT.
RICH PEOPLE REALLY ARE SCARY.
...AREN'T *YOU* ONE OF THEM? THOSE "RICH PEOPLE" ?

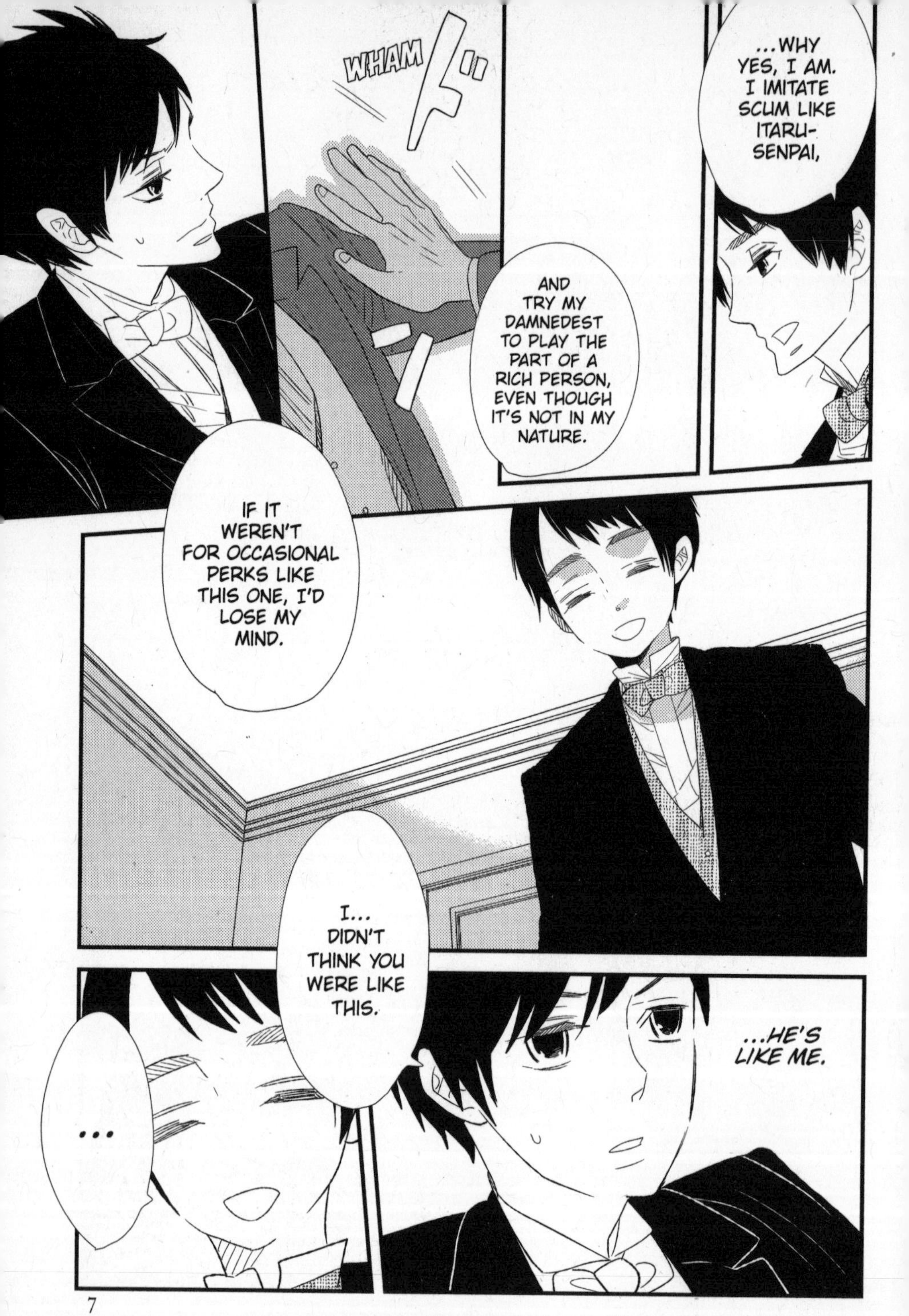
...WHY YES, I AM. I IMITATE SCUM LIKE ITARU-SENPAI,
AND TRY MY DAMNEDEST TO PLAY THE PART OF A RICH PERSON, EVEN THOUGH IT'S NOT IN MY NATURE.
WHAM
IF IT WEREN'T FOR OCCASIONAL PERKS LIKE THIS ONE, I'D LOSE MY MIND.
I... DIDN'T THINK YOU WERE LIKE THIS.
...HE'S LIKE ME.
...

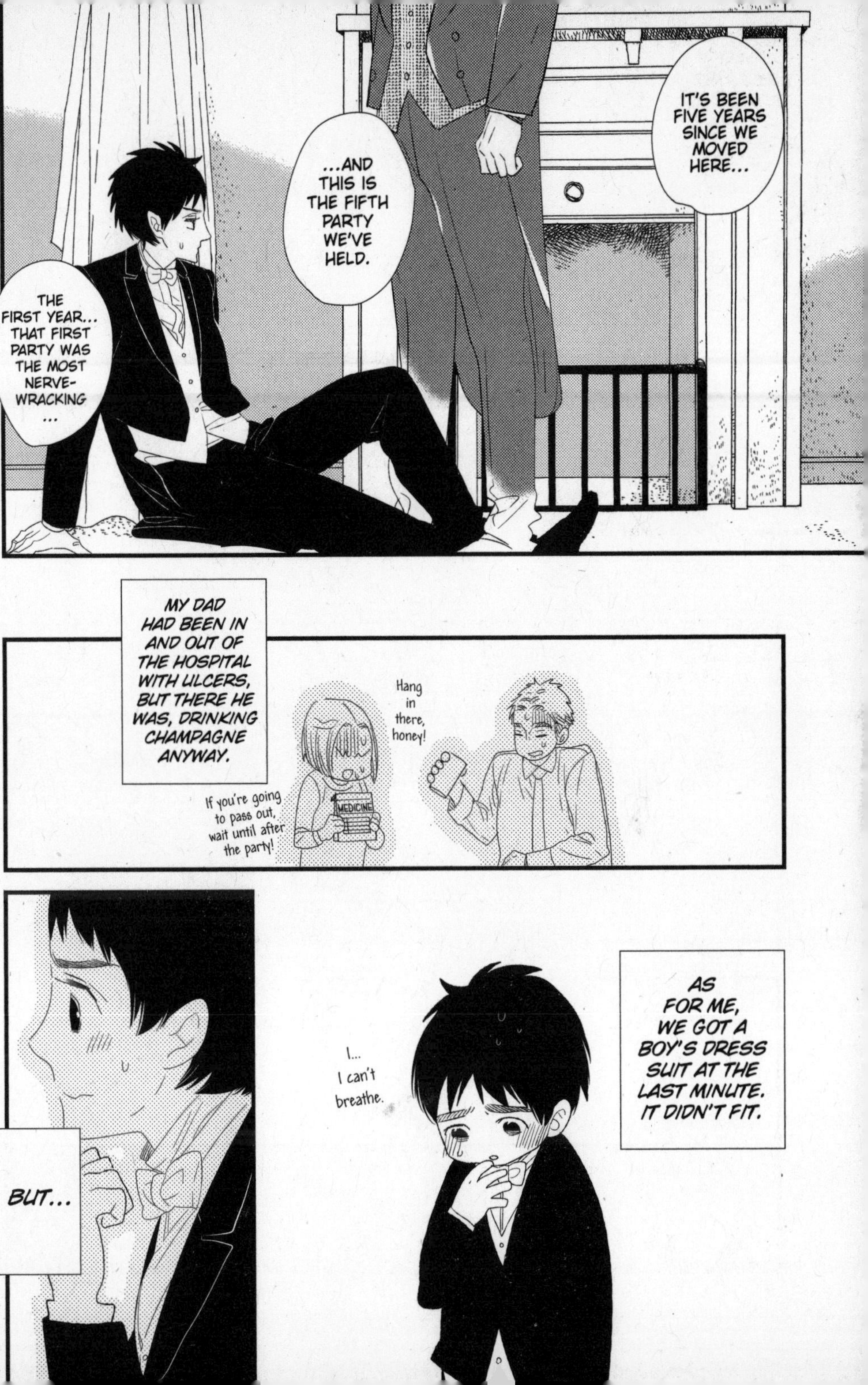
IT'S BEEN FIVE YEARS SINCE WE MOVED HERE...
...AND THIS IS THE FIFTH PARTY WE'VE HELD.
THE FIRST YEAR... THAT FIRST PARTY WAS THE MOST NERVE-WRACKING ...
MY DAD HAD BEEN IN AND OUT OF THE HOSPITAL WITH ULCERS, BUT THERE HE WAS, DRINKING CHAMPAGNE ANYWAY.
Hang in there, honey!
MEDICINE
If you're going to pass out, wait until after the party!
AS FOR ME, WE GOT A BOY'S DRESS SUIT AT THE LAST MINUTE. IT DIDN'T FIT.
I... I can't breathe.
BUT...

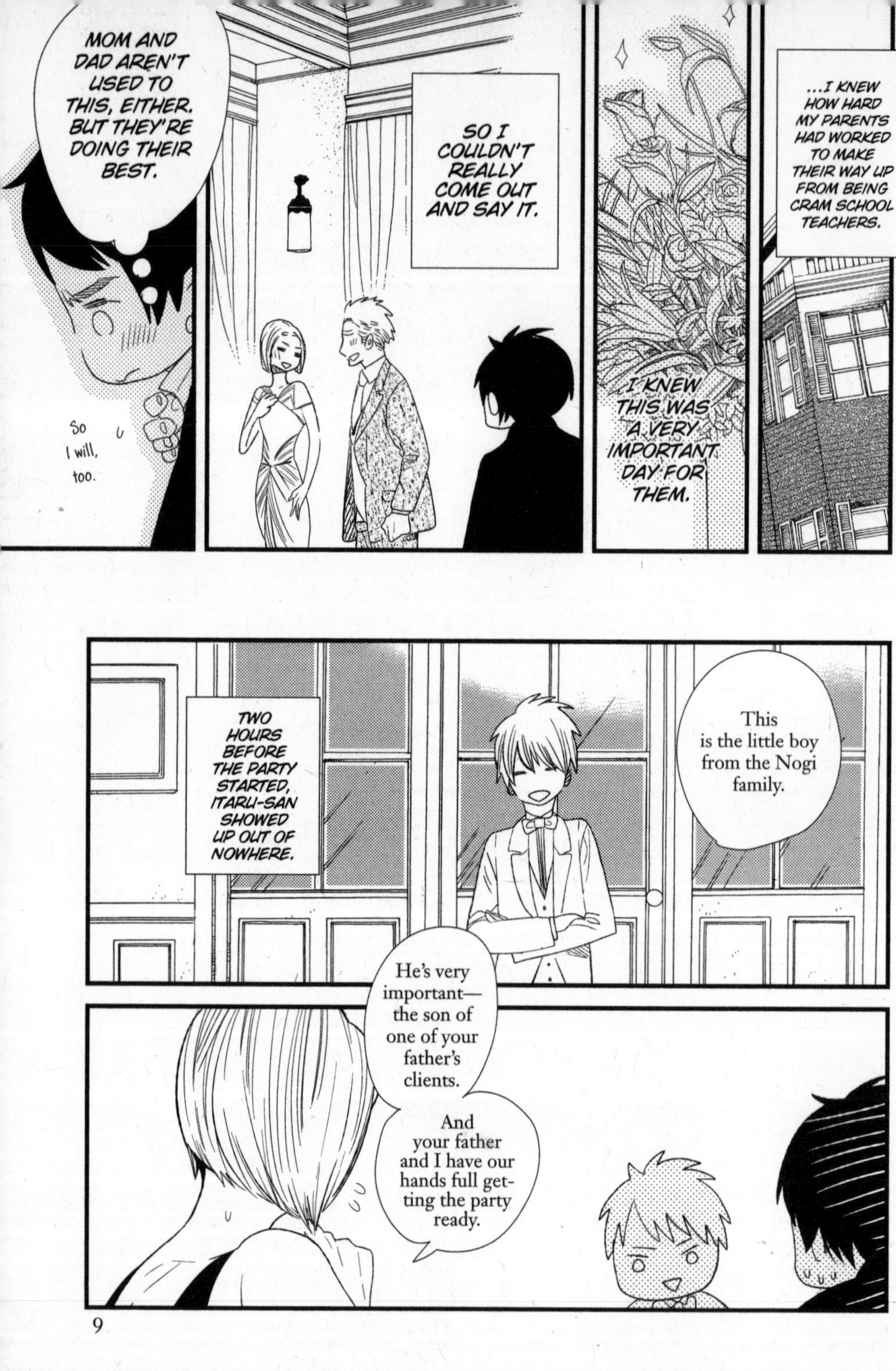

...I KNEW HOW HARD MY PARENTS HAD WORKED TO MAKE THEIR WAY UP FROM BEING CRAM SCHOOL TEACHERS.
I KNEW THIS WAS A VERY IMPORTANT DAY FOR THEM.
SO I COULDN'T REALLY COME OUT AND SAY IT.
MOM AND DAD AREN'T USED TO THIS, EITHER. BUT THEY'RE DOING THEIR BEST.
So I will, too.
This is the little boy from the Nogi family.
TWO HOURS BEFORE THE PARTY STARTED, ITARU-SAN SHOWED UP OUT OF NOWHERE.
He's very important—the son of one of your father's clients.
And your father and I have our hands full getting the party ready.

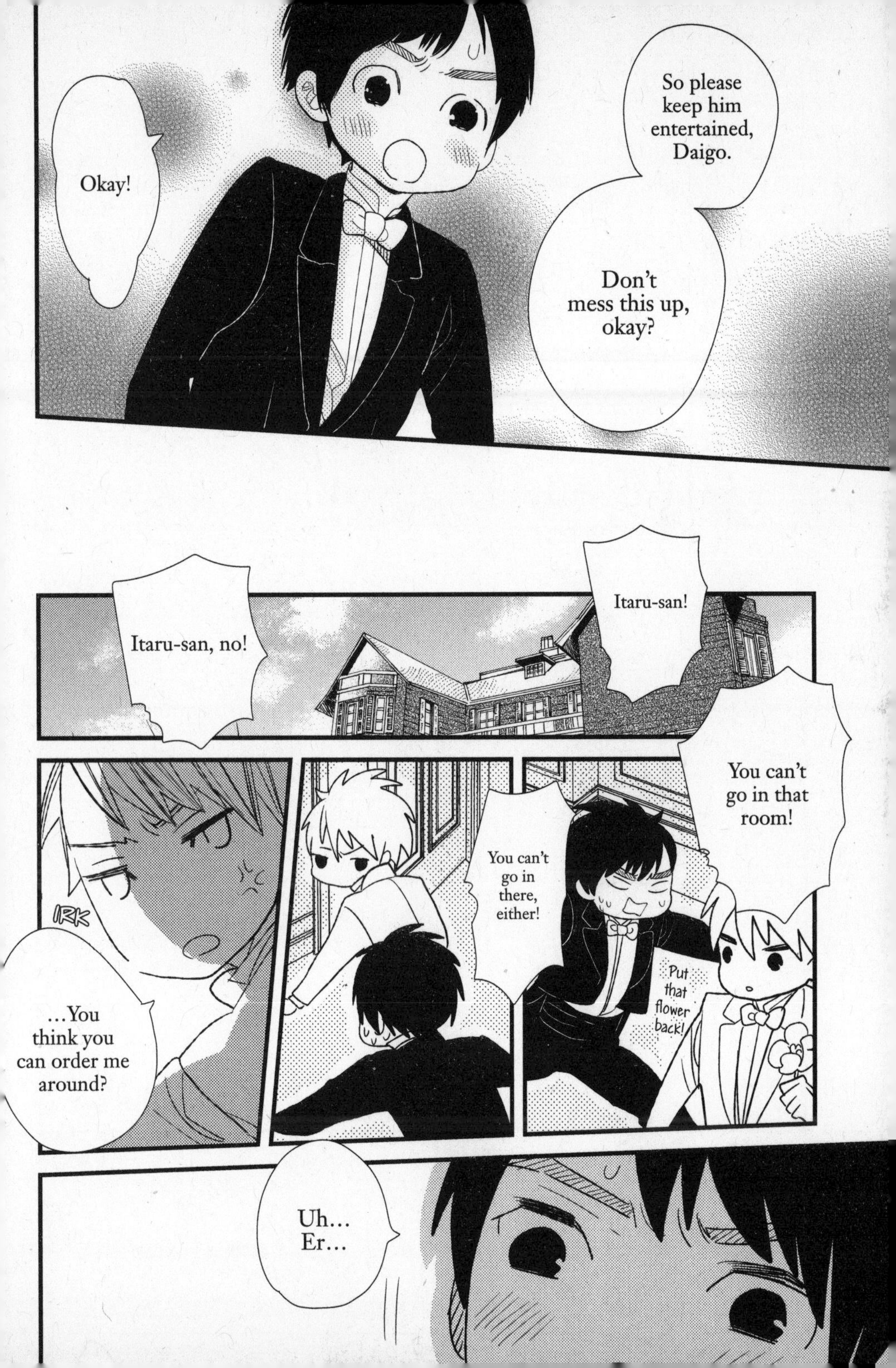
So please keep him entertained, Daigo.
Don't mess this up, okay?
Okay!
Itaru-san!
Itaru-san, no!
You can't go in that room!
Put that flower back!
You can't go in there, either!
IRK
…You think you can order me around?
Uh… Er…

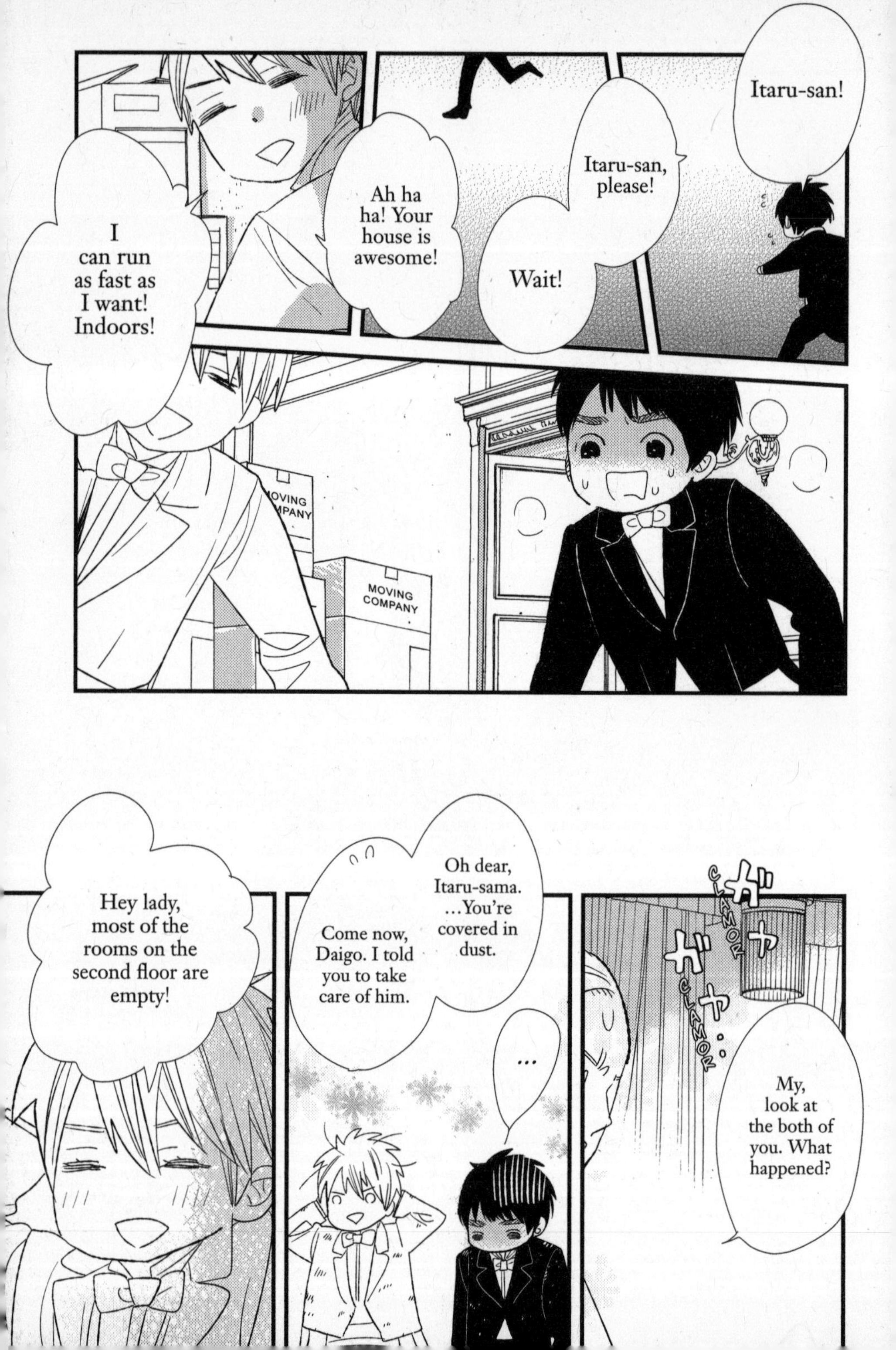
Itaru-san!
Itaru-san, please!
Wait!
Ah ha ha! Your house is awesome!
I can run as fast as I want! Indoors!
MOVING COMPANY
MOVING COMPANY
CLAMOR
CLAMOR
My, look at the both of you. What happened?
Oh dear, Itaru-sama. …You're covered in dust.
…
Come now, Daigo. I told you to take care of him.
Hey lady, most of the rooms on the second floor are empty!

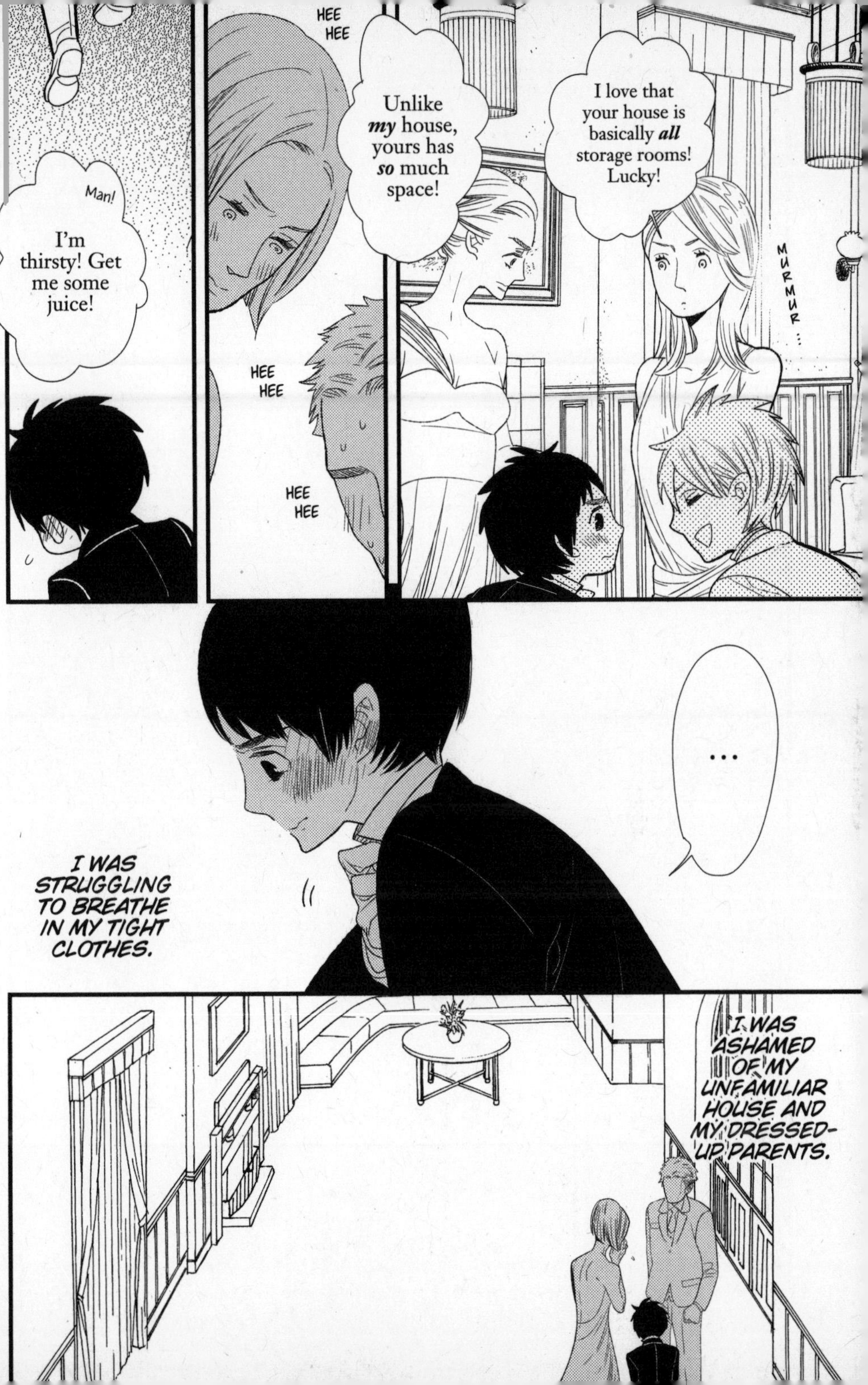
I love that your house is basically *all* storage rooms! Lucky!
MURMUR...
HEE HEE
Unlike *my* house, yours has *so* much space!
HEE HEE
HEE HEE
Man!
I'm thirsty! Get me some juice!
...
I WAS STRUGGLING TO BREATHE IN MY TIGHT CLOTHES.
I WAS ASHAMED OF MY UNFAMILIAR HOUSE AND MY DRESSED-UP PARENTS.

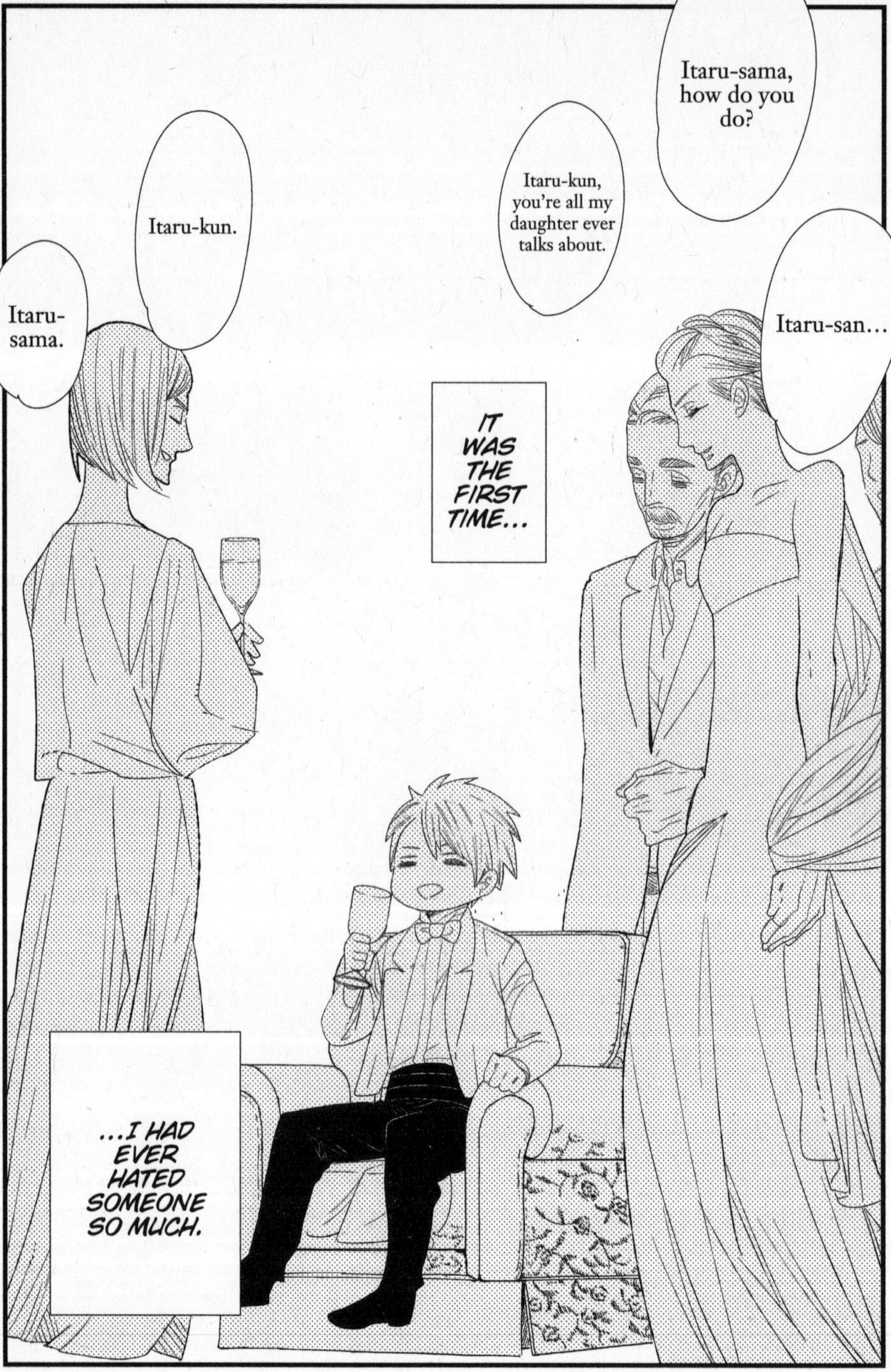
Itaru-sama, how do you do?
Itaru-san…
Itaru-kun, you're all my daughter ever talks about.
IT WAS THE FIRST TIME…
Itaru-kun.
Itaru-sama.
…I HAD EVER HATED SOMEONE SO MUCH.

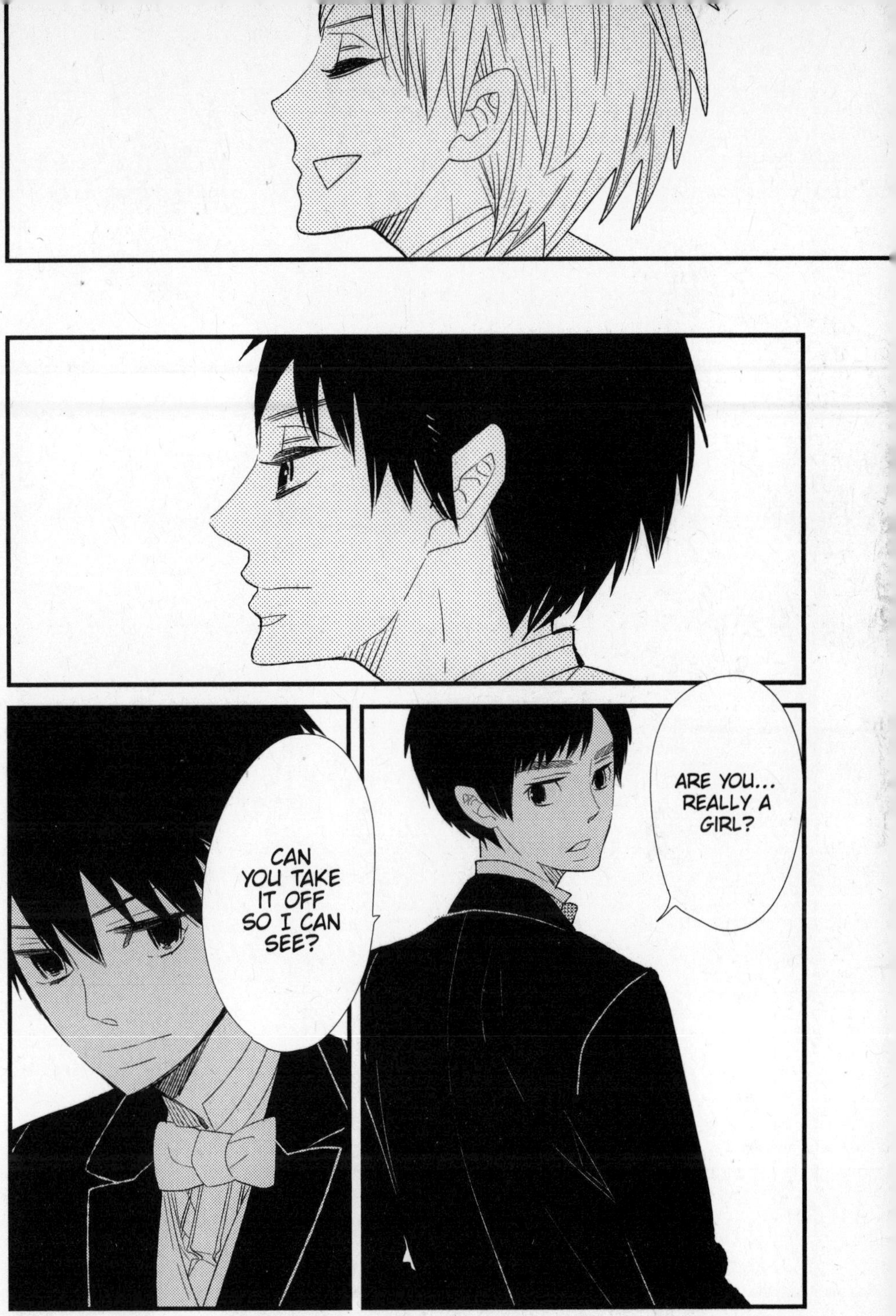
ARE YOU... REALLY A GIRL?
CAN YOU TAKE IT OFF SO I CAN SEE?

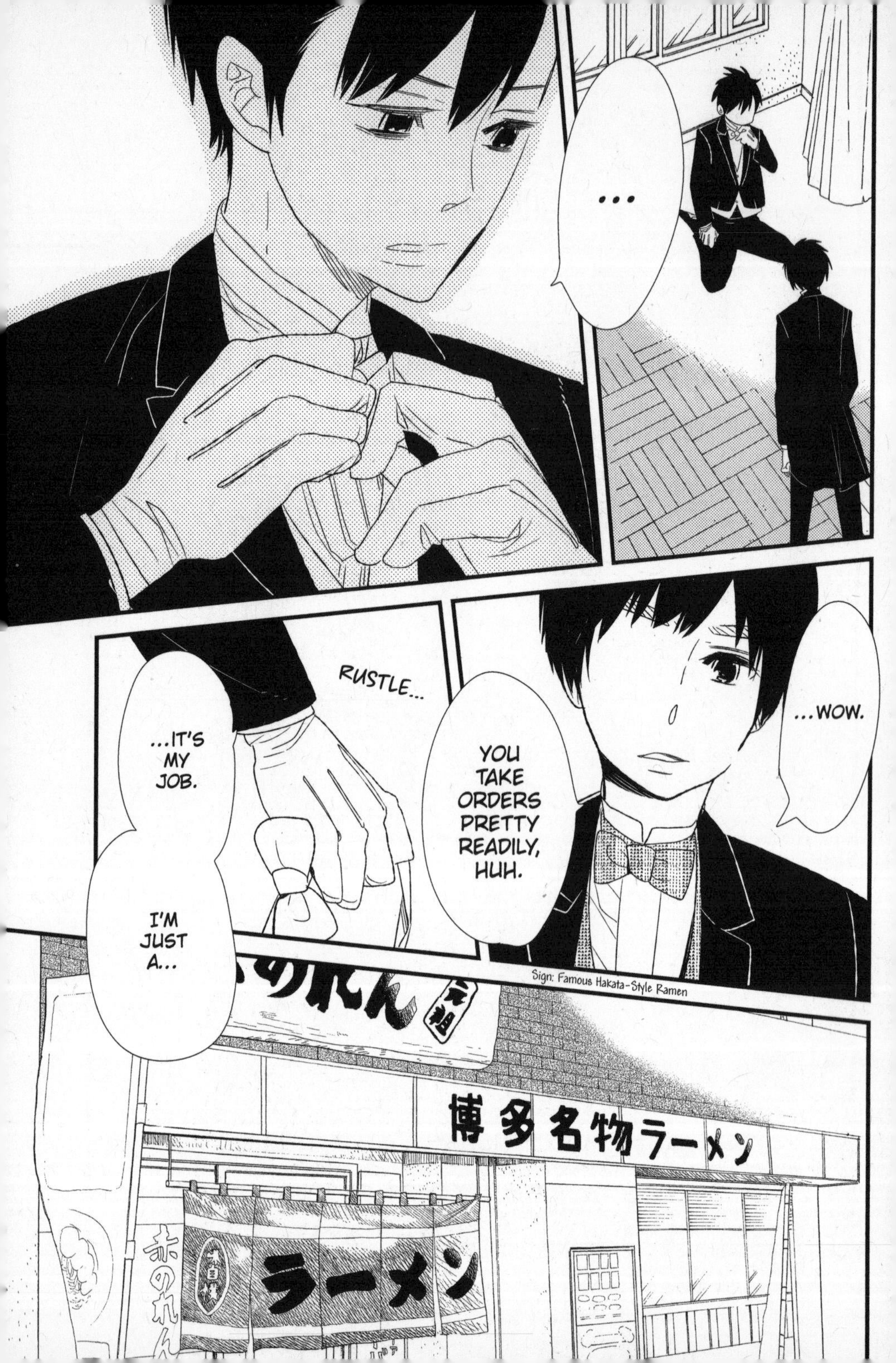
...
...WOW.
YOU TAKE ORDERS PRETTY READILY, HUH.
RUSTLE...
...IT'S MY JOB.
I'M JUST A...
Sign: Famous Hakata-Style Ramen
博多名物ラーメン
ラーメン
赤のれん
元祖

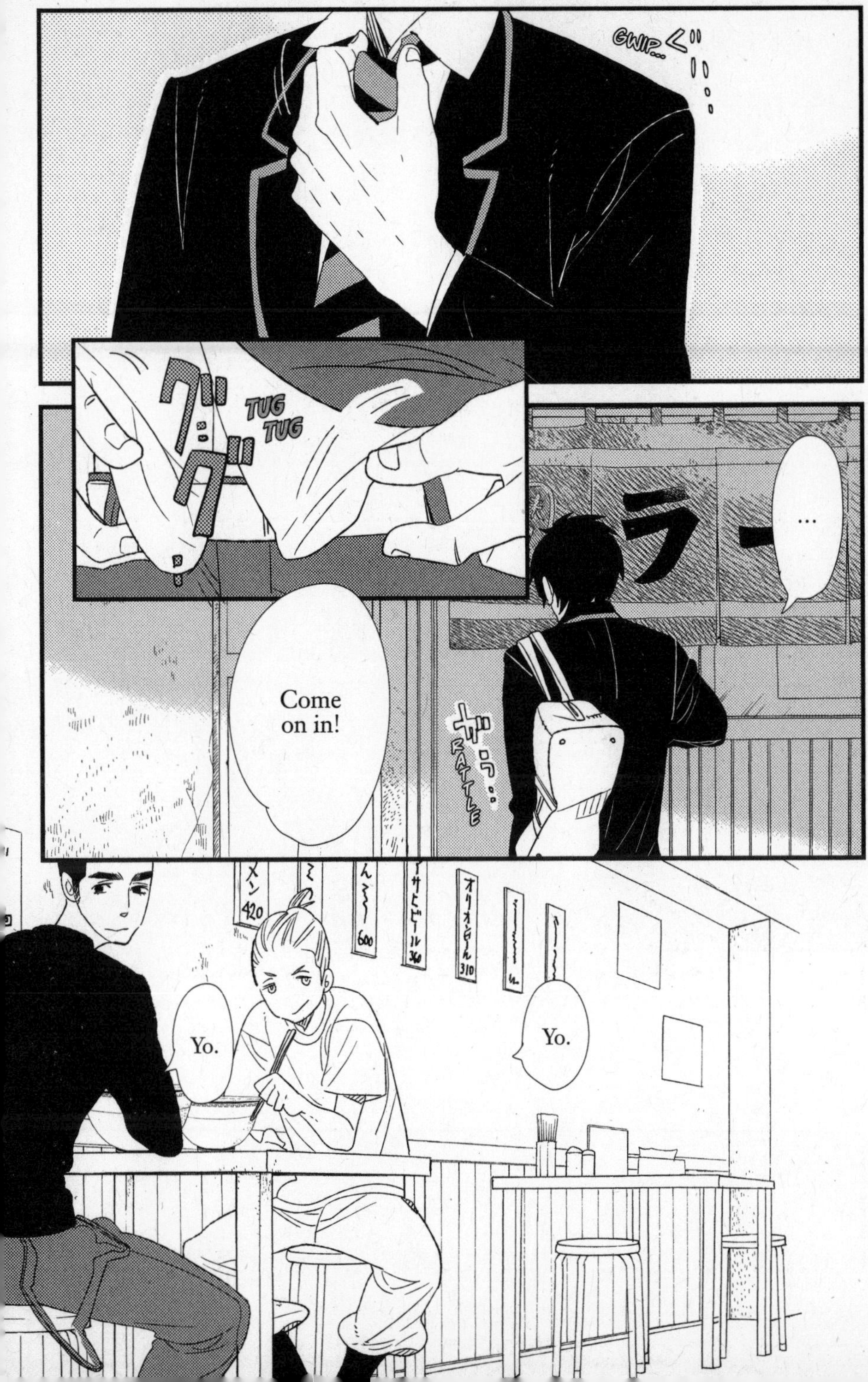
GWIP...
…
TUG TUG
Come on in!
RATTLE
Yo.
Yo.

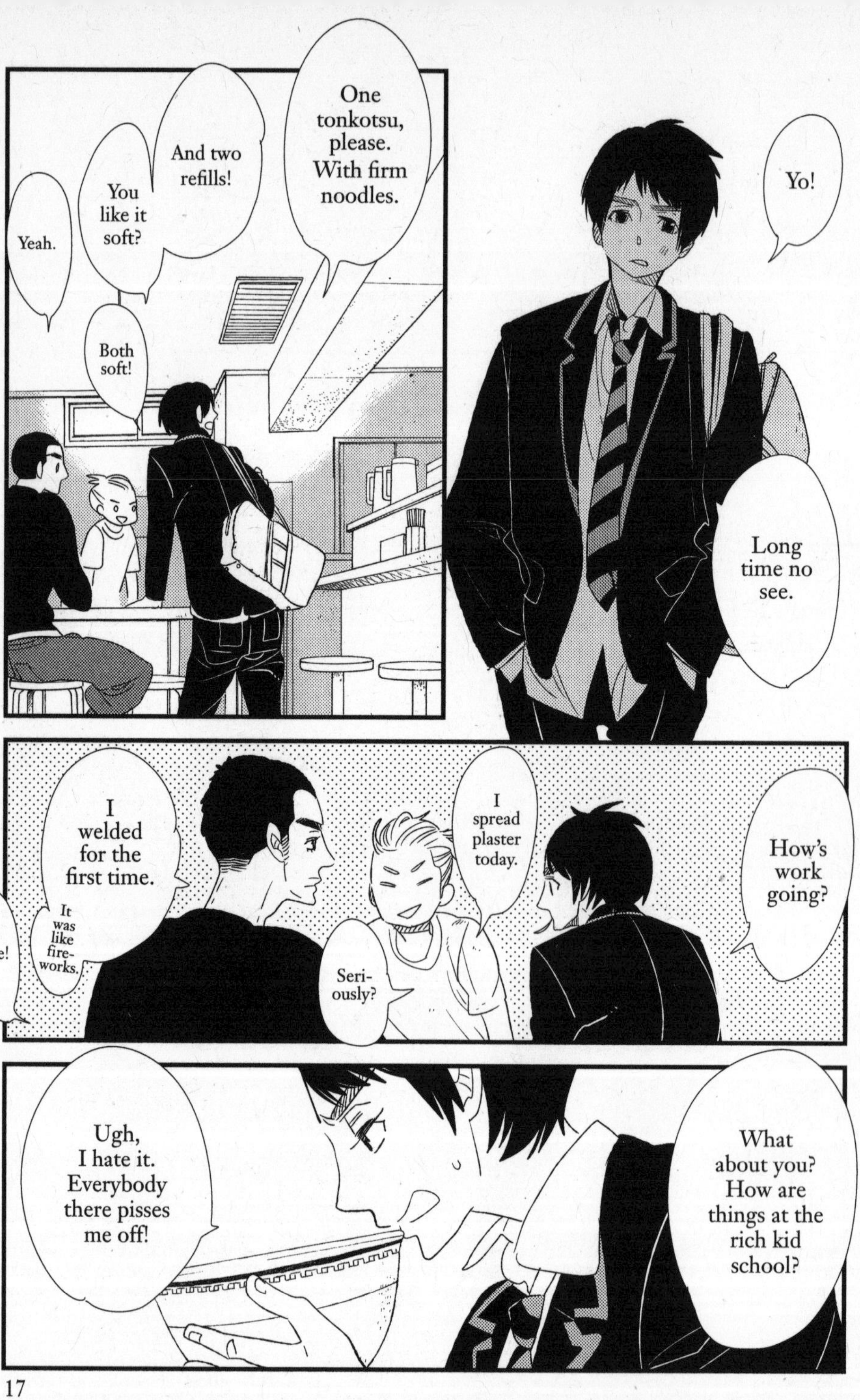

Yo!
Long time no see.
One tonkotsu, please. With firm noodles.
And two refills!
You like it soft?
Yeah.
Both soft!
How's work going?
I spread plaster today.
Seriously?
I welded for the first time.
It was like fire-works.
Nice!
What about you? How are things at the rich kid school?
Ugh, I hate it. Everybody there pisses me off!

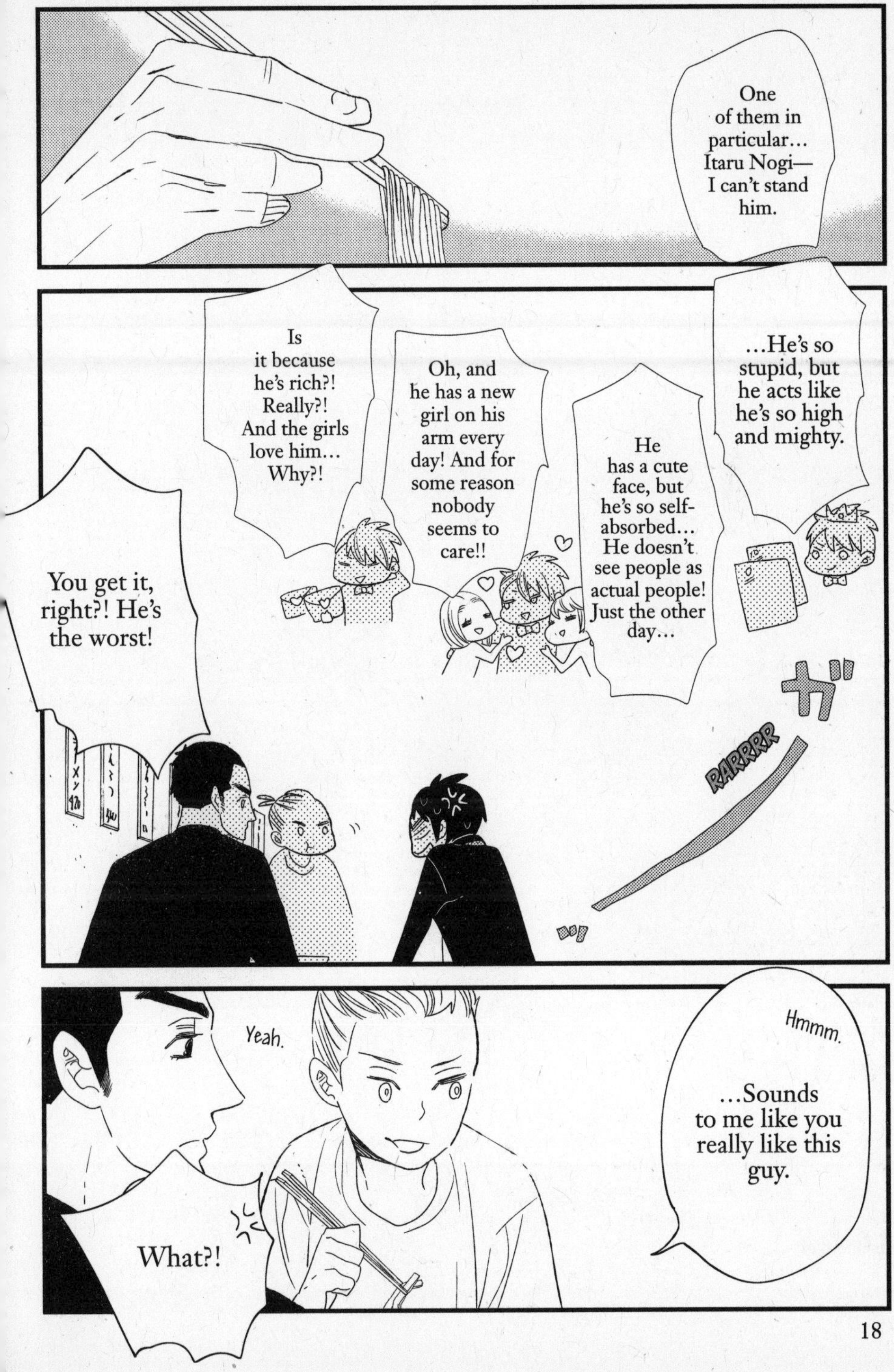

One of them in particular… Itaru Nogi— I can't stand him.
…He's so stupid, but he acts like he's so high and mighty.
He has a cute face, but he's so self-absorbed… He doesn't see people as actual people! Just the other day…
Oh, and he has a new girl on his arm every day! And for some reason nobody seems to care!!
Is it because he's rich?! Really?! And the girls love him… Why?!
RARRRR
You get it, right?! He's the worst!
Hmmm.
…Sounds to me like you really like this guy.
Yeah.
What?!

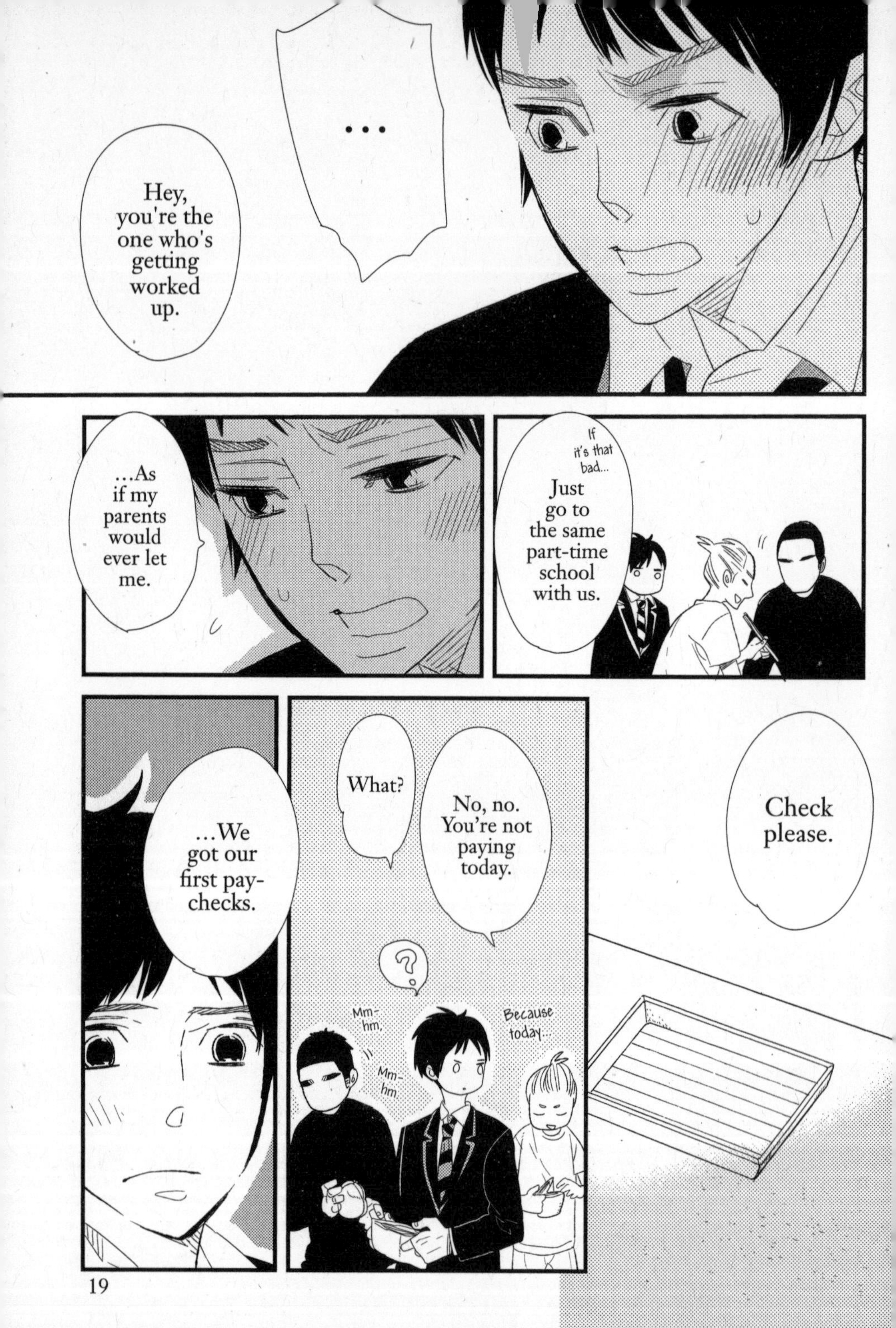
...
Hey, you're the one who's getting worked up.
If it's that bad...
Just go to the same part-time school with us.
...As if my parents would ever let me.
Check please.
No, no. You're not paying today.
What?
?
Because today...
Mm-hm,
Mm-hm
...We got our first pay-checks.

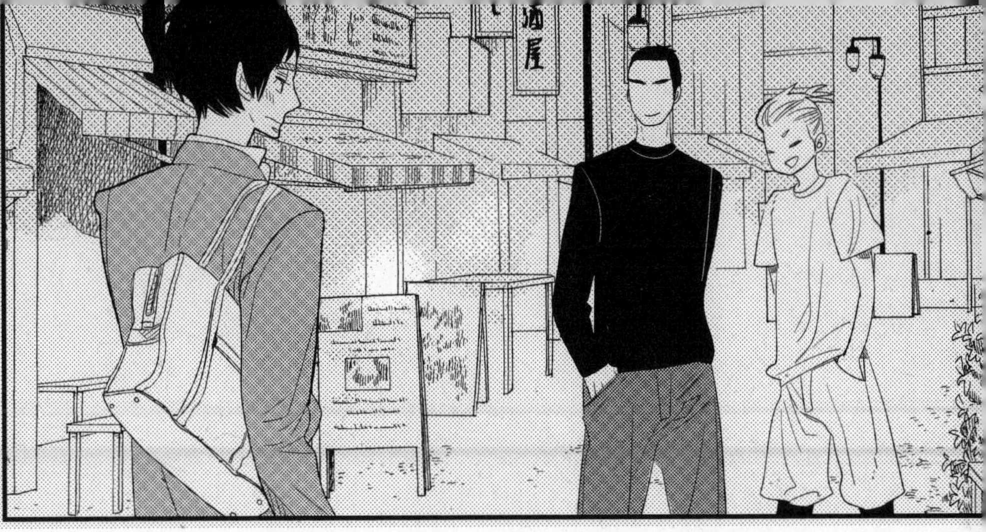

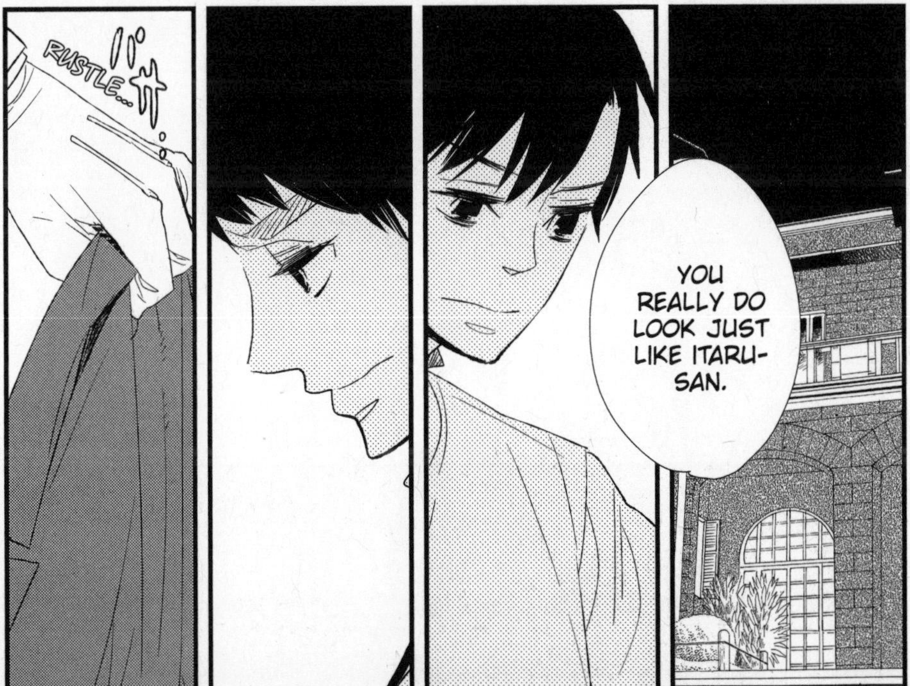
YOU REALLY DO LOOK JUST LIKE ITARU-SAN.
パサ
RUSTLE...

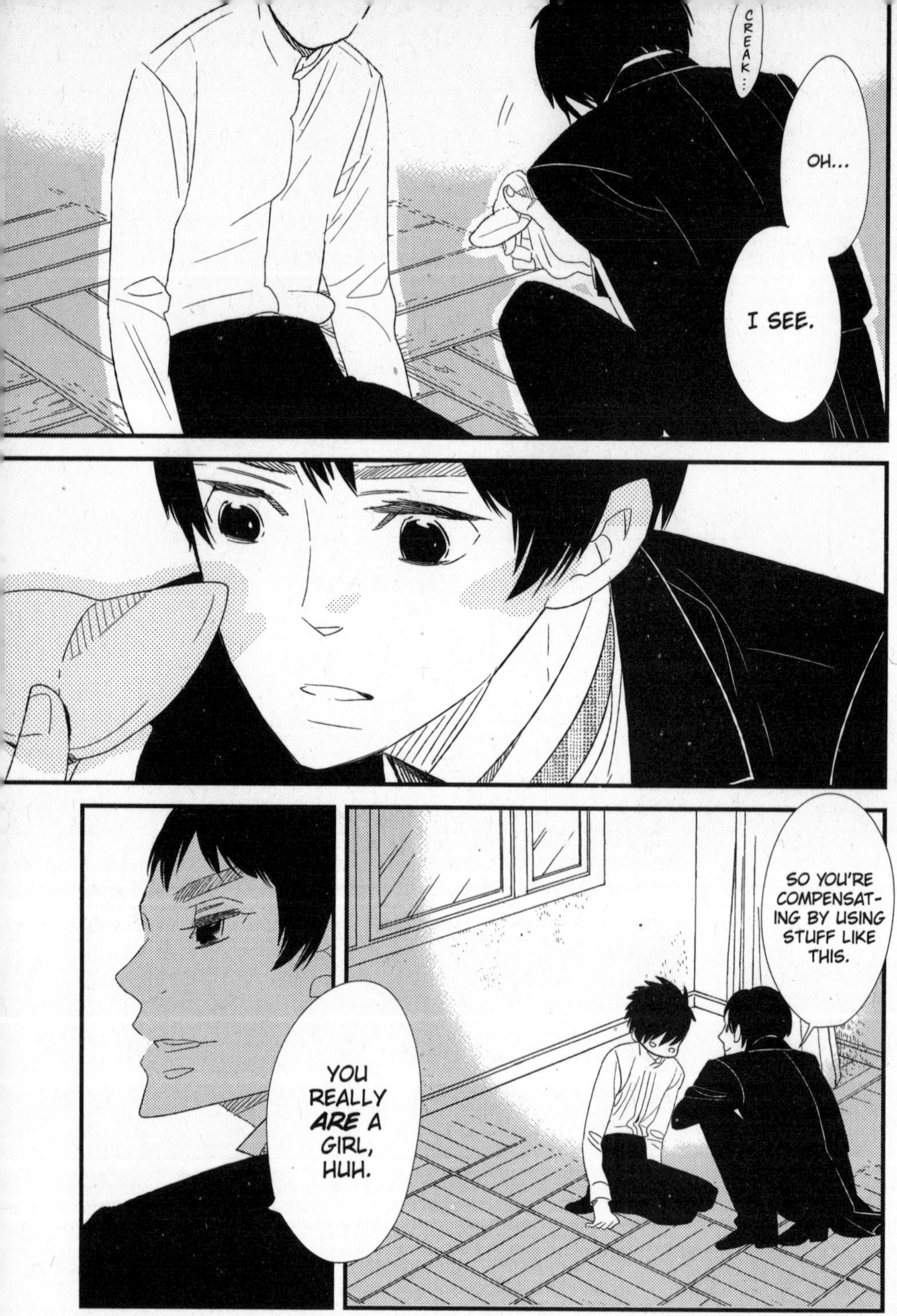
CREAK...
OH...
I SEE.
SO YOU'RE COMPENSATING BY USING STUFF LIKE THIS.
YOU REALLY ARE A GIRL, HUH.

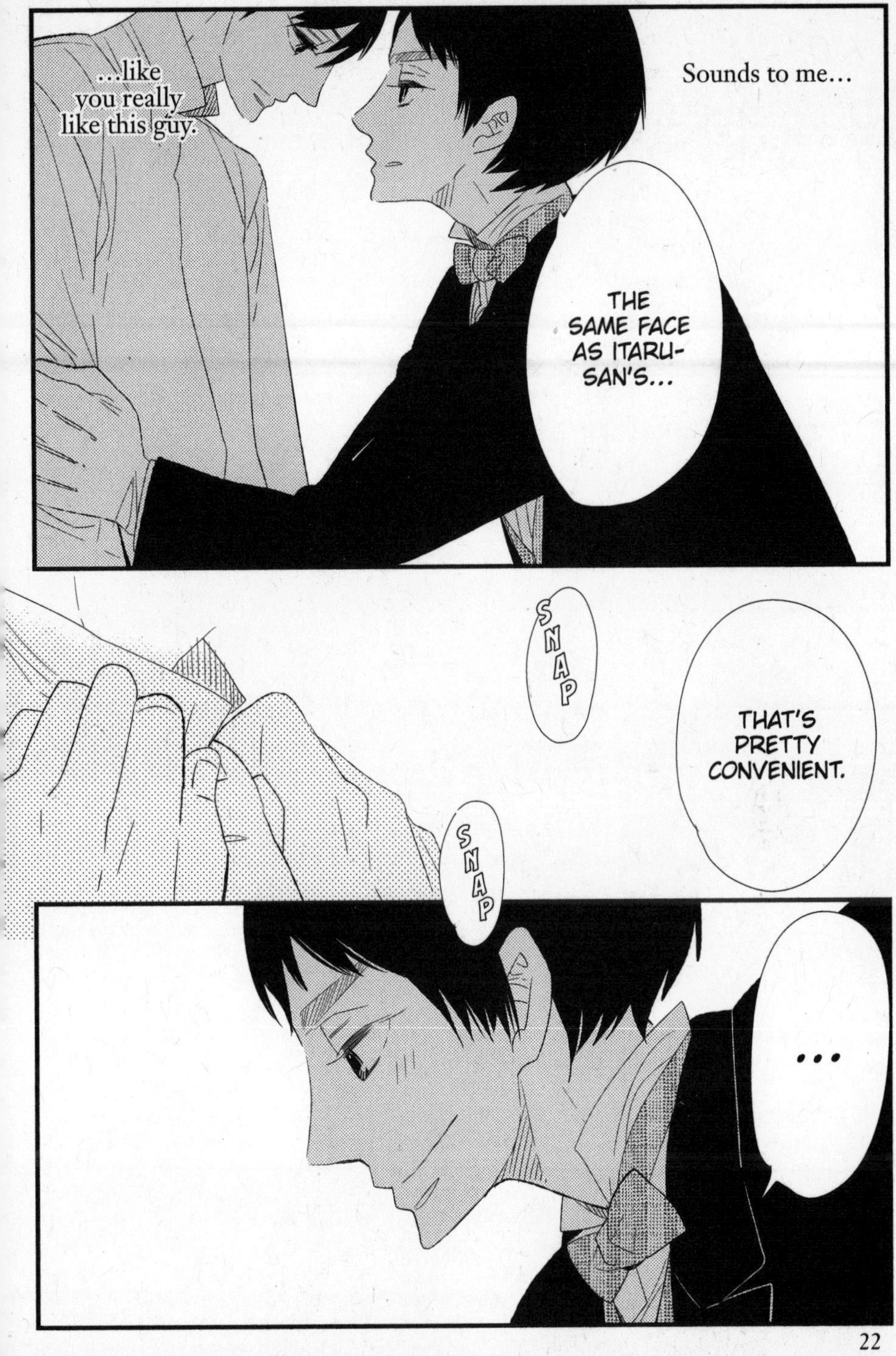
Sounds to me…
…like you really like this guy.
THE SAME FACE AS ITARU-SAN'S…
THAT'S PRETTY CONVENIENT.
SNAP
SNAP
…

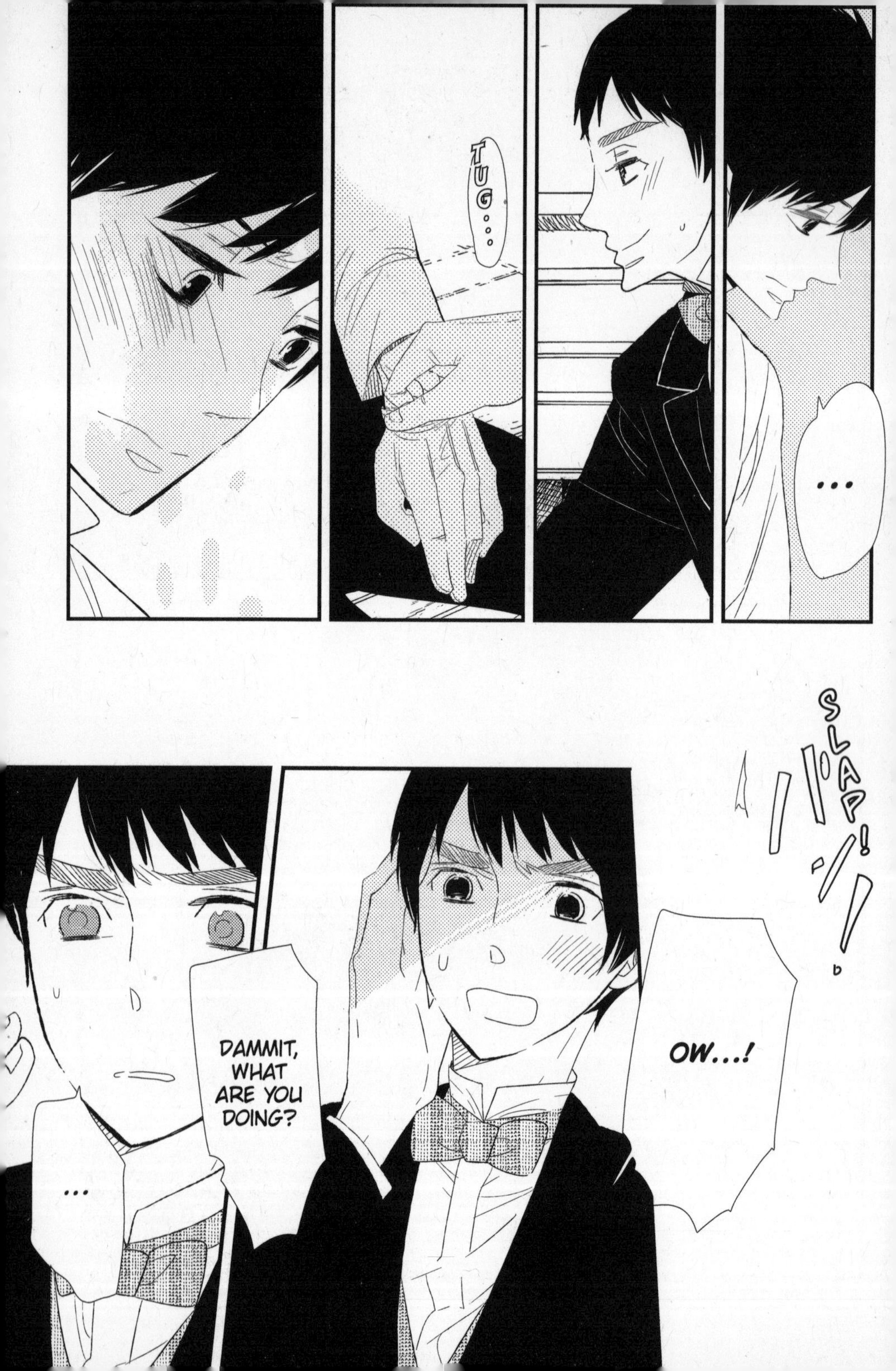
...
TUG...
SLAP!!
OW...!
DAMMIT, WHAT ARE YOU DOING?
...

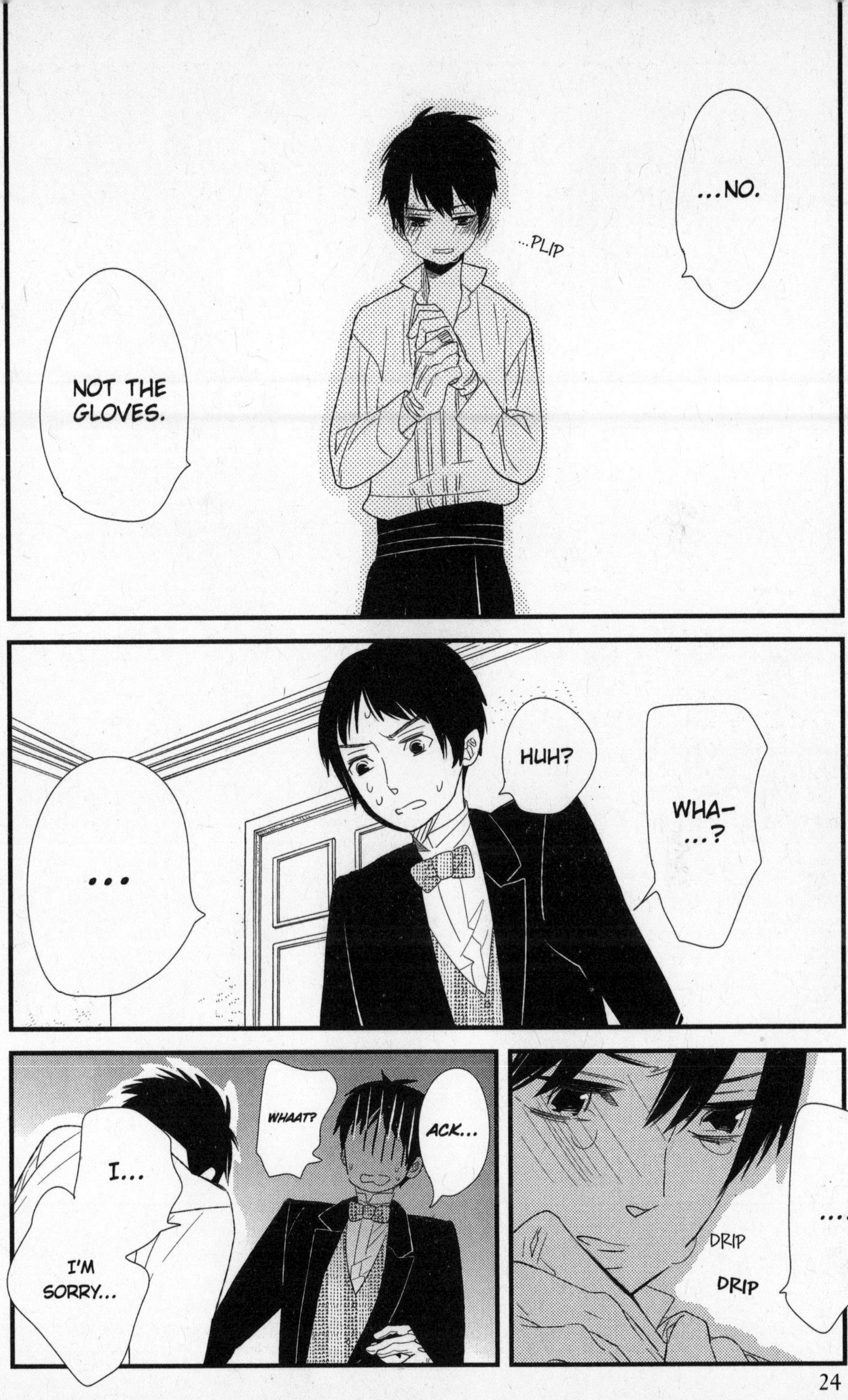
...NO.
...PLIP
NOT THE GLOVES.
WHA- ...?
HUH?
...
...!
DRIP
DRIP
ACK...
WHAAT?
I...
I'M SORRY...

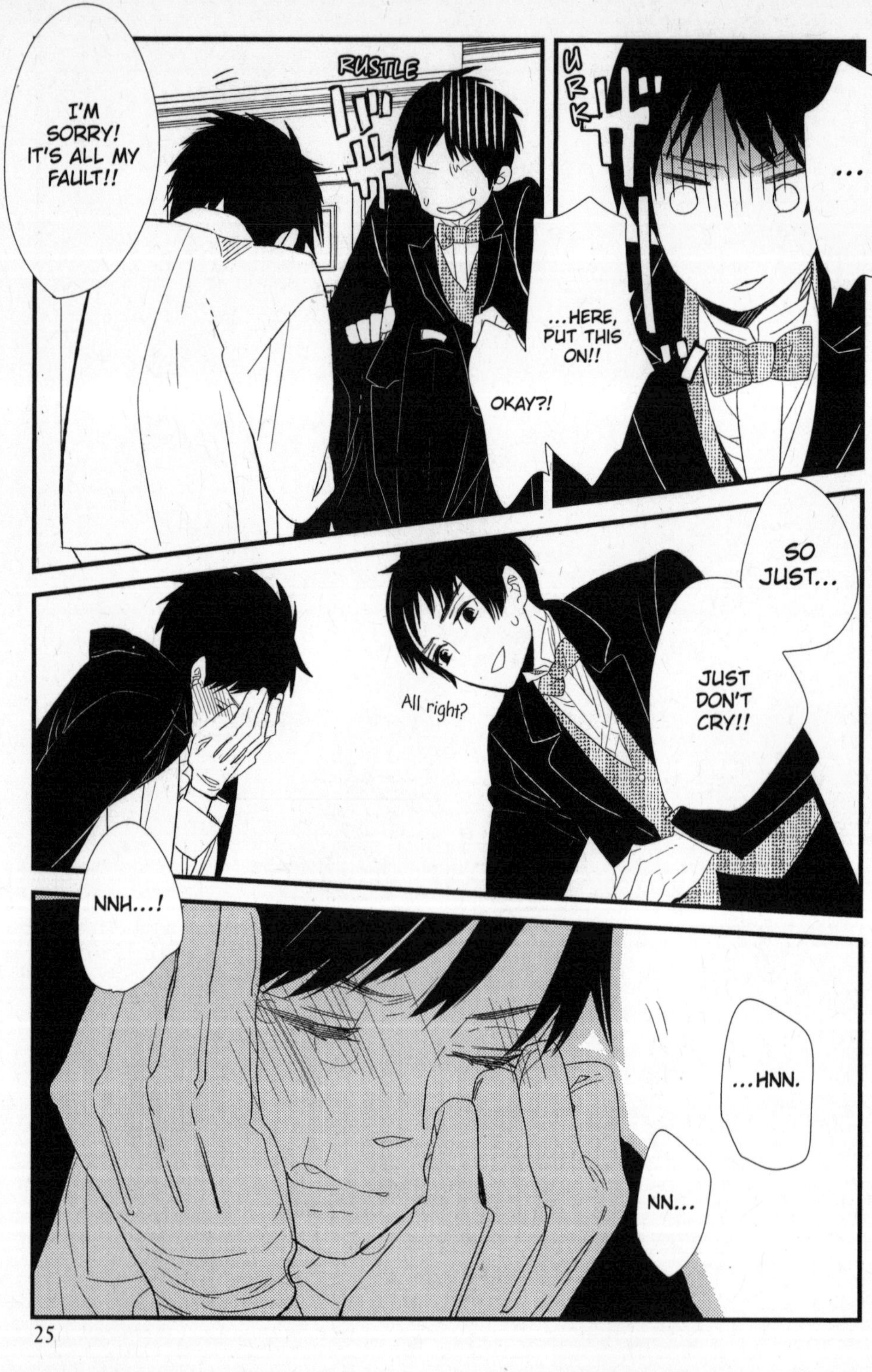
URK
...
...HERE, PUT THIS ON!!
OKAY?!
RUSTLE
I'M SORRY! IT'S ALL MY FAULT!!
SO JUST...
JUST DON'T CRY!!
All right?
...HNN.
NN...
NNH...!

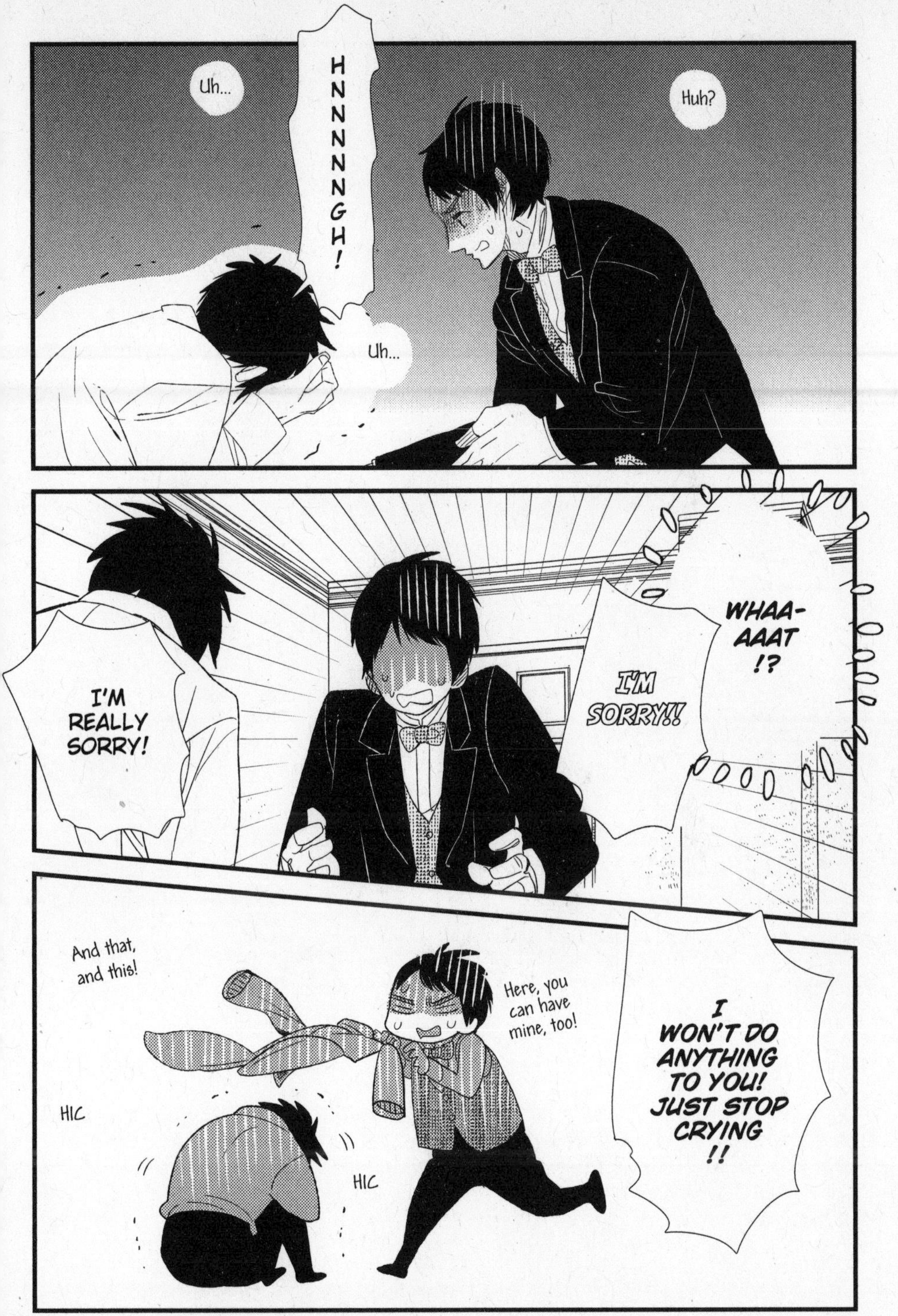
Huh?
HNNNNNNGH!
Uh...
Uh...
WHAA-AAAT!?
I'M SORRY!!
I'M REALLY SORRY!
I WON'T DO ANYTHING TO YOU! JUST STOP CRYING!!
Here, you can have mine, too!
And that, and this!
HIC
HIC

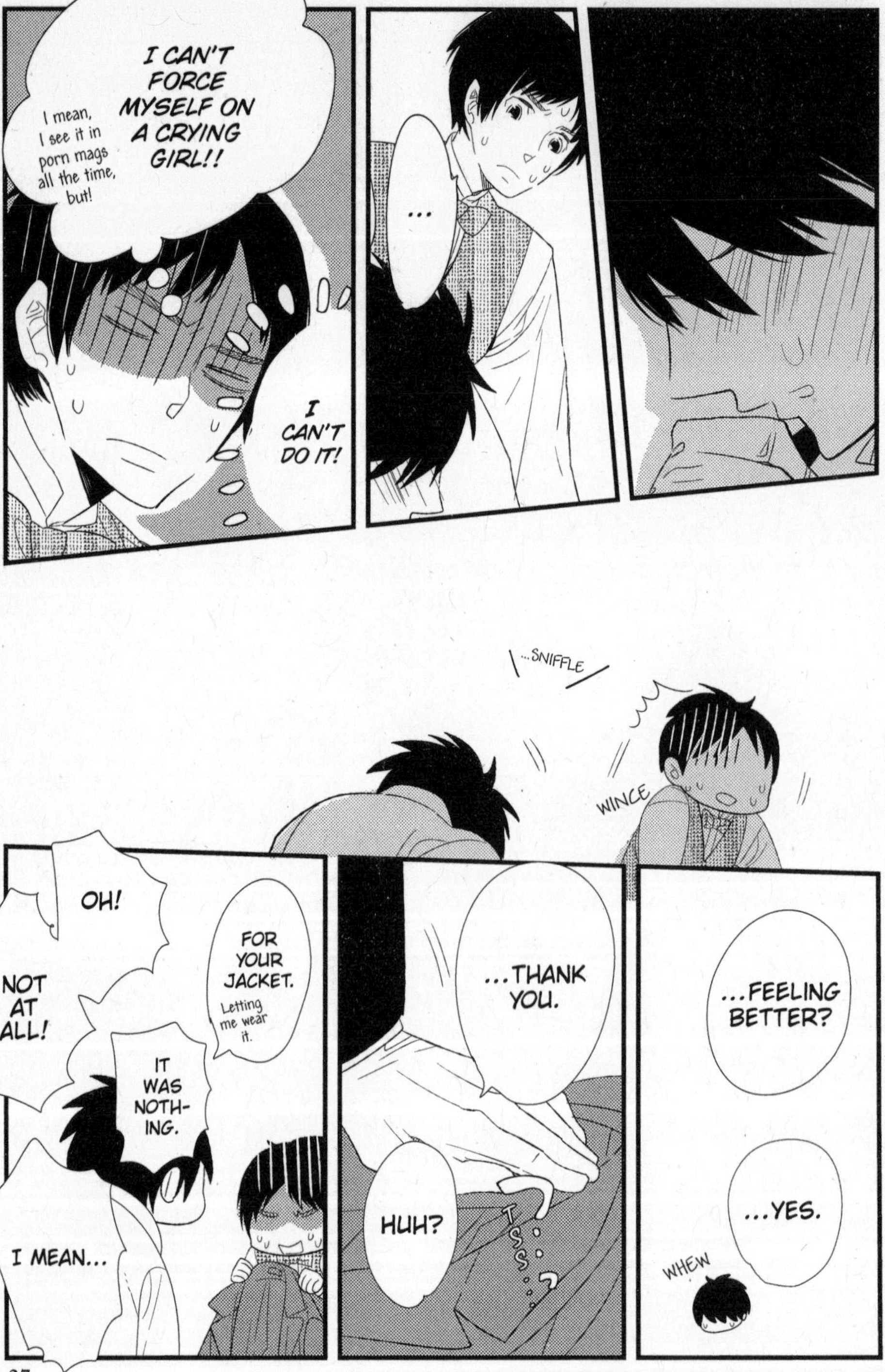
...
I CAN'T FORCE MYSELF ON A CRYING GIRL!!
I mean, I see it in porn mags all the time, but!
I CAN'T DO IT!
...SNIFFLE
WINCE
...FEELING BETTER?
...YES.
WHEW
...THANK YOU.
HUH?
TSS
FOR YOUR JACKET.
Letting me wear it.
OH!
NOT AT ALL!
IT WAS NOTH-ING.
I MEAN...

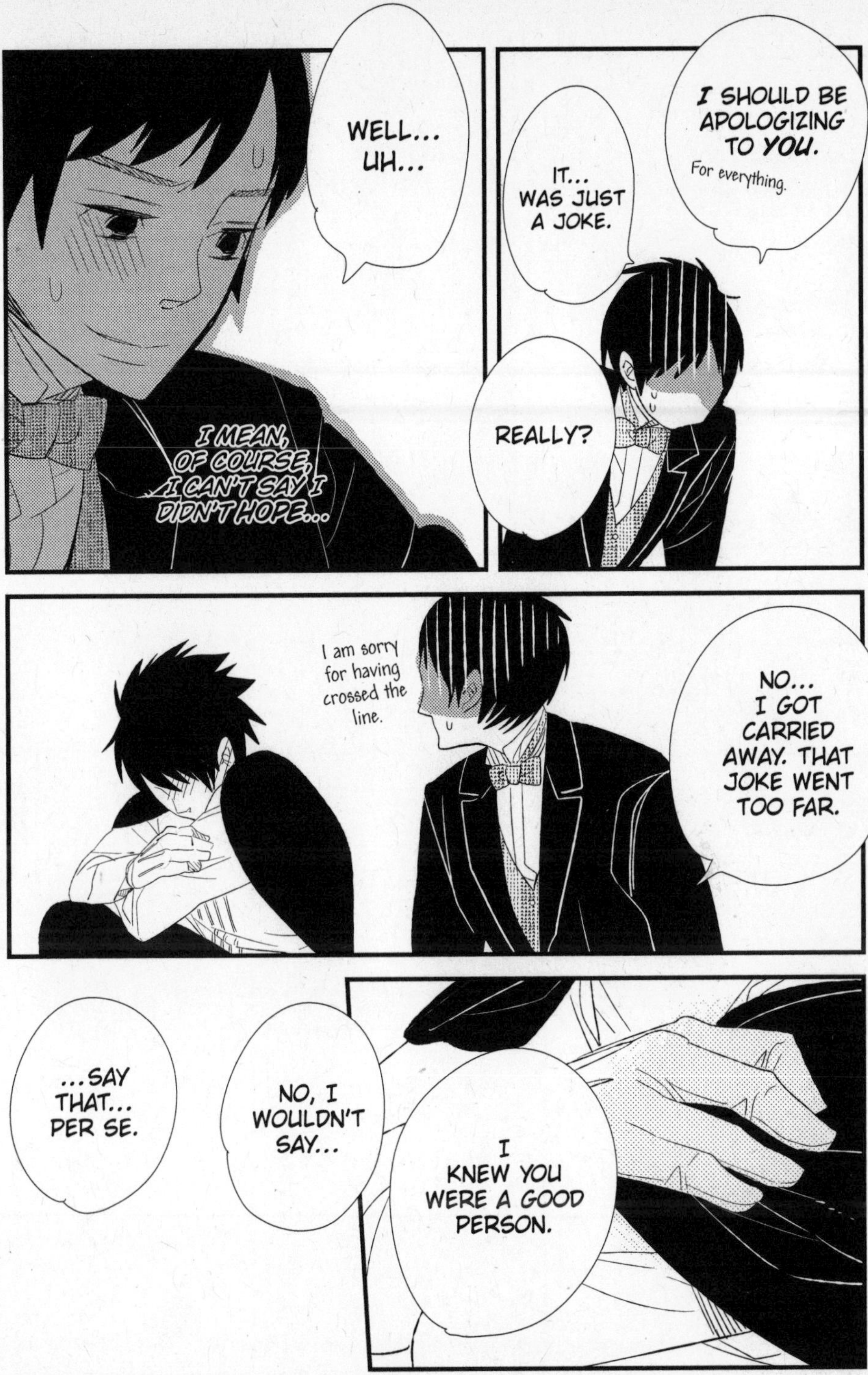
I SHOULD BE APOLOGIZING TO YOU.
For everything.
IT... WAS JUST A JOKE.
REALLY?
WELL... UH...
I MEAN, OF COURSE, I CAN'T SAY I DIDN'T HOPE...
NO... I GOT CARRIED AWAY. THAT JOKE WENT TOO FAR.
I am sorry for having crossed the line.
I KNEW YOU WERE A GOOD PERSON.
NO, I WOULDN'T SAY...
...SAY THAT... PER SE.

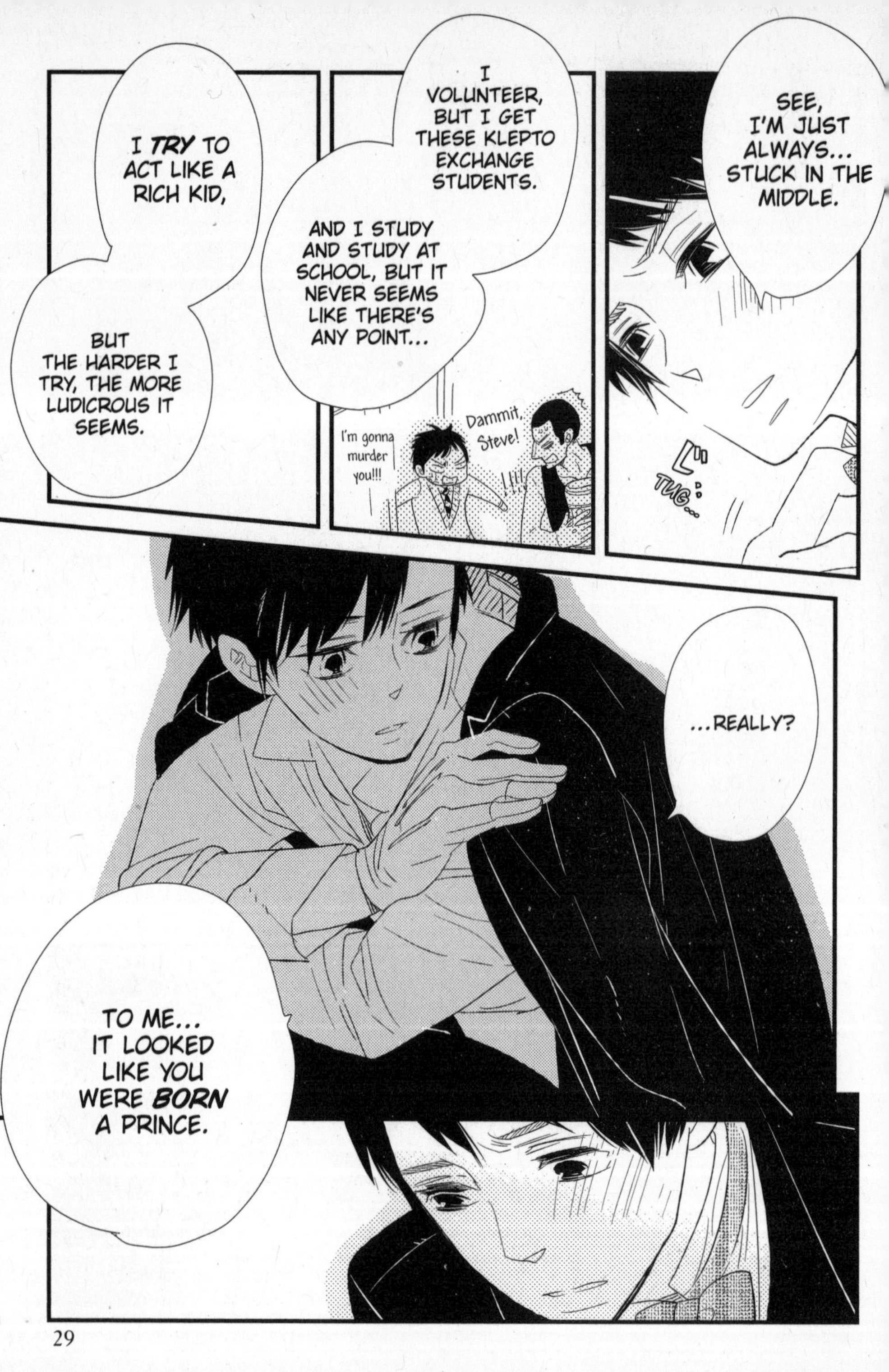
SEE, I'M JUST ALWAYS... STUCK IN THE MIDDLE.
TUG...
I VOLUNTEER, BUT I GET THESE KLEPTO EXCHANGE STUDENTS.
AND I STUDY AND STUDY AT SCHOOL, BUT IT NEVER SEEMS LIKE THERE'S ANY POINT...
Dammit, Steve!
I'm gonna murder you!!!
I *TRY* TO ACT LIKE A RICH KID,
BUT THE HARDER I TRY, THE MORE LUDICROUS IT SEEMS.
...REALLY?
TO ME... IT LOOKED LIKE YOU WERE *BORN* A PRINCE.

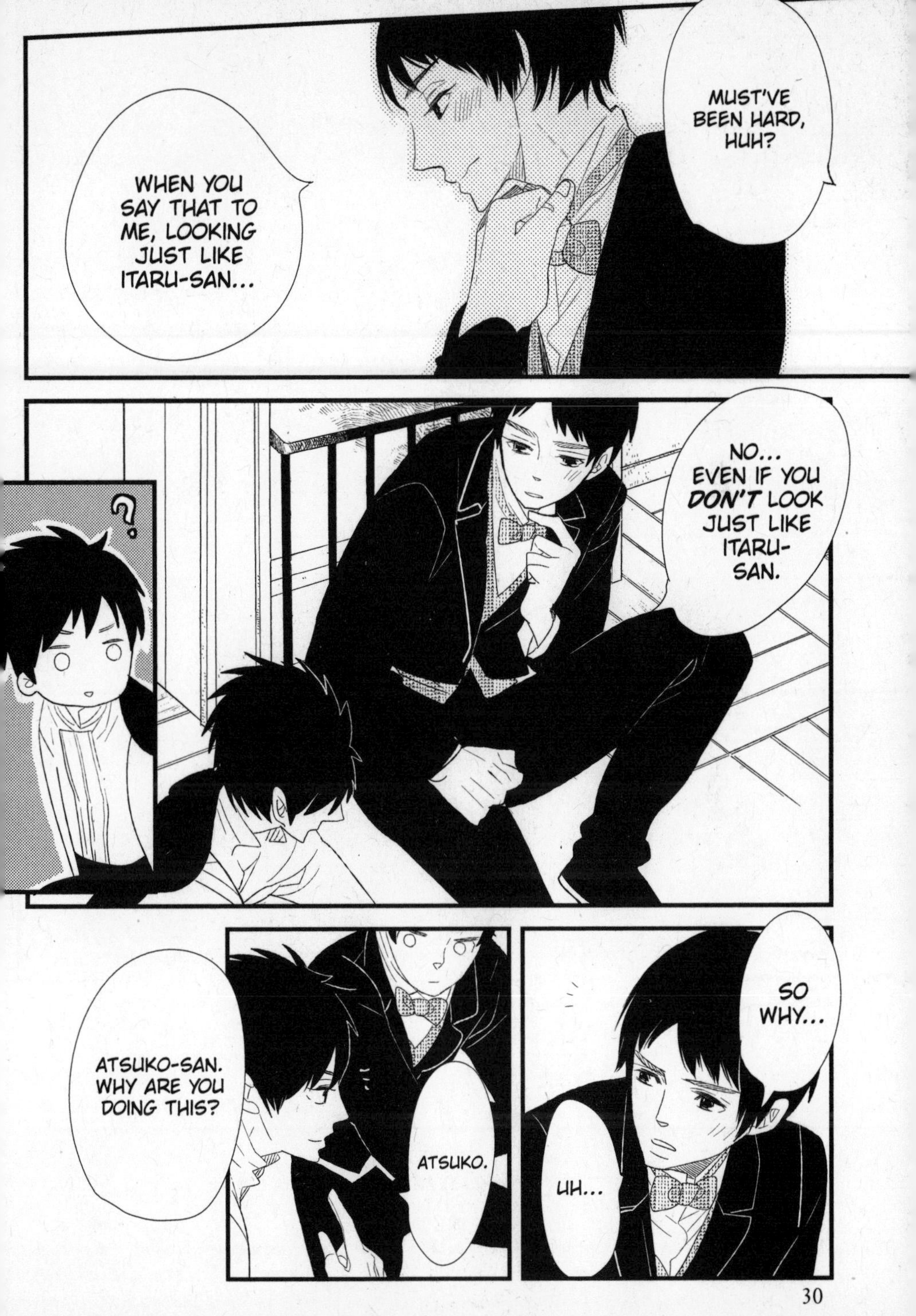
MUST'VE BEEN HARD, HUH?
WHEN YOU SAY THAT TO ME, LOOKING JUST LIKE ITARU-SAN...
NO... EVEN IF YOU DON'T LOOK JUST LIKE ITARU-SAN.
?
SO WHY...
UH...
ATSUKO-SAN. WHY ARE YOU DOING THIS?
ATSUKO.

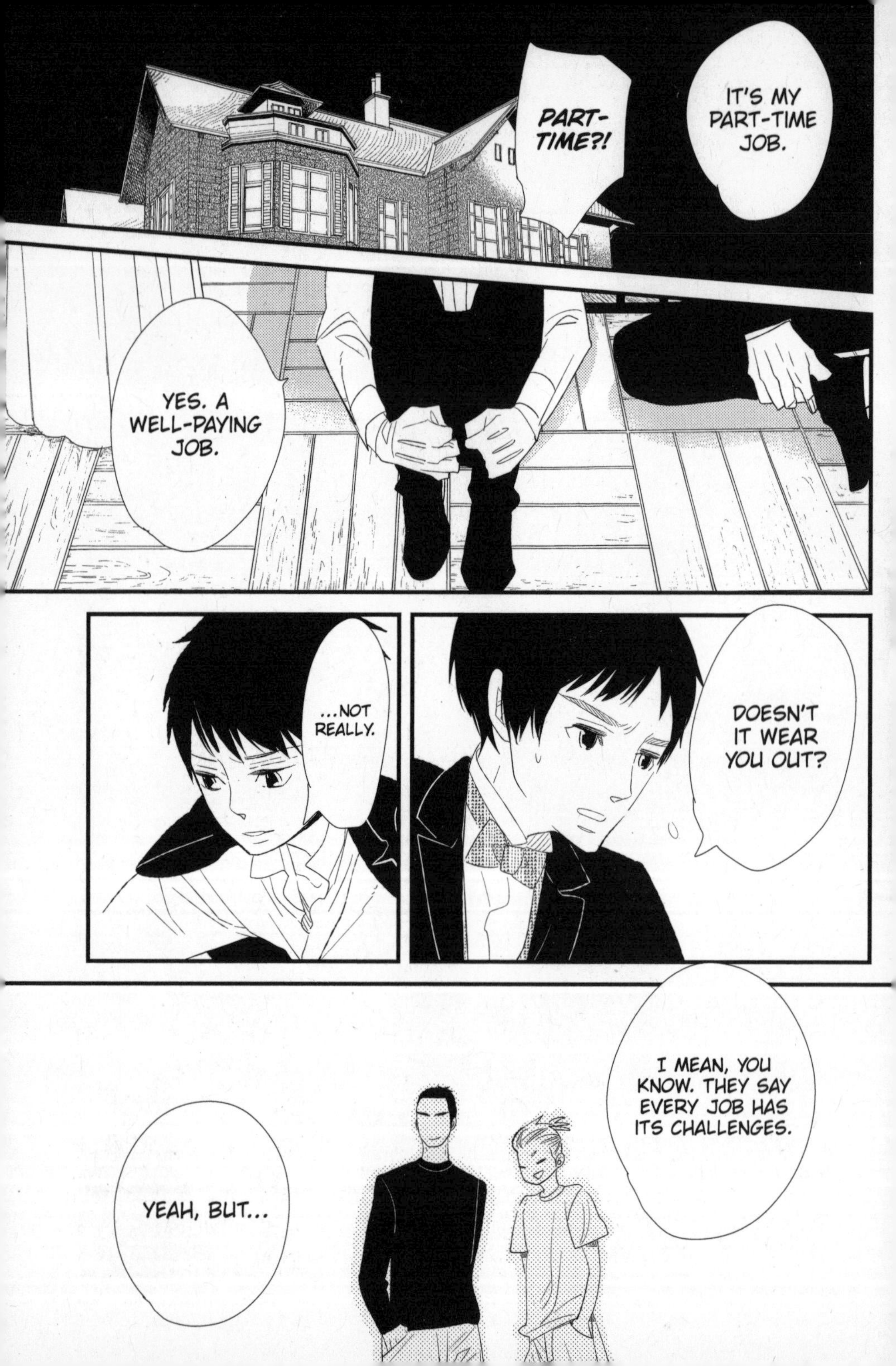
IT'S MY PART-TIME JOB.
PART-TIME?!
YES. A WELL-PAYING JOB.
DOESN'T IT WEAR YOU OUT?
...NOT REALLY.
I MEAN, YOU KNOW. THEY SAY EVERY JOB HAS ITS CHALLENGES.
YEAH, BUT...

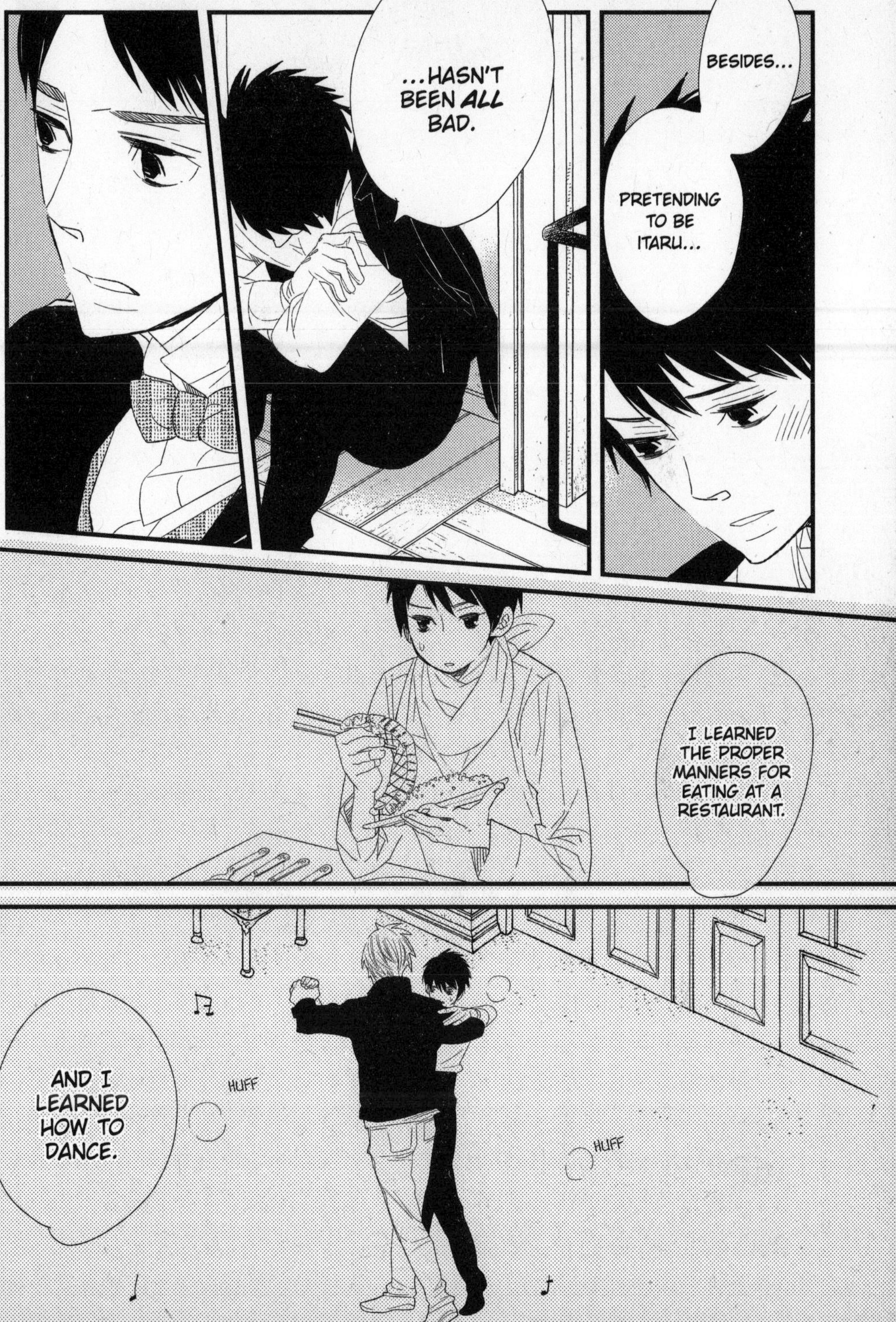
BESIDES...
PRETENDING TO BE ITARU...
...HASN'T BEEN ALL BAD.
I LEARNED THE PROPER MANNERS FOR EATING AT A RESTAURANT.
HUFF
HUFF
AND I LEARNED HOW TO DANCE.

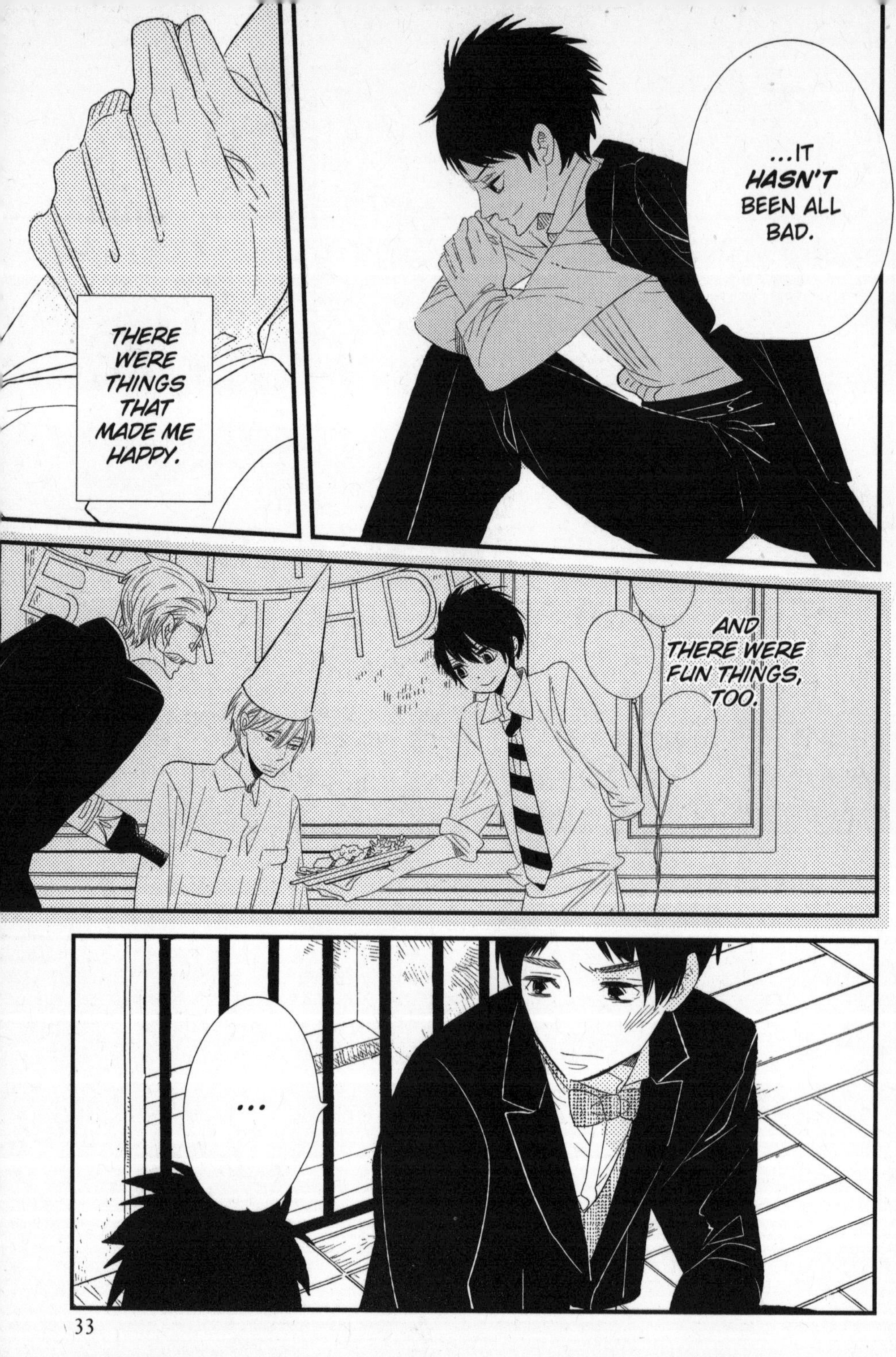
...IT HASN'T BEEN ALL BAD.
THERE WERE THINGS THAT MADE ME HAPPY.
AND THERE WERE FUN THINGS, TOO.
...

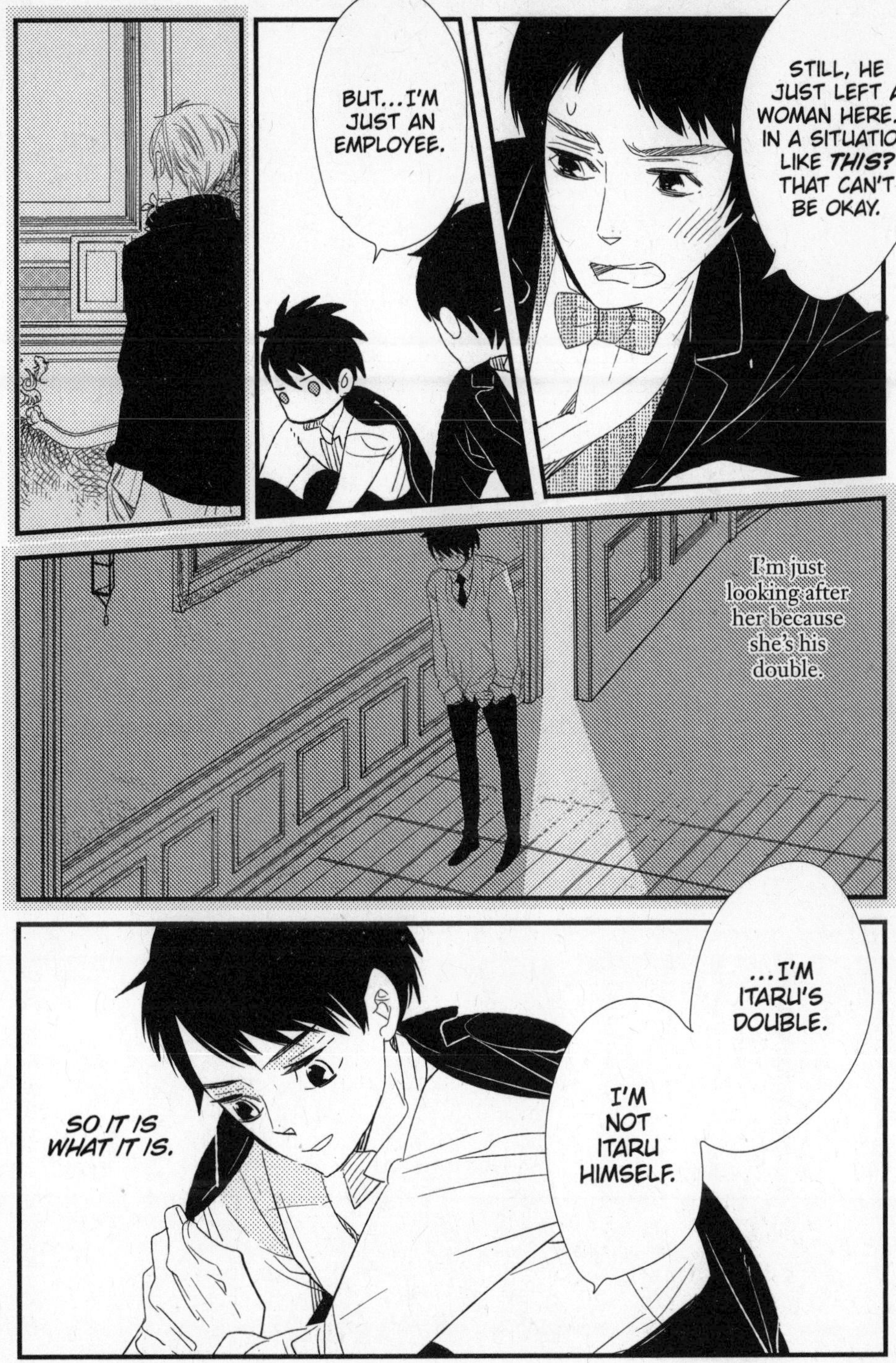
STILL, HE JUST LEFT A WOMAN HERE... IN A SITUATION LIKE *THIS?* THAT CAN'T BE OKAY.
BUT...I'M JUST AN EMPLOYEE.
I'm just looking after her because she's his double.
...I'M ITARU'S DOUBLE.
I'M NOT ITARU HIMSELF.
SO IT IS WHAT IT IS.

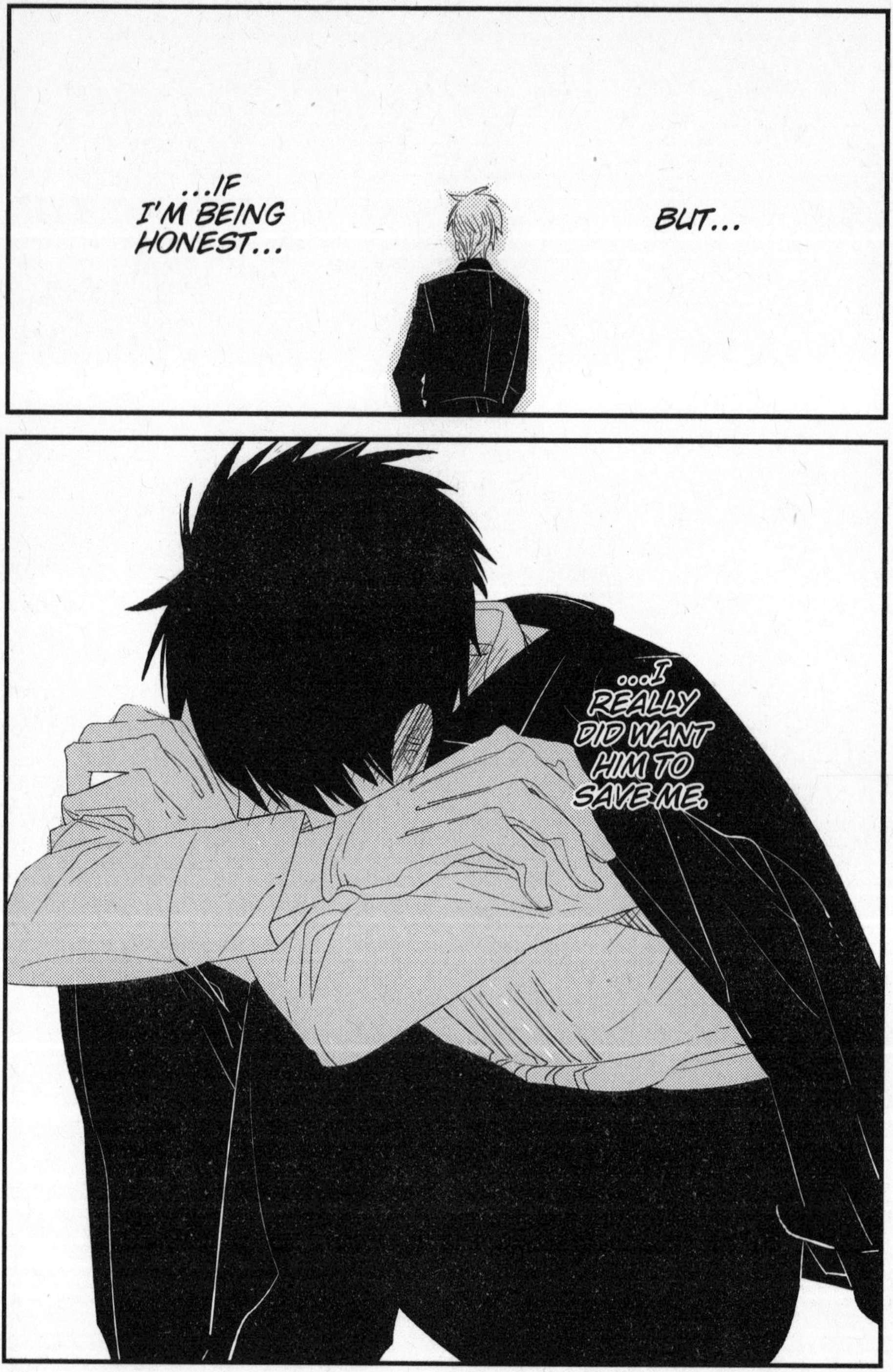
BUT...
...IF I'M BEING HONEST...
...I REALLY DID WANT HIM TO SAVE ME.

the prince in his dark days
nico yamanaka

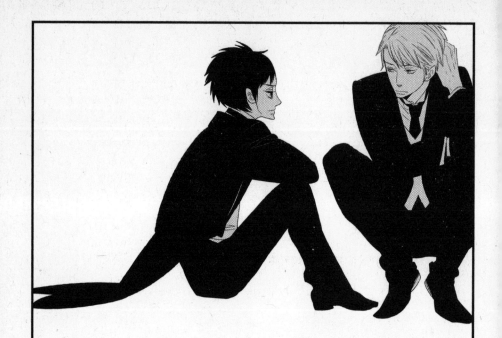

chapter
II

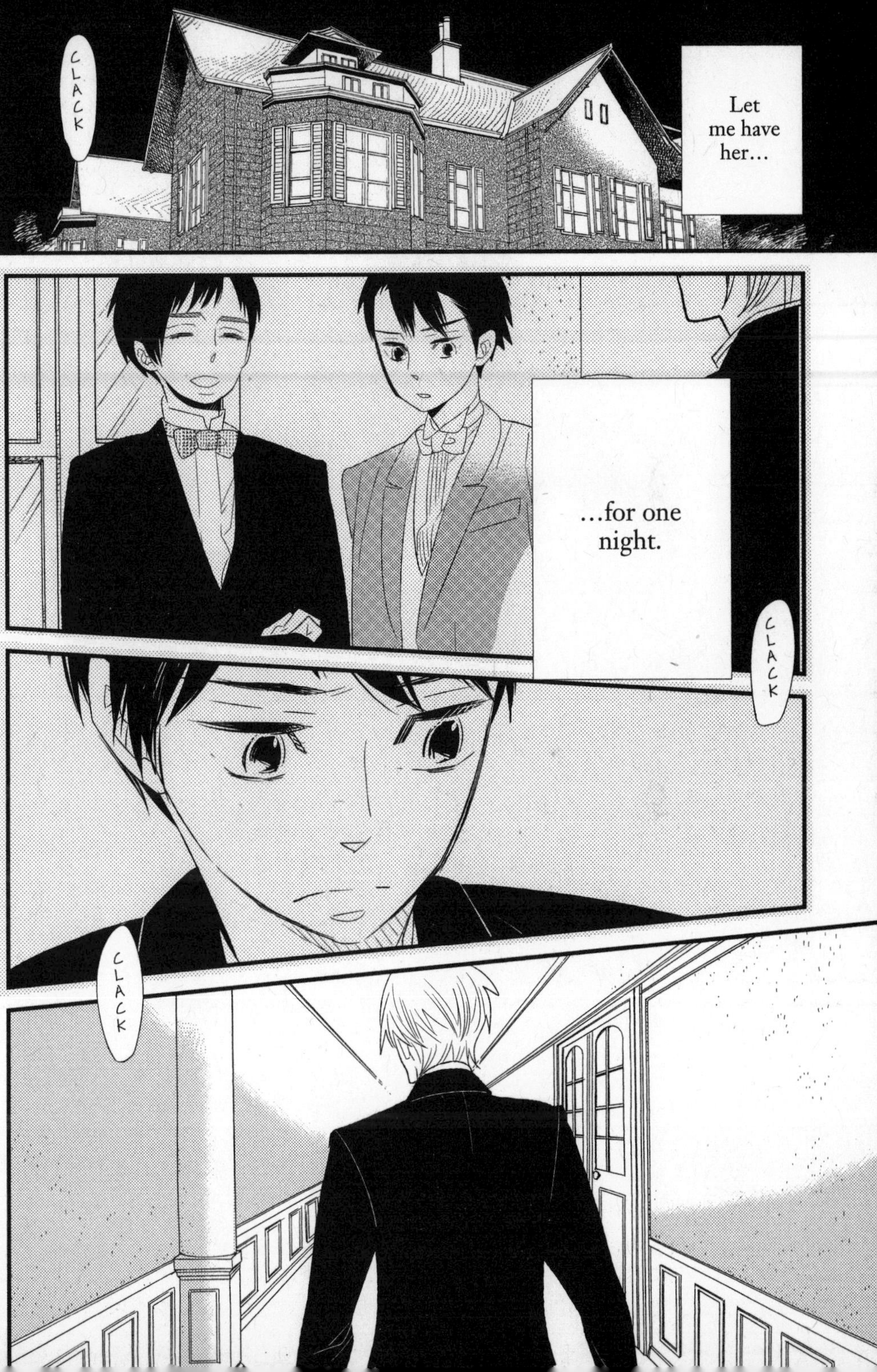

Let me have her…
CLACK
…for one night.
CLACK
CLACK

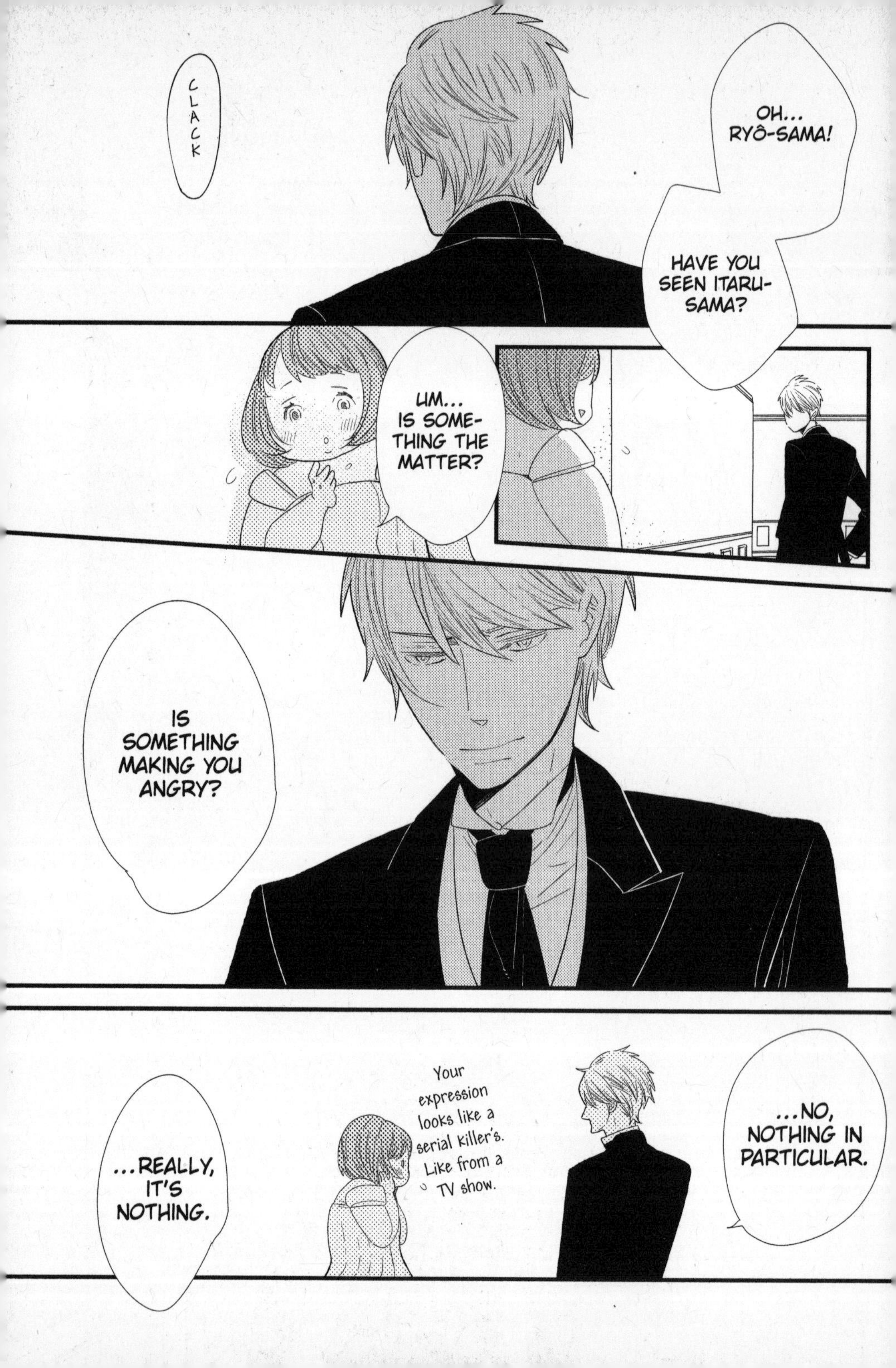
OH... RYÔ-SAMA!
HAVE YOU SEEN ITARU-SAMA?
CLACK
UM... IS SOME-THING THE MATTER?
IS SOMETHING MAKING YOU ANGRY?
...NO, NOTHING IN PARTICULAR.
Your expression looks like a serial killer's. Like from a TV show.
...REALLY, IT'S NOTHING.

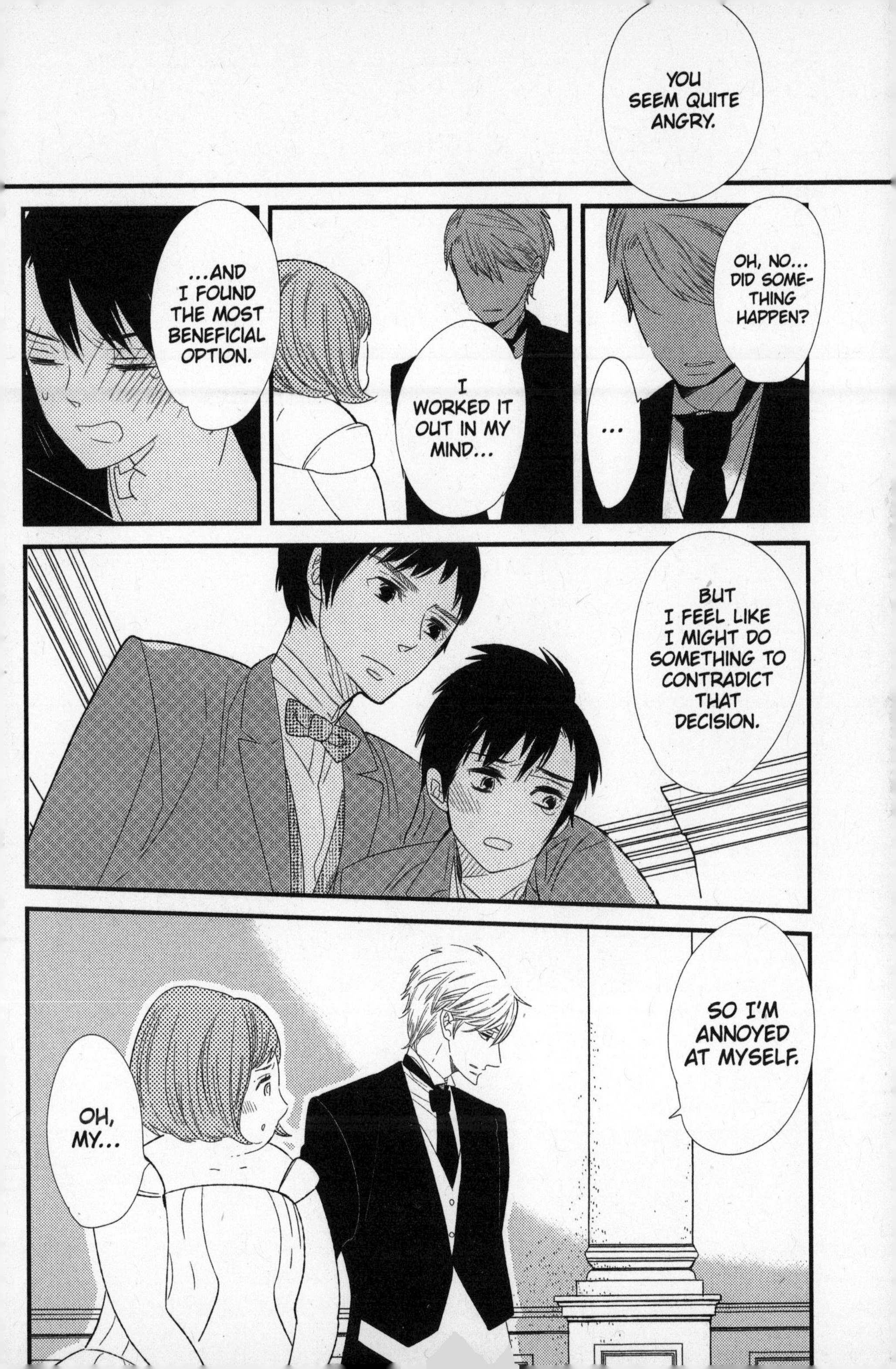
YOU SEEM QUITE ANGRY.
OH, NO... DID SOMETHING HAPPEN?
...
I WORKED IT OUT IN MY MIND...
...AND I FOUND THE MOST BENEFICIAL OPTION.
BUT I FEEL LIKE I MIGHT DO SOMETHING TO CONTRADICT THAT DECISION.
SO I'M ANNOYED AT MYSELF.
OH, MY...

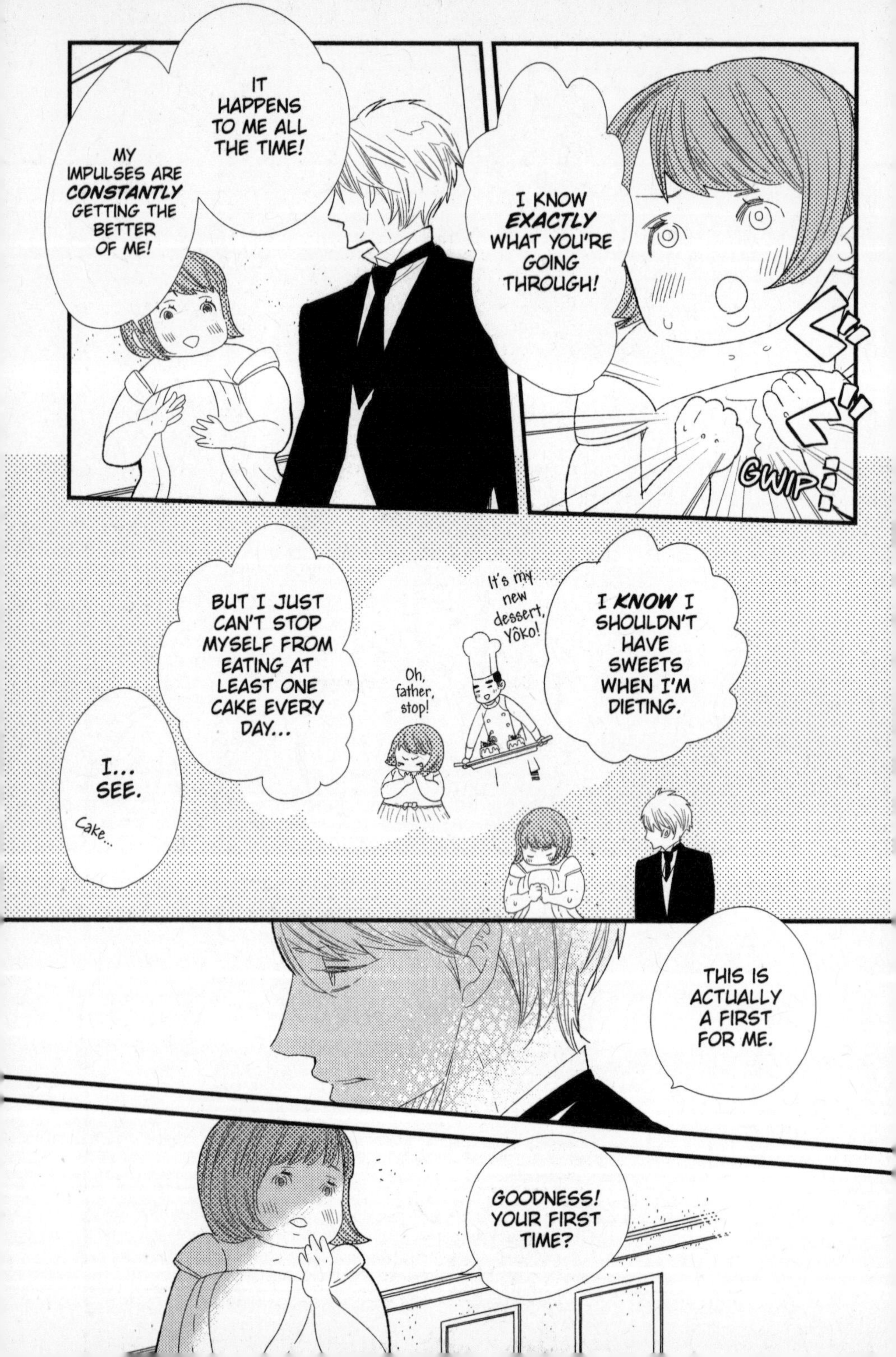
I KNOW EXACTLY WHAT YOU'RE GOING THROUGH!
GWIP!
IT HAPPENS TO ME ALL THE TIME!
MY IMPULSES ARE CONSTANTLY GETTING THE BETTER OF ME!
I KNOW I SHOULDN'T HAVE SWEETS WHEN I'M DIETING.
It's my new dessert, Yôko!
Oh, father, stop!
BUT I JUST CAN'T STOP MYSELF FROM EATING AT LEAST ONE CAKE EVERY DAY...
I... SEE.
Cake...
THIS IS ACTUALLY A FIRST FOR ME.
GOODNESS! YOUR FIRST TIME?

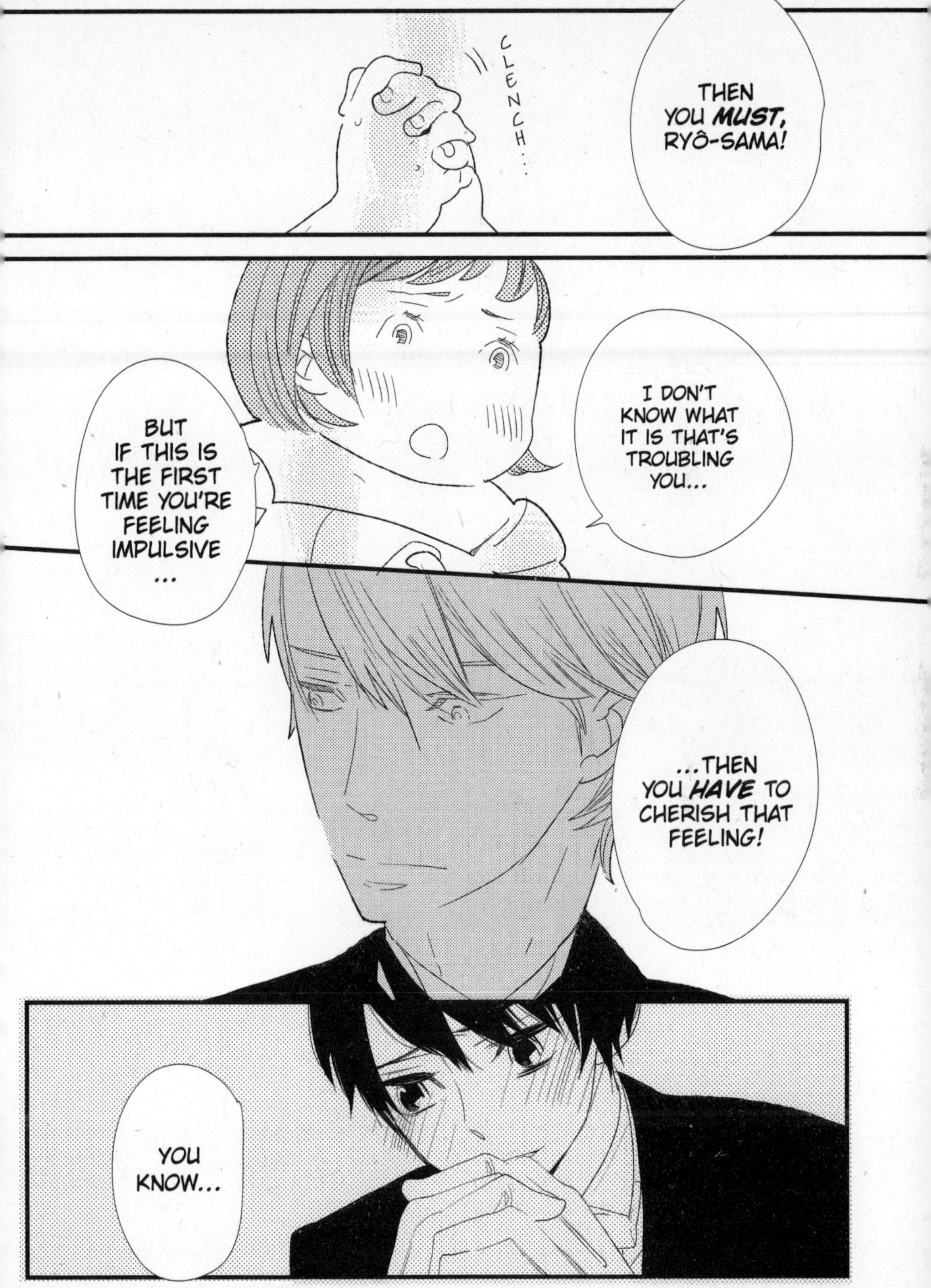
THEN YOU MUST, RYÔ-SAMA!
CLENCH...
I DON'T KNOW WHAT IT IS THAT'S TROUBLING YOU...
BUT IF THIS IS THE FIRST TIME YOU'RE FEELING IMPULSIVE ...
...THEN YOU HAVE TO CHERISH THAT FEELING!
YOU KNOW...

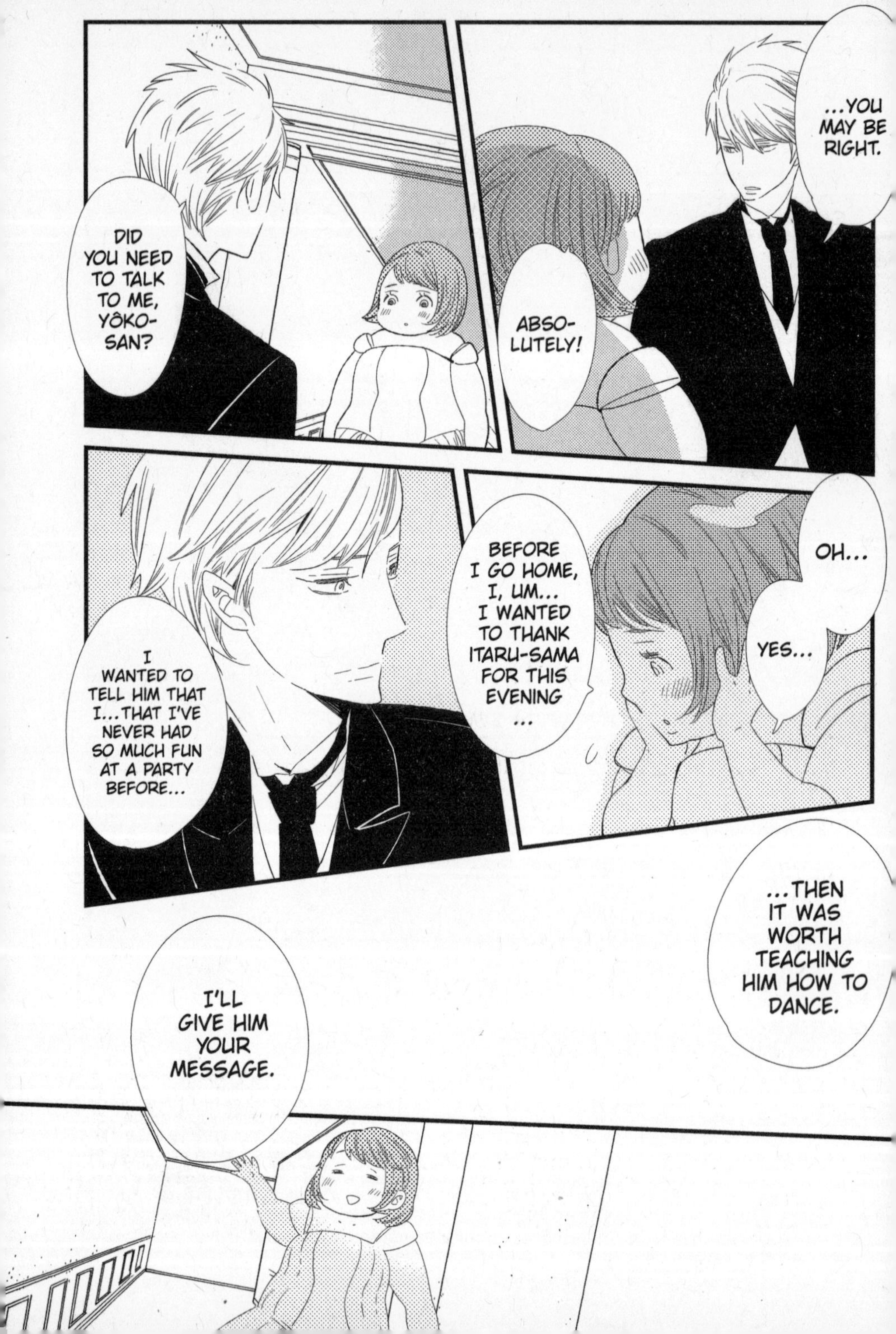
...YOU MAY BE RIGHT.
ABSO-LUTELY!
DID YOU NEED TO TALK TO ME, YÔKO-SAN?
OH...
YES...
BEFORE I GO HOME, I, UM... I WANTED TO THANK ITARU-SAMA FOR THIS EVENING...
I WANTED TO TELL HIM THAT I...THAT I'VE NEVER HAD SO MUCH FUN AT A PARTY BEFORE...
...THEN IT WAS WORTH TEACHING HIM HOW TO DANCE.
I'LL GIVE HIM YOUR MESSAGE.

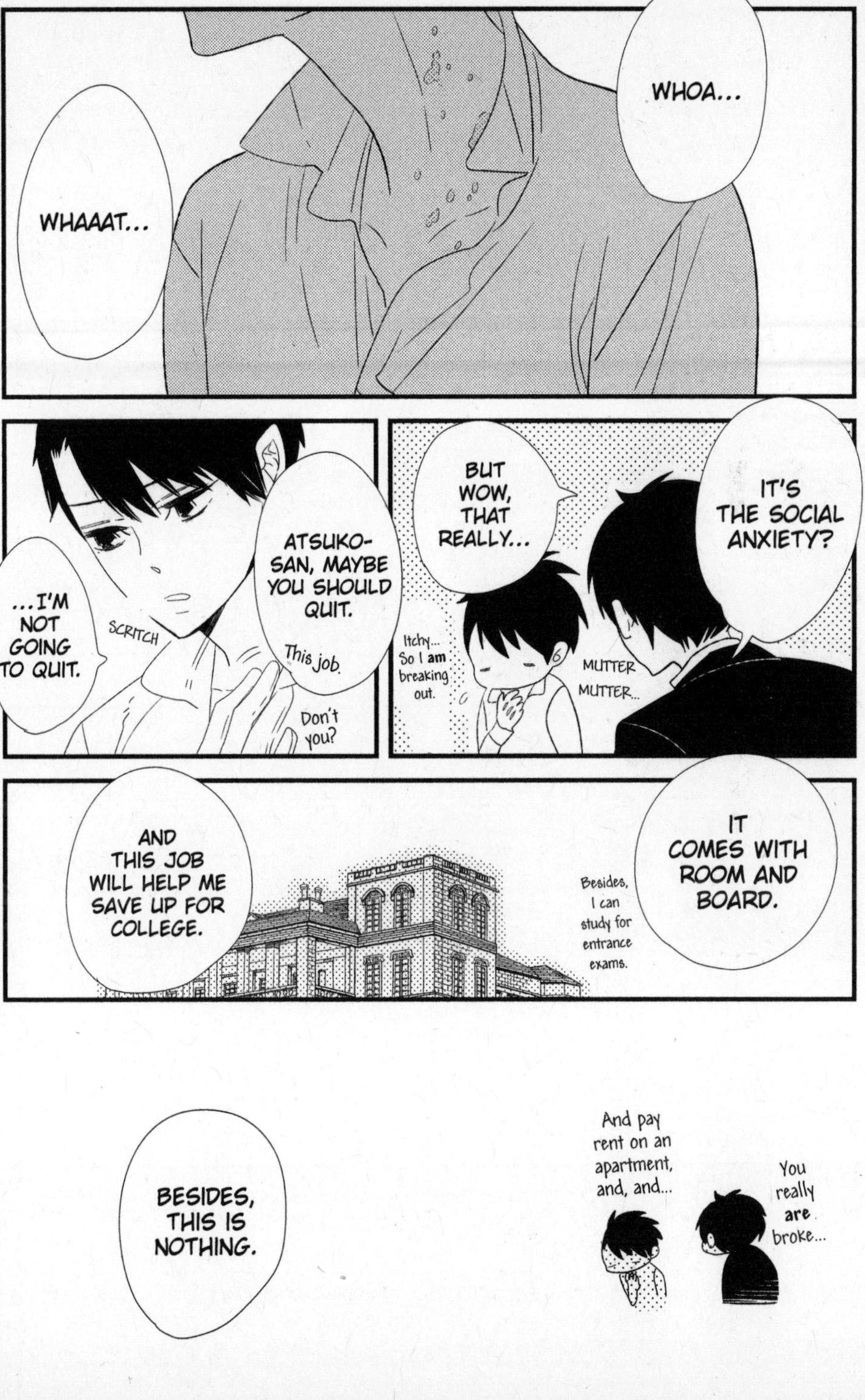
WHOA...
WHAAAT...
IT'S THE SOCIAL ANXIETY?
MUTTER MUTTER...
BUT WOW, THAT REALLY...
Itchy... So I am breaking out.
ATSUKO-SAN, MAYBE YOU SHOULD QUIT.
This job.
Don't you?
SCRITCH
...I'M NOT GOING TO QUIT.
IT COMES WITH ROOM AND BOARD.
Besides, I can study for entrance exams.
AND THIS JOB WILL HELP ME SAVE UP FOR COLLEGE.
You really are broke...
And pay rent on an apartment, and, and...
BESIDES, THIS IS NOTHING.

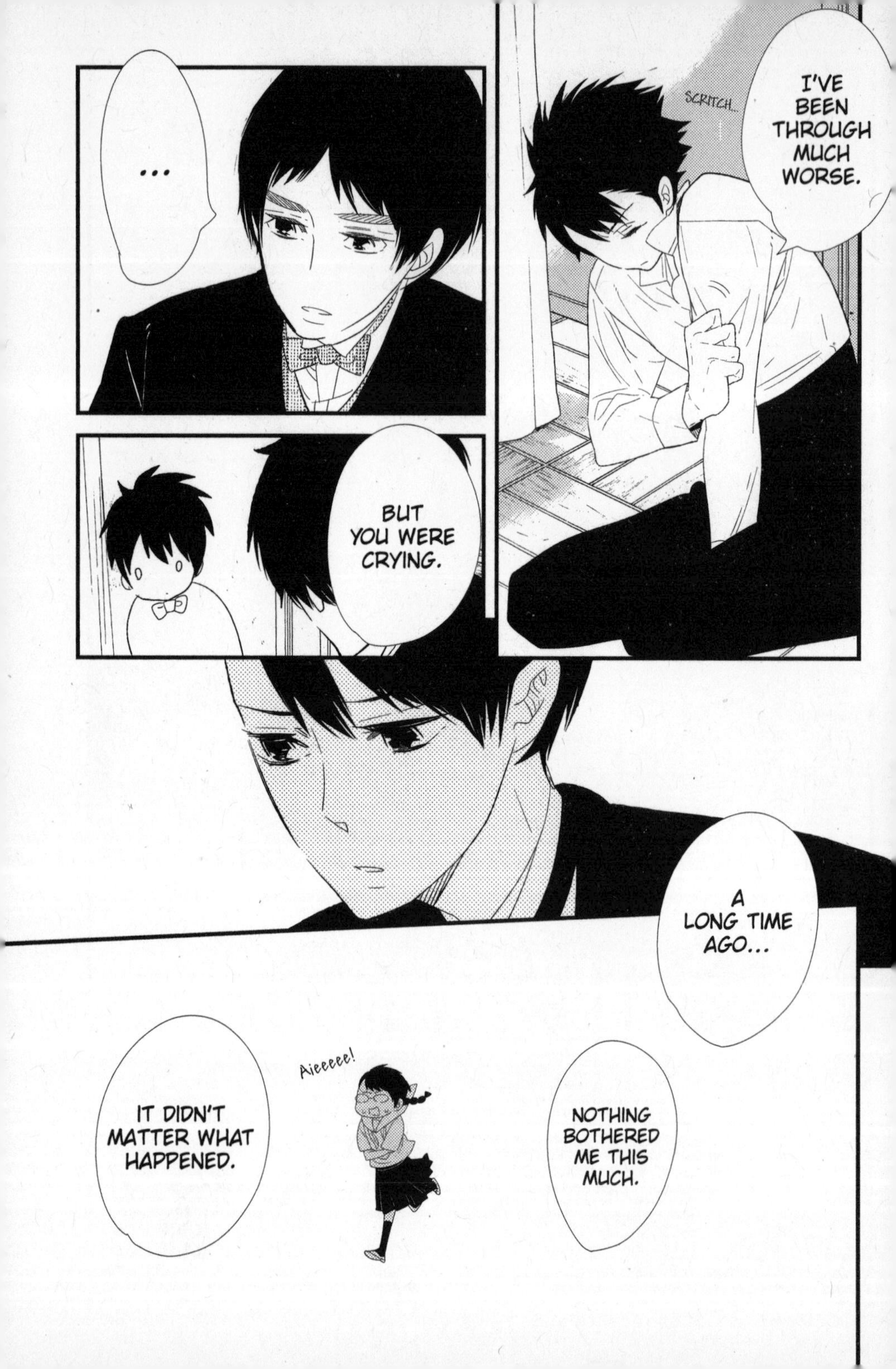
I'VE BEEN THROUGH MUCH WORSE.
SCRITCH...
...
BUT YOU WERE CRYING.
A LONG TIME AGO...
NOTHING BOTHERED ME THIS MUCH.
Aieeeee!
IT DIDN'T MATTER WHAT HAPPENED.

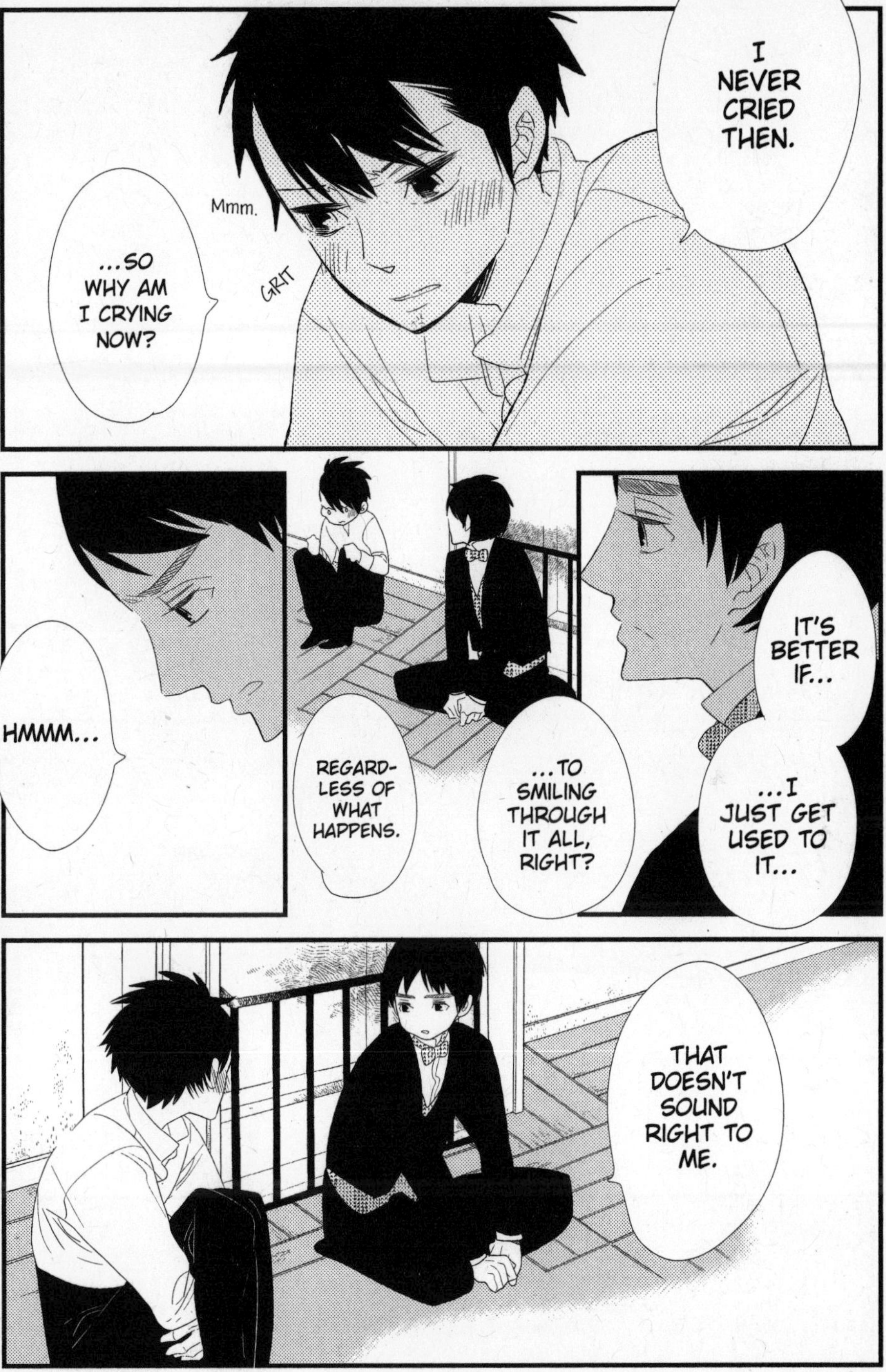
I NEVER CRIED THEN.
Mmm.
GRIT
...SO WHY AM I CRYING NOW?
IT'S BETTER IF...
...I JUST GET USED TO IT...
...TO SMILING THROUGH IT ALL, RIGHT?
REGARDLESS OF WHAT HAPPENS.
HMMM...
THAT DOESN'T SOUND RIGHT TO ME.

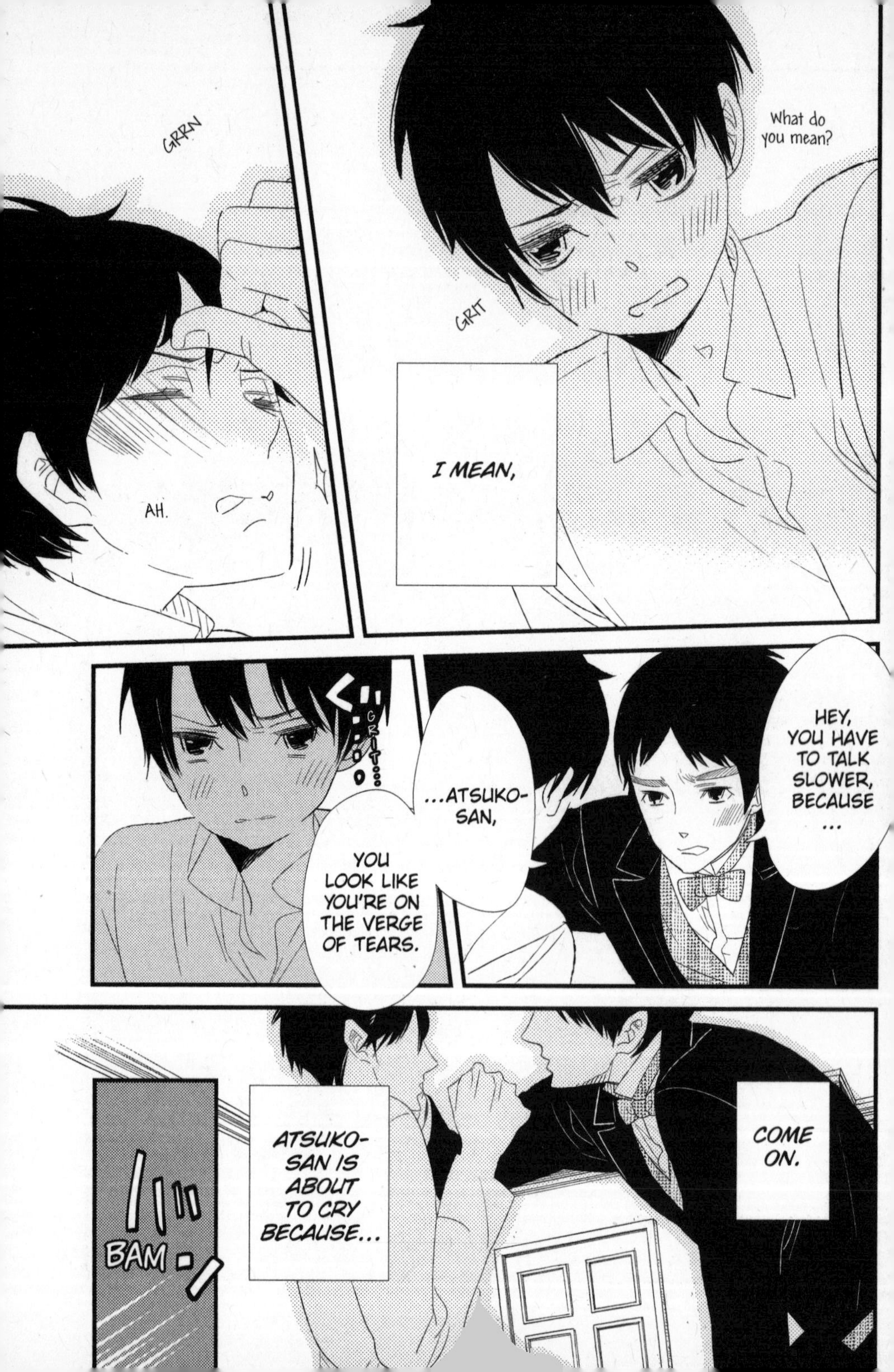
What do you mean?
GRIT
I MEAN,
GRRN
AH.
HEY, YOU HAVE TO TALK SLOWER, BECAUSE ...
...ATSUKO-SAN,
YOU LOOK LIKE YOU'RE ON THE VERGE OF TEARS.
GRIT...
COME ON.
ATSUKO-SAN IS ABOUT TO CRY BECAUSE...
BAM

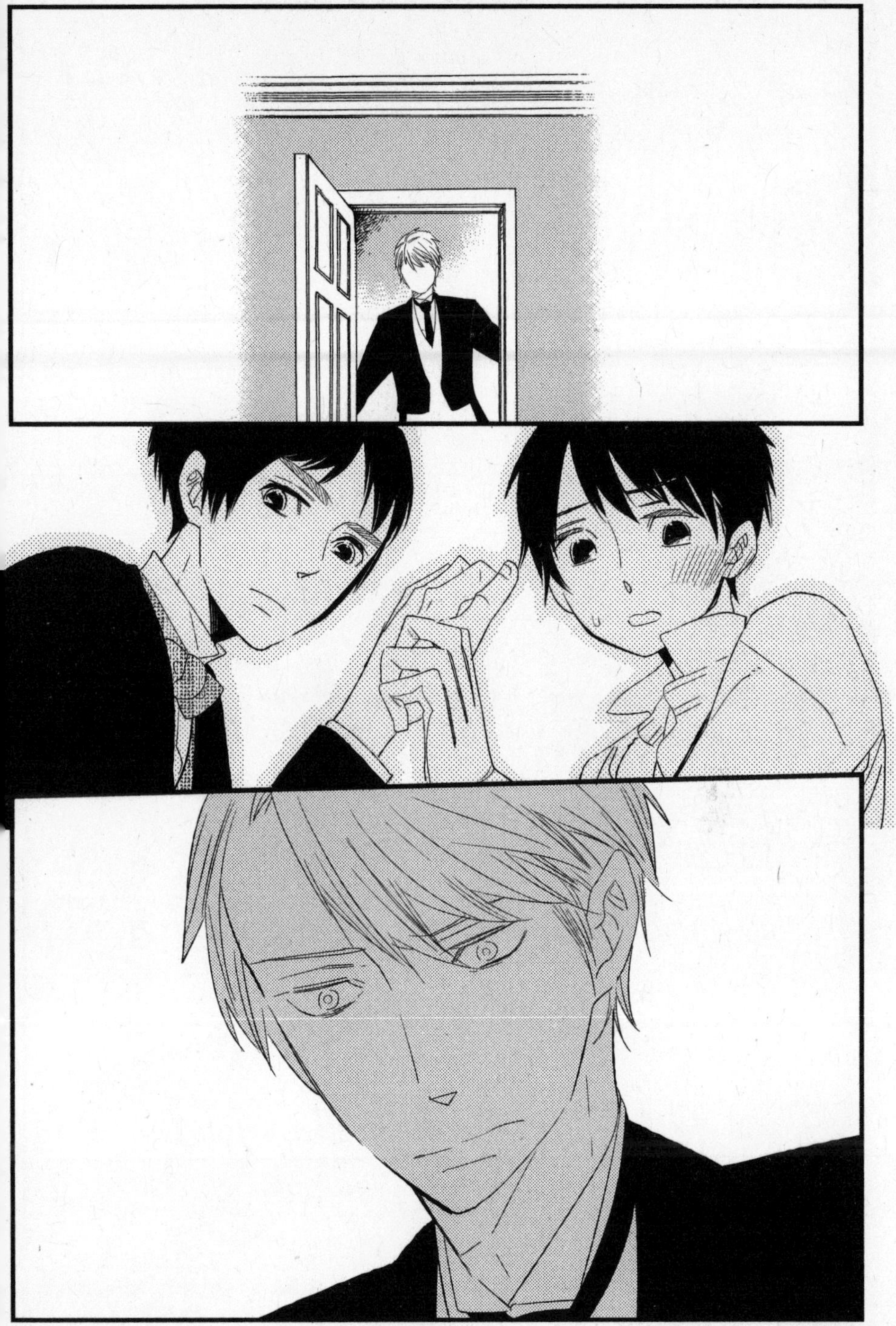

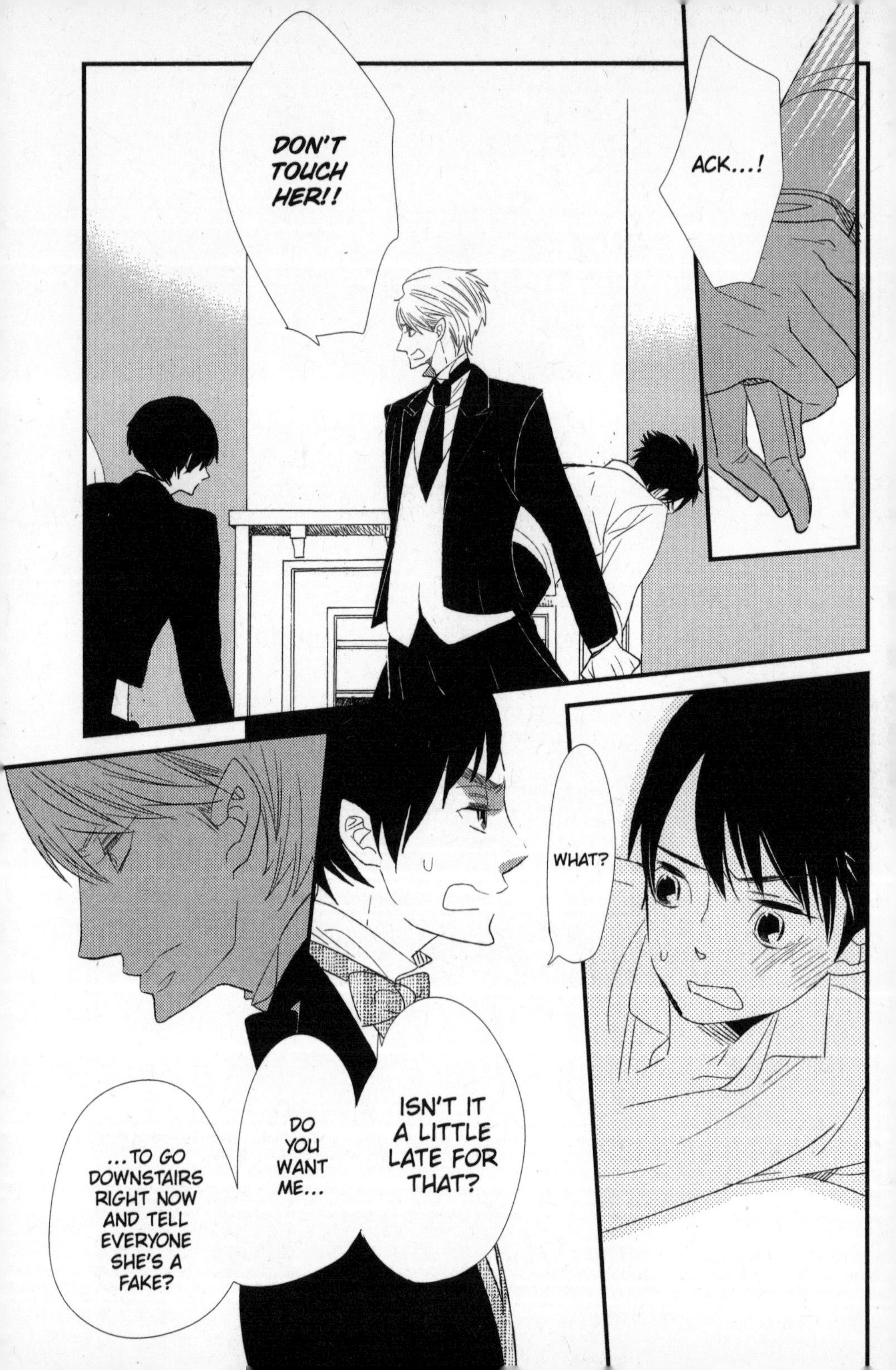
ACK...!
DON'T TOUCH HER!!
WHAT?
ISN'T IT A LITTLE LATE FOR THAT?
DO YOU WANT ME...
...TO GO DOWNSTAIRS RIGHT NOW AND TELL EVERYONE SHE'S A FAKE?

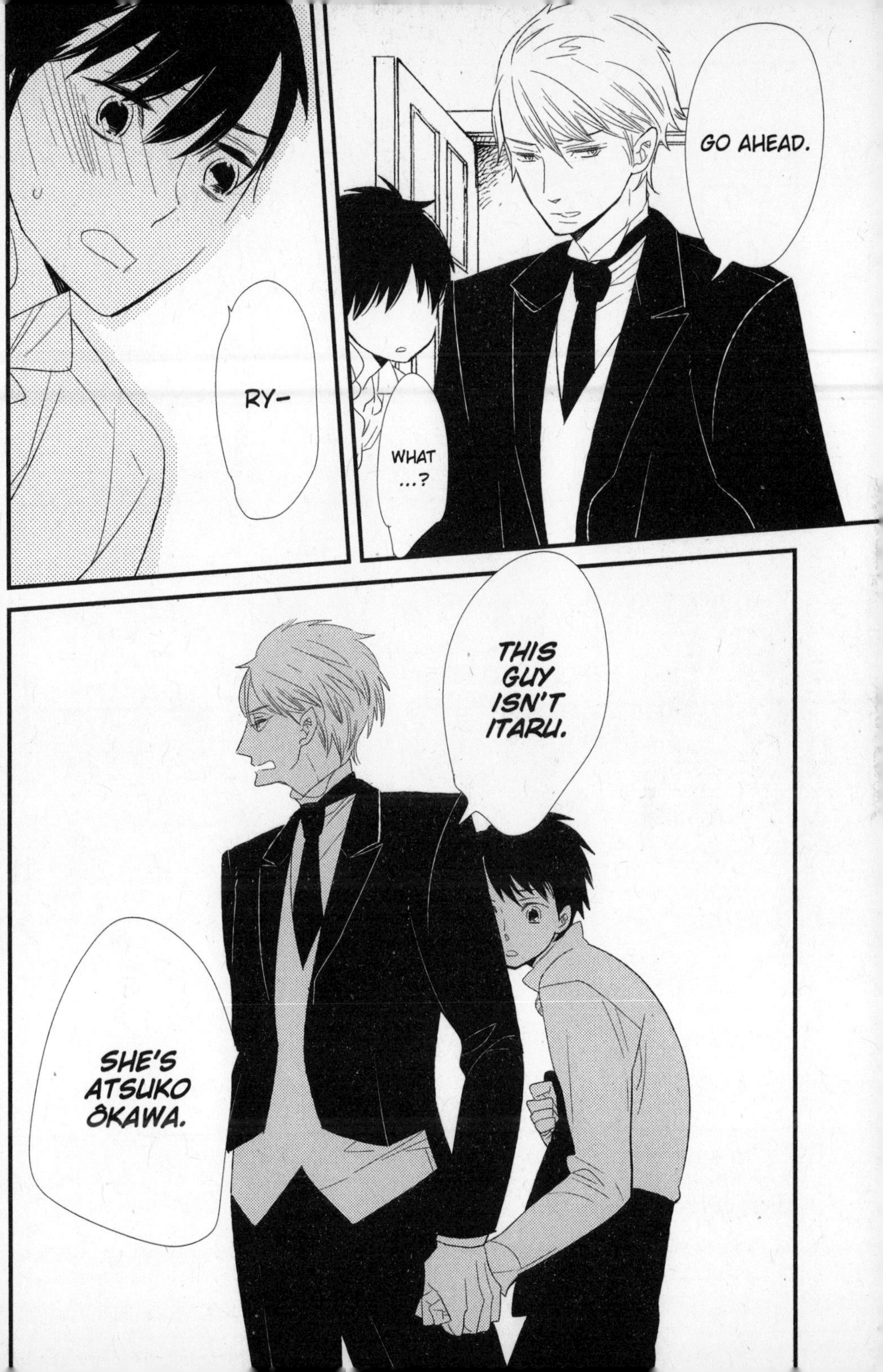
GO AHEAD.
WHAT ...?
RY-
THIS GUY ISN'T ITARU.
SHE'S ATSUKO ŌKAWA.

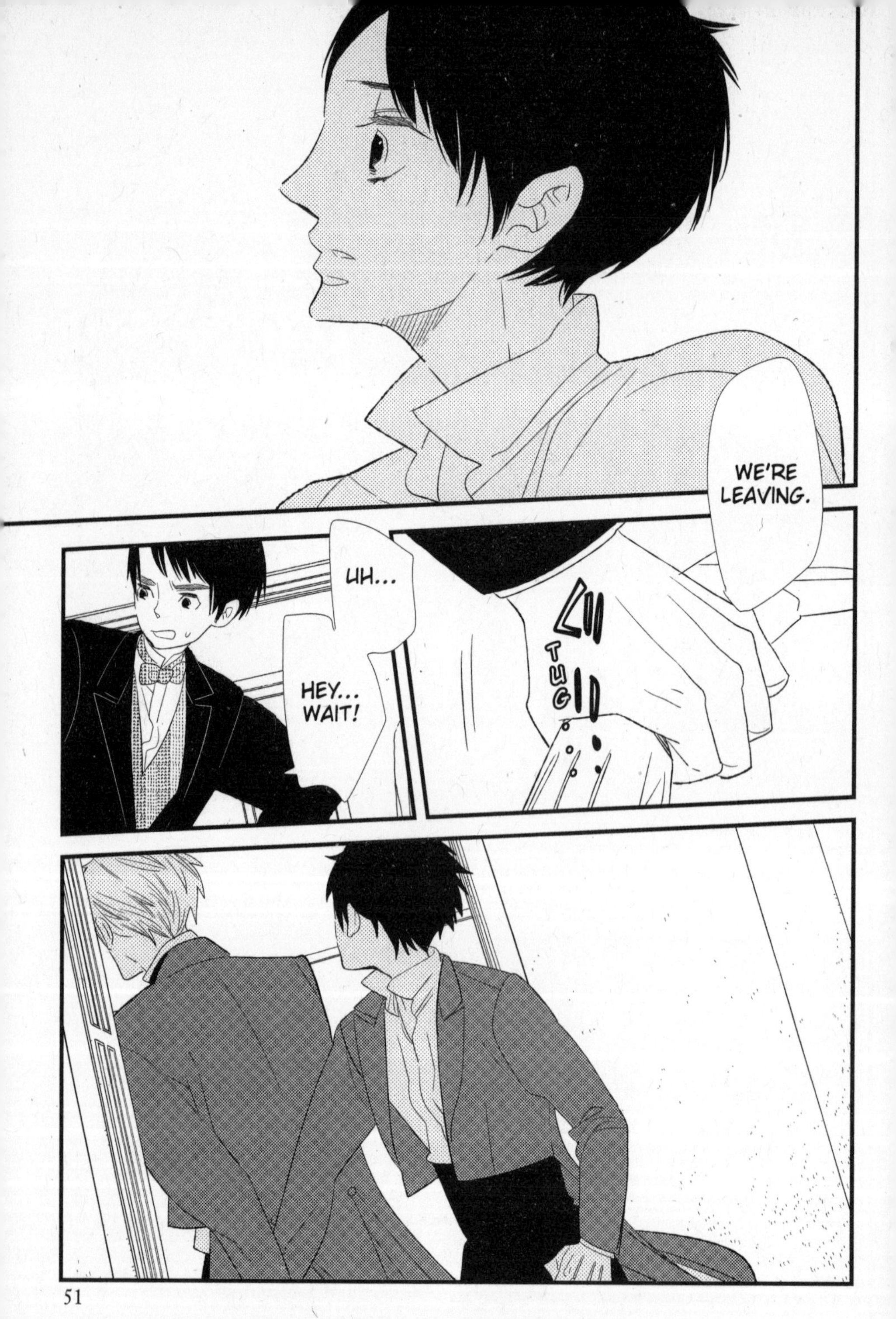
WE'RE LEAVING.
TUG
UH...
HEY... WAIT!

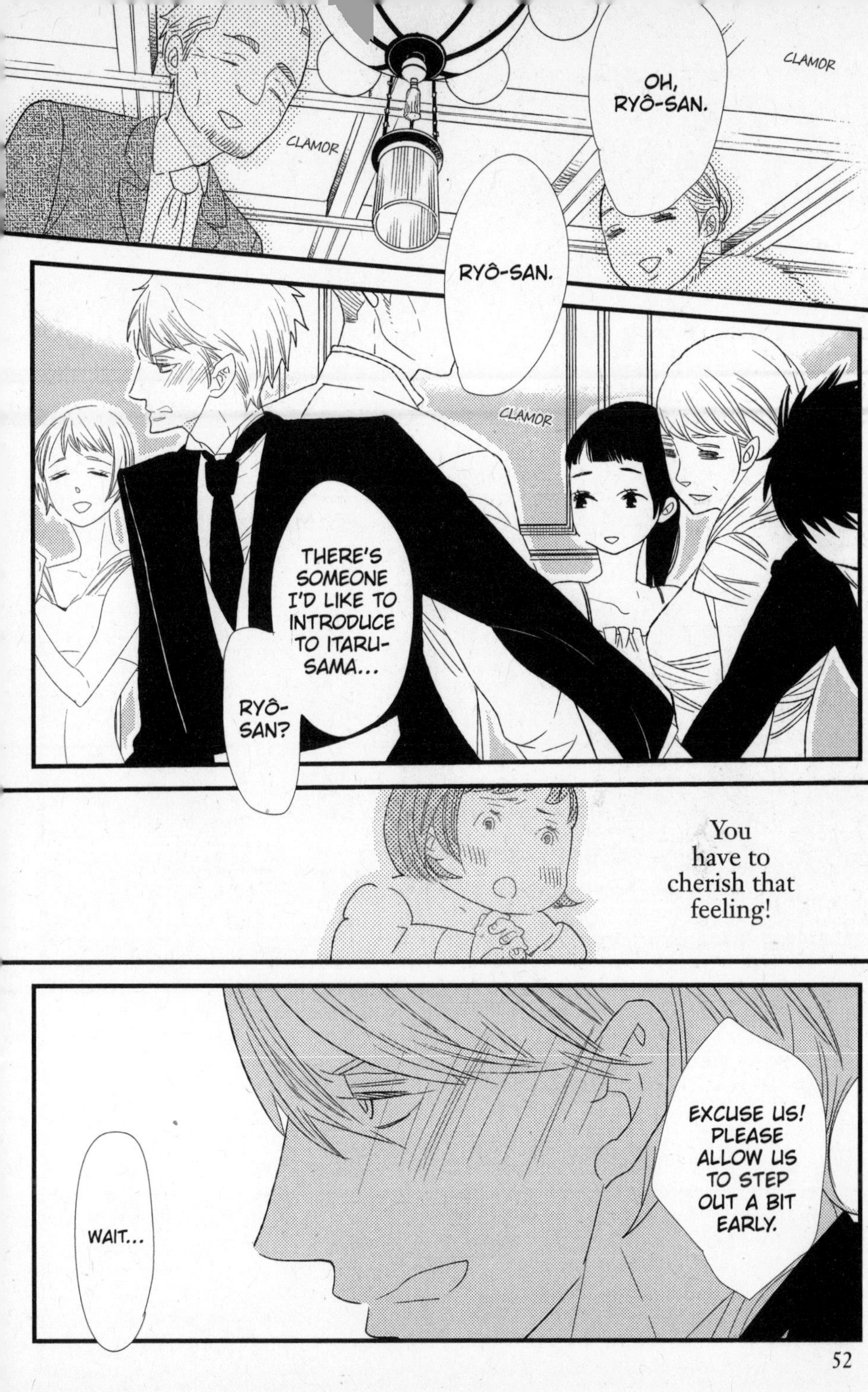
CLAMOR
OH, RYÔ-SAN.
RYÔ-SAN.
CLAMOR
CLAMOR
THERE'S SOMEONE I'D LIKE TO INTRODUCE TO ITARU-SAMA...
RYÔ-SAN?
You have to cherish that feeling!
EXCUSE US! PLEASE ALLOW US TO STEP OUT A BIT EARLY.
WAIT...

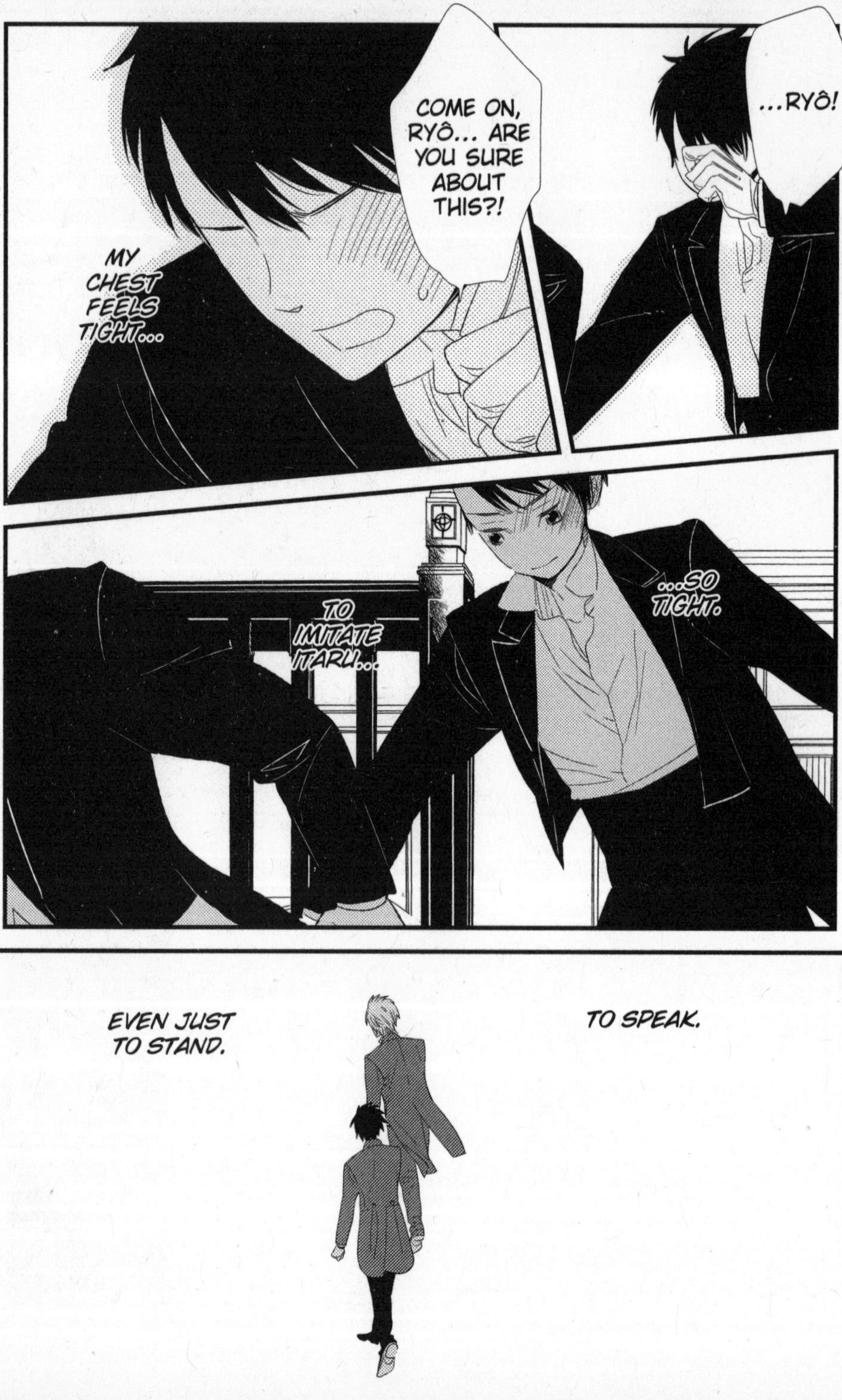
...RYÔ!
COME ON, RYÔ... ARE YOU SURE ABOUT THIS?!
MY CHEST FEELS TIGHT...
...SO TIGHT.
TO IMITATE ITARU...
TO SPEAK.
EVEN JUST TO STAND.

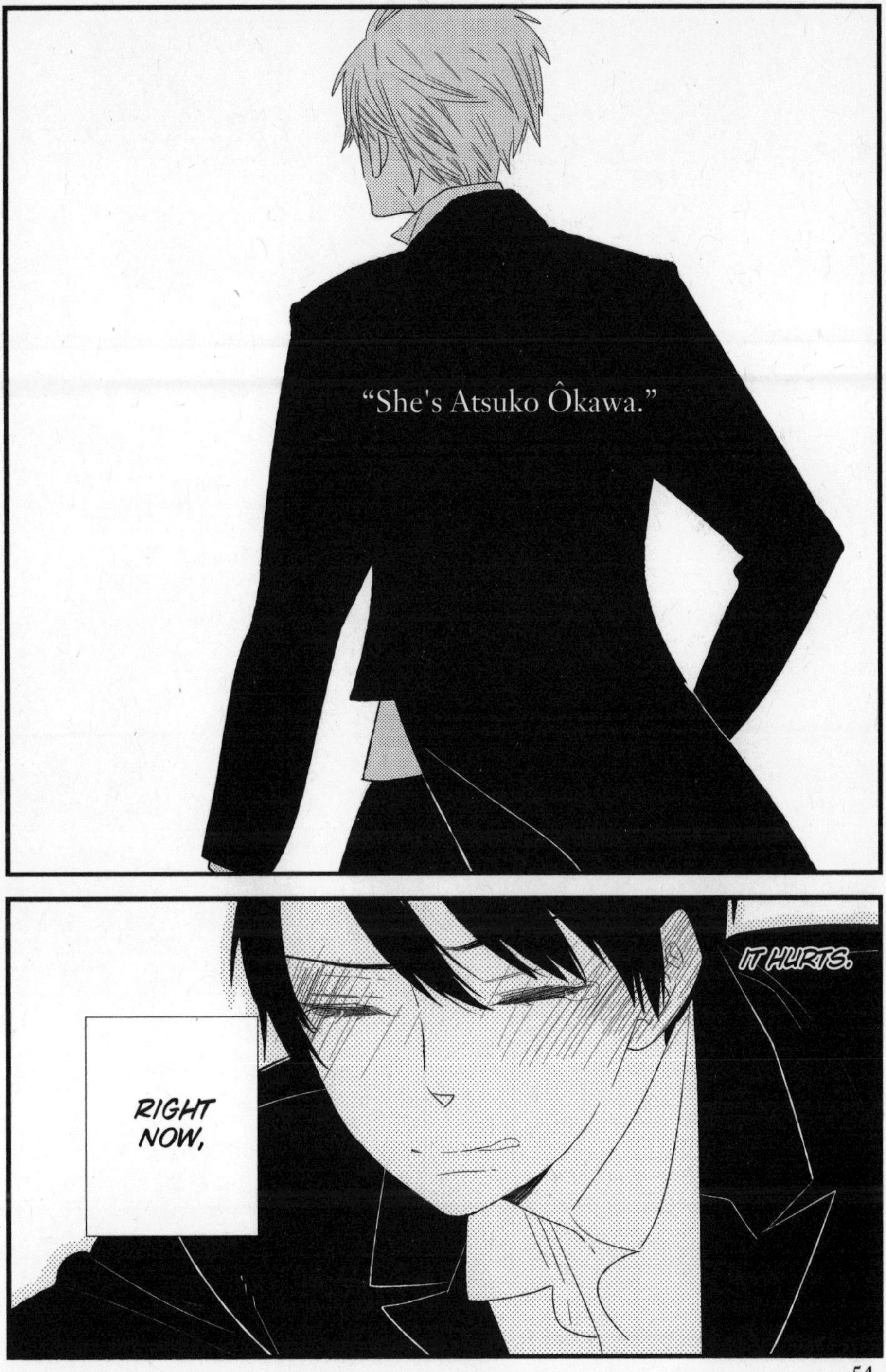
"She's Atsuko Ôkawa."
IT HURTS.
RIGHT NOW,

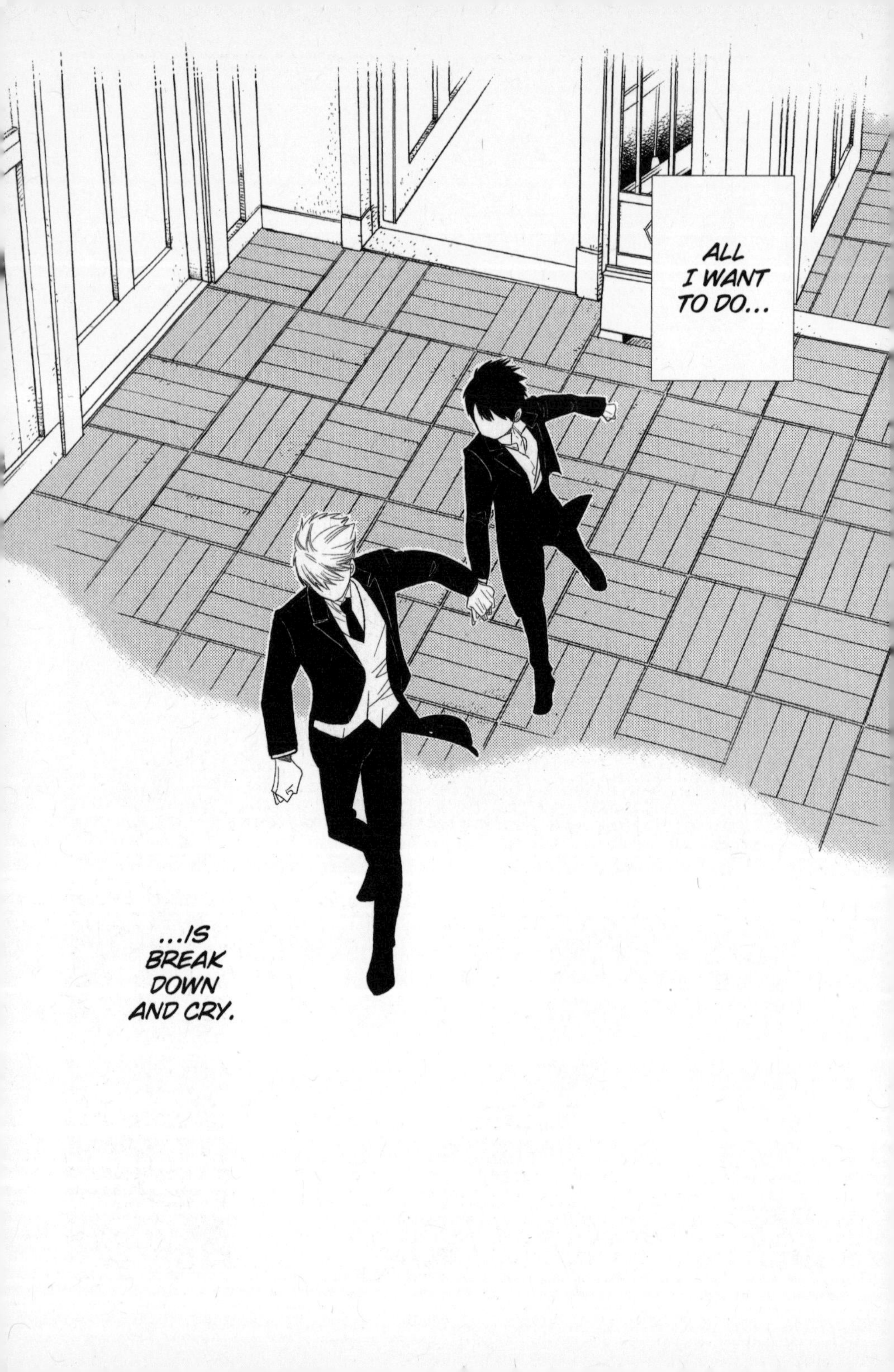
ALL I WANT TO DO...
...IS BREAK DOWN AND CRY.

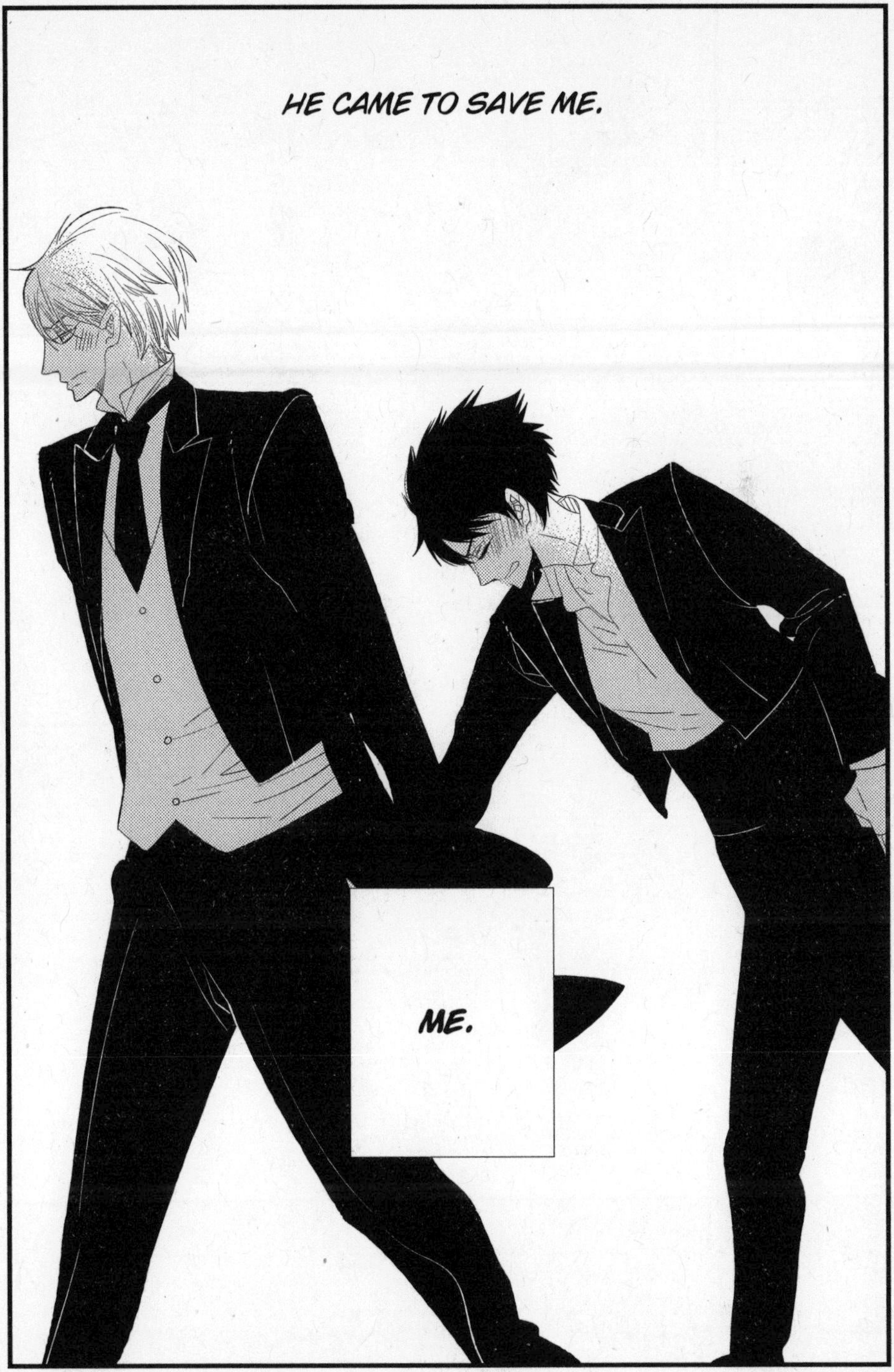
HE CAME TO SAVE ME.
ME.

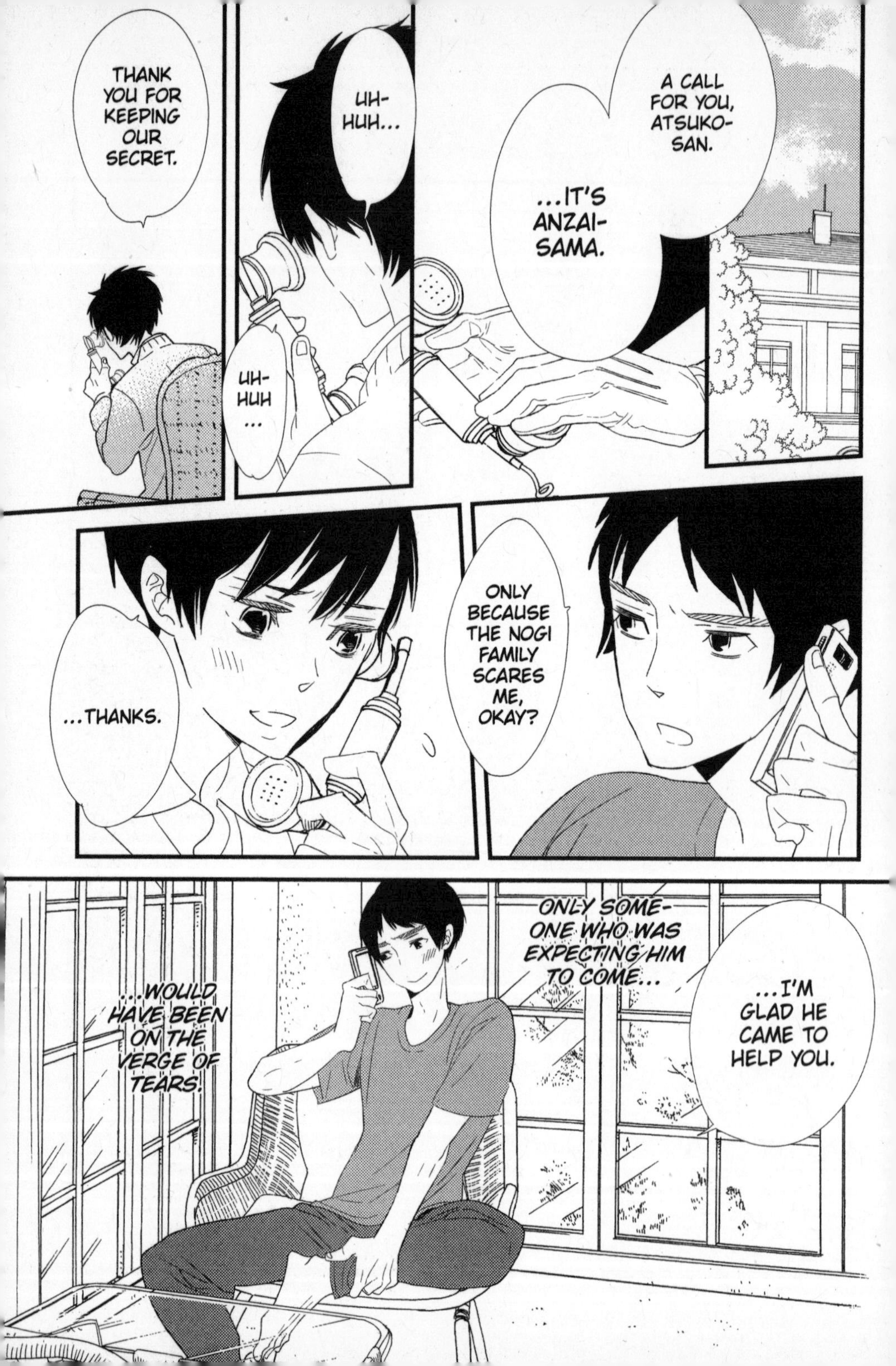
A CALL FOR YOU, ATSUKO-SAN.
...IT'S ANZAI-SAMA.
UH-HUH...
UH-HUH ...
THANK YOU FOR KEEPING OUR SECRET.
ONLY BECAUSE THE NOGI FAMILY SCARES ME, OKAY?
...THANKS.
...I'M GLAD HE CAME TO HELP YOU.
ONLY SOME-ONE WHO WAS EXPECTING HIM TO COME...
...WOULD HAVE BEEN ON THE VERGE OF TEARS.

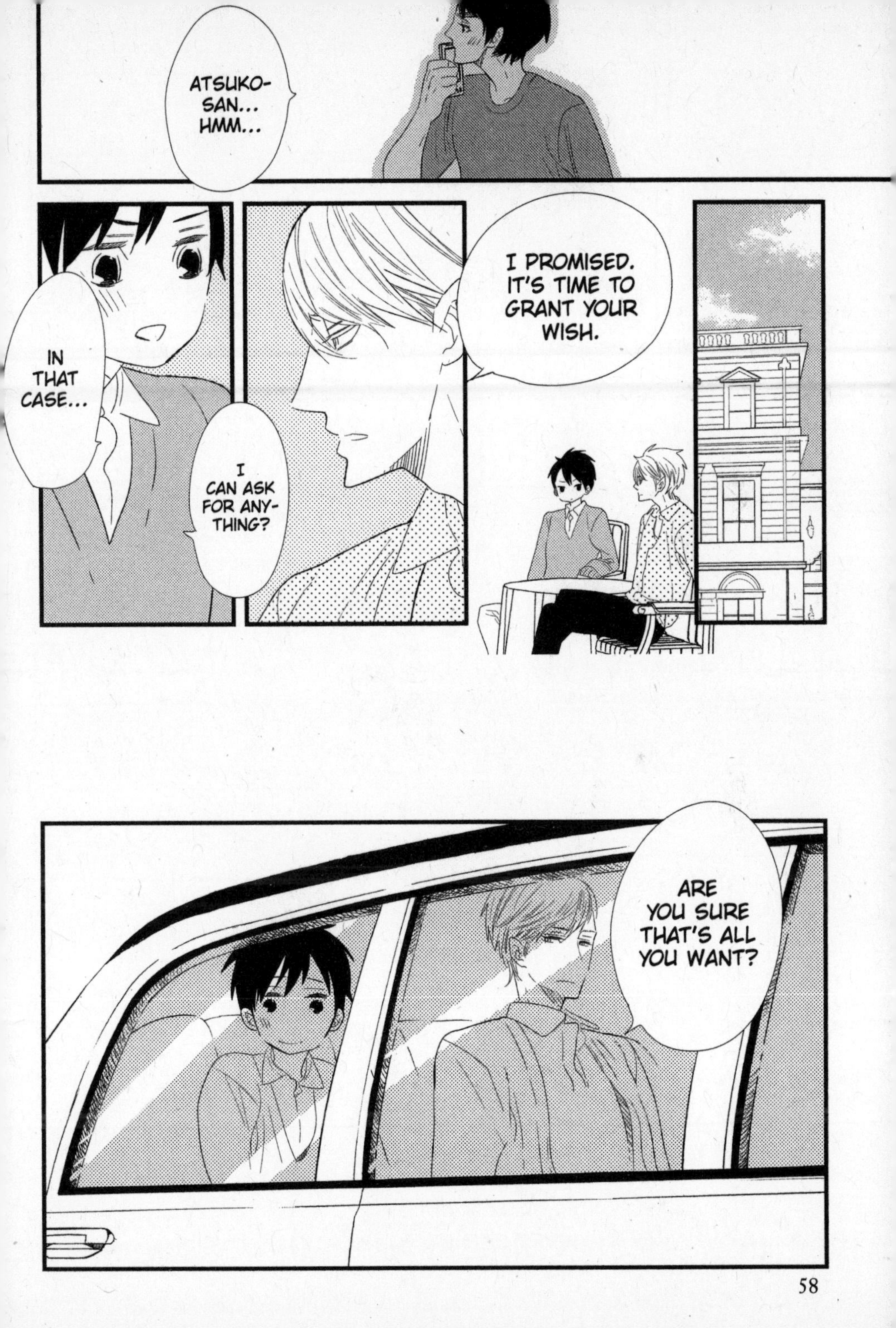
ATSUKO-SAN... HMM...
I PROMISED. IT'S TIME TO GRANT YOUR WISH.
I CAN ASK FOR ANYTHING?
IN THAT CASE...
ARE YOU SURE THAT'S ALL YOU WANT?

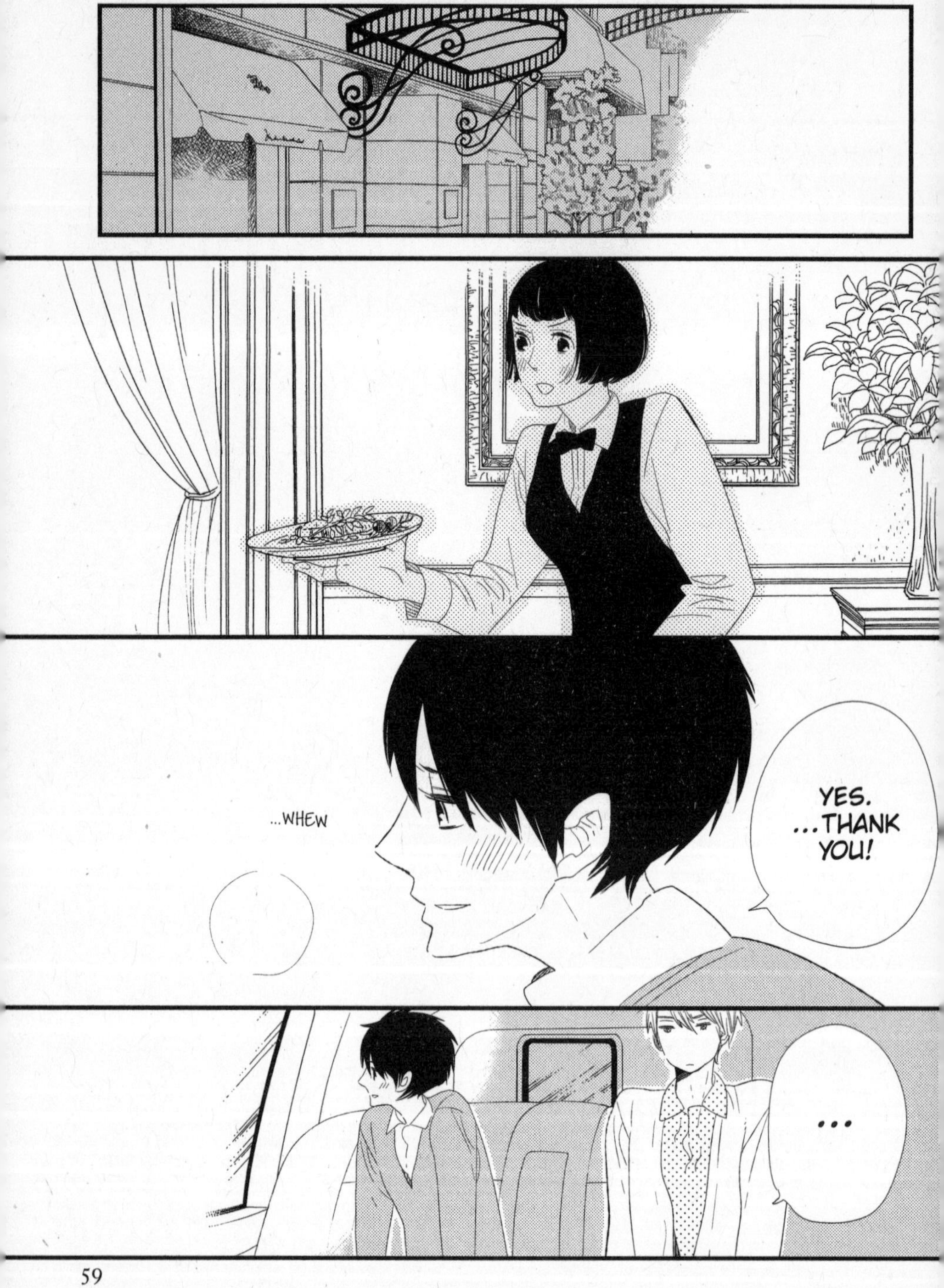
YES. ...THANK YOU!
...WHEW
...

the prince in his dark days
nico yamanaka

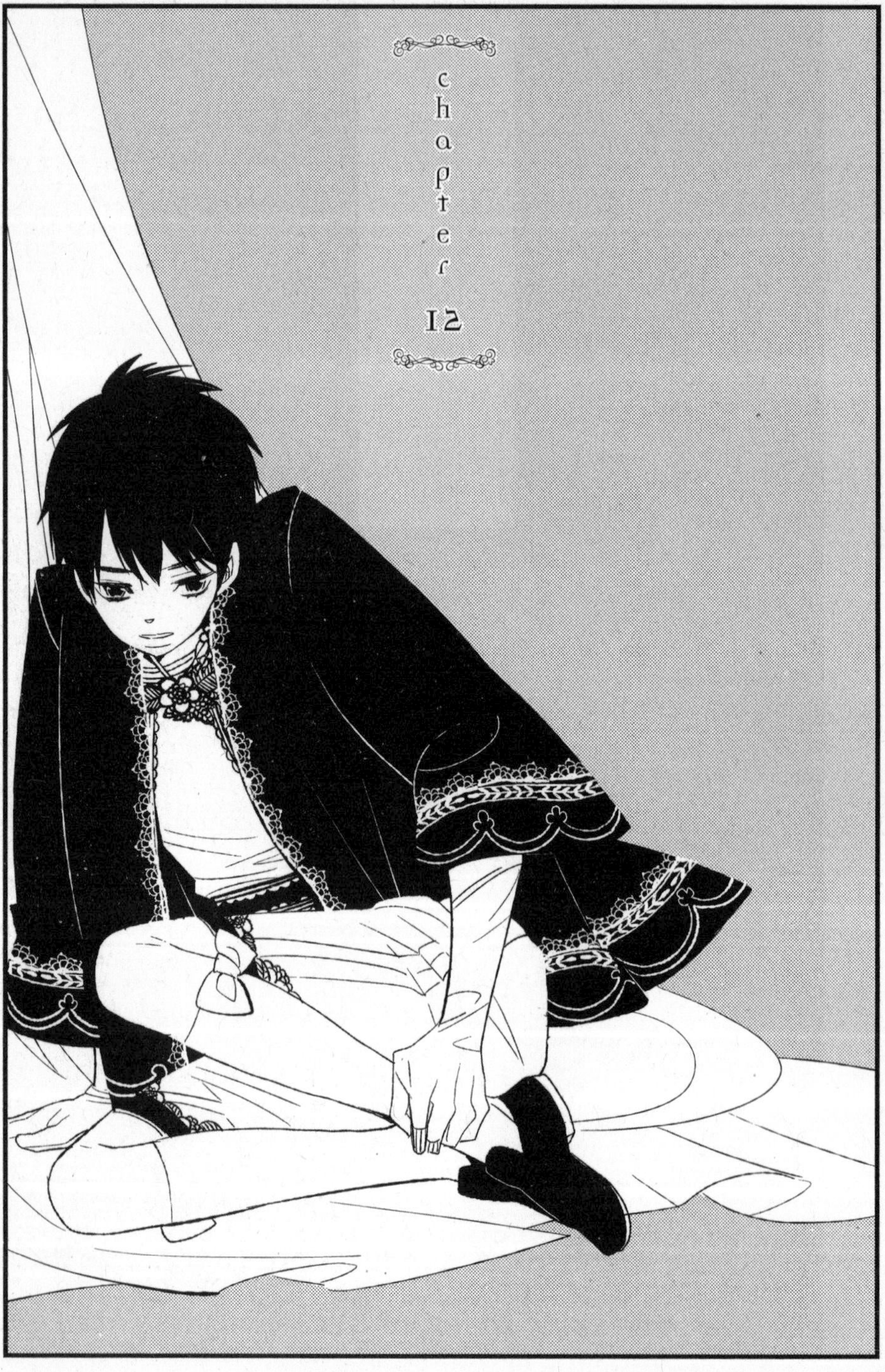
chapter 12

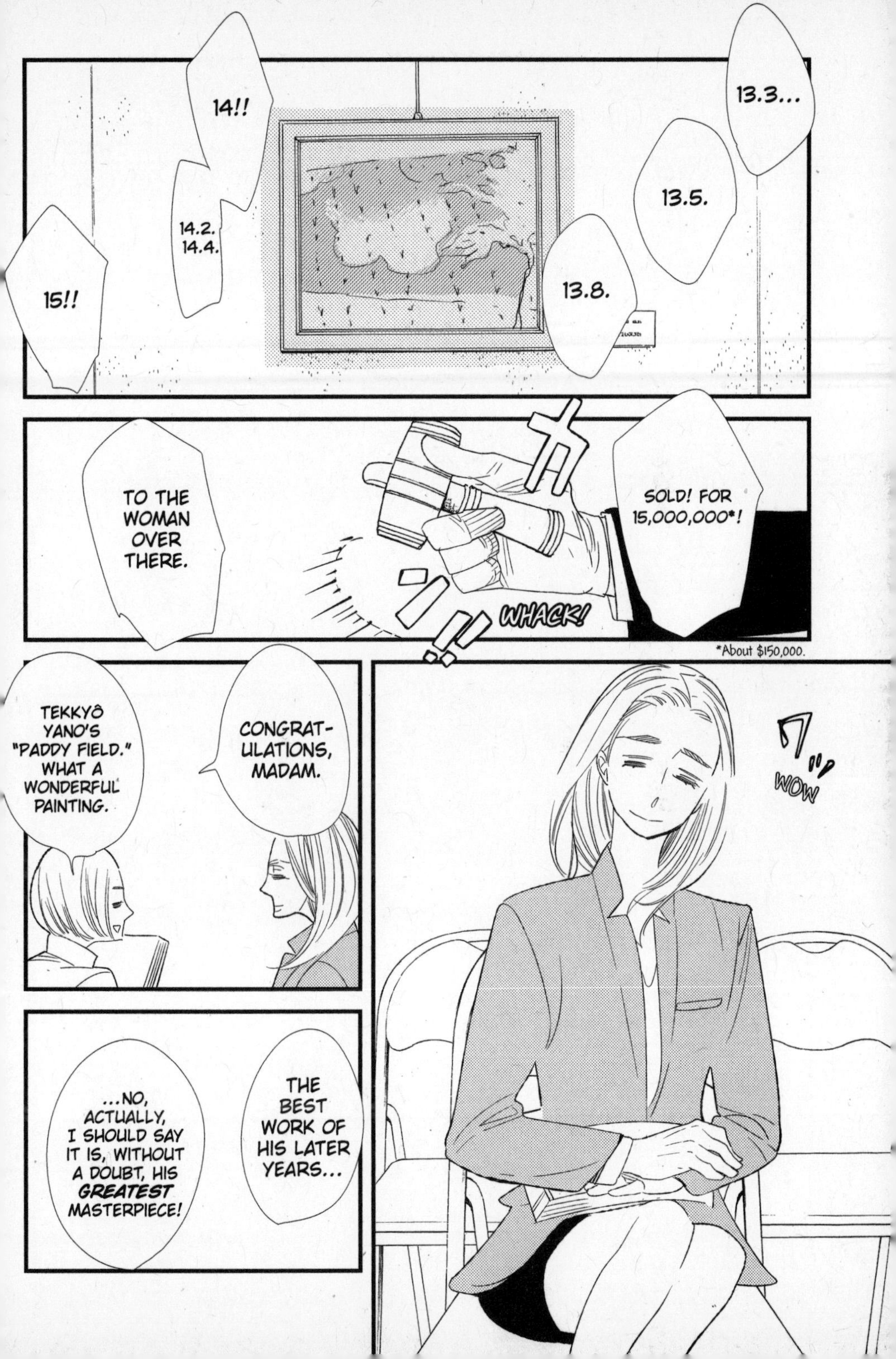
13.3...
13.5.
13.8.
14.2. 14.4.
14!!
15!!
SOLD! FOR 15,000,000*!
WHACK!
TO THE WOMAN OVER THERE.
WOW
CONGRATULATIONS, MADAM.
TEKKYÔ YANO'S "PADDY FIELD." WHAT A WONDERFUL PAINTING.
THE BEST WORK OF HIS LATER YEARS...
...NO, ACTUALLY, I SHOULD SAY IT IS, WITHOUT A DOUBT, HIS *GREATEST* MASTERPIECE!

*About $150,000.

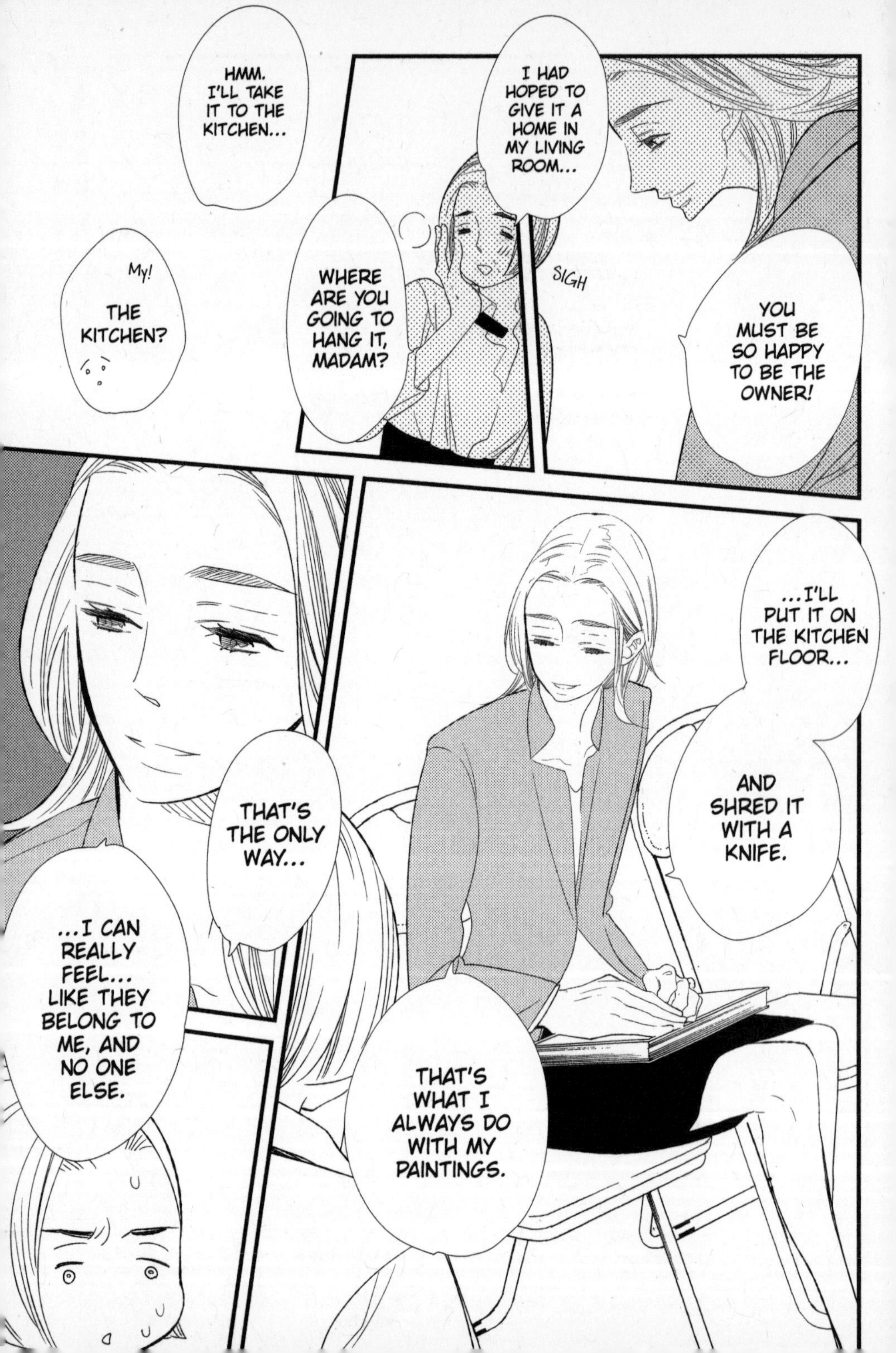
YOU MUST BE SO HAPPY TO BE THE OWNER!
I HAD HOPED TO GIVE IT A HOME IN MY LIVING ROOM...
SIGH
WHERE ARE YOU GOING TO HANG IT, MADAM?
HMM. I'LL TAKE IT TO THE KITCHEN...
My!
THE KITCHEN?
...I'LL PUT IT ON THE KITCHEN FLOOR...
AND SHRED IT WITH A KNIFE.
THAT'S WHAT I ALWAYS DO WITH MY PAINTINGS.
THAT'S THE ONLY WAY...
...I CAN REALLY FEEL... LIKE THEY BELONG TO ME, AND NO ONE ELSE.

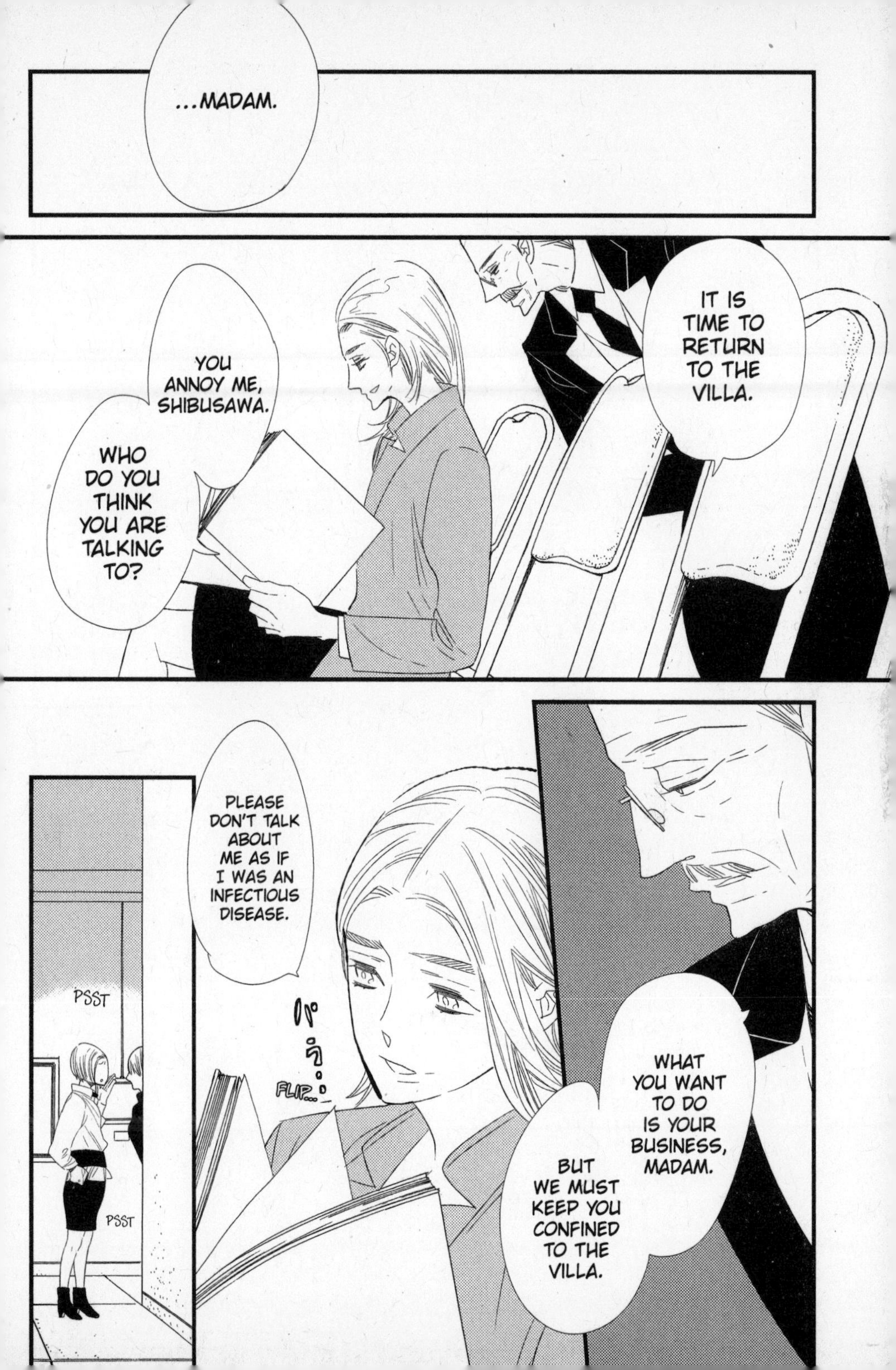
...MADAM.
IT IS TIME TO RETURN TO THE VILLA.
YOU ANNOY ME, SHIBUSAWA.
WHO DO YOU THINK YOU ARE TALKING TO?
WHAT YOU WANT TO DO IS YOUR BUSINESS, MADAM.
BUT WE MUST KEEP YOU CONFINED TO THE VILLA.
PLEASE DON'T TALK ABOUT ME AS IF I WAS AN INFECTIOUS DISEASE.
FLIP...
PSST
PSST

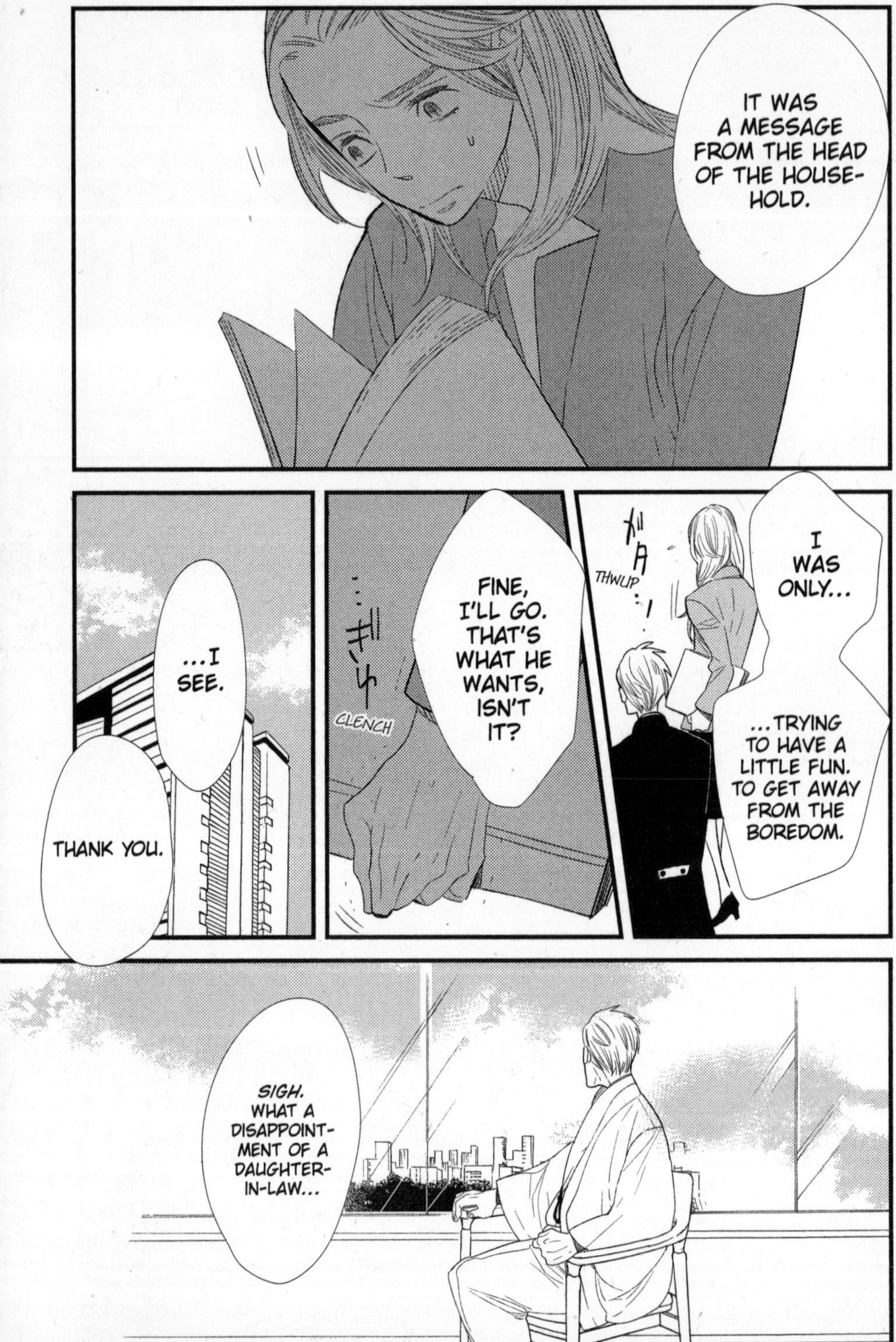
IT WAS A MESSAGE FROM THE HEAD OF THE HOUSE-HOLD.
THWUP
I WAS ONLY...
...TRYING TO HAVE A LITTLE FUN. TO GET AWAY FROM THE BOREDOM.
CLENCH
FINE, I'LL GO. THAT'S WHAT HE WANTS, ISN'T IT?
...I SEE.
THANK YOU.
SIGH. WHAT A DISAPPOINT-MENT OF A DAUGHTER-IN-LAW...

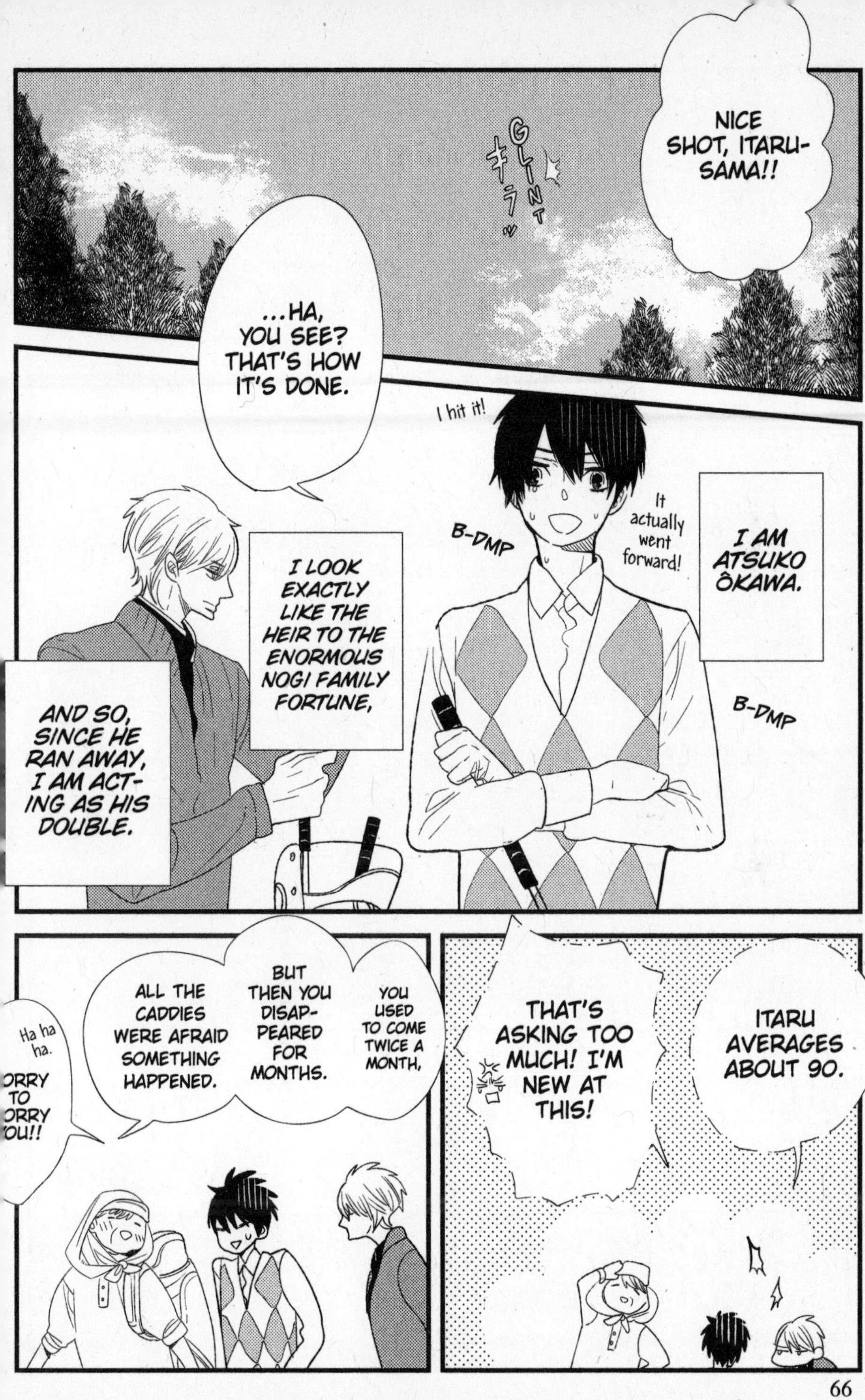
NICE SHOT, ITARU-SAMA!!
GLINT
...HA, YOU SEE? THAT'S HOW IT'S DONE.
I hit it!
It actually went forward!
B-DMP
B-DMP
I AM ATSUKO ÔKAWA.
I LOOK EXACTLY LIKE THE HEIR TO THE ENORMOUS NOGI FAMILY FORTUNE,
AND SO, SINCE HE RAN AWAY, I AM ACTING AS HIS DOUBLE.
ITARU AVERAGES ABOUT 90.
THAT'S ASKING TOO MUCH! I'M NEW AT THIS!
YOU USED TO COME TWICE A MONTH,
BUT THEN YOU DISAPPEARED FOR MONTHS.
ALL THE CADDIES WERE AFRAID SOMETHING HAPPENED.
Ha ha ha.

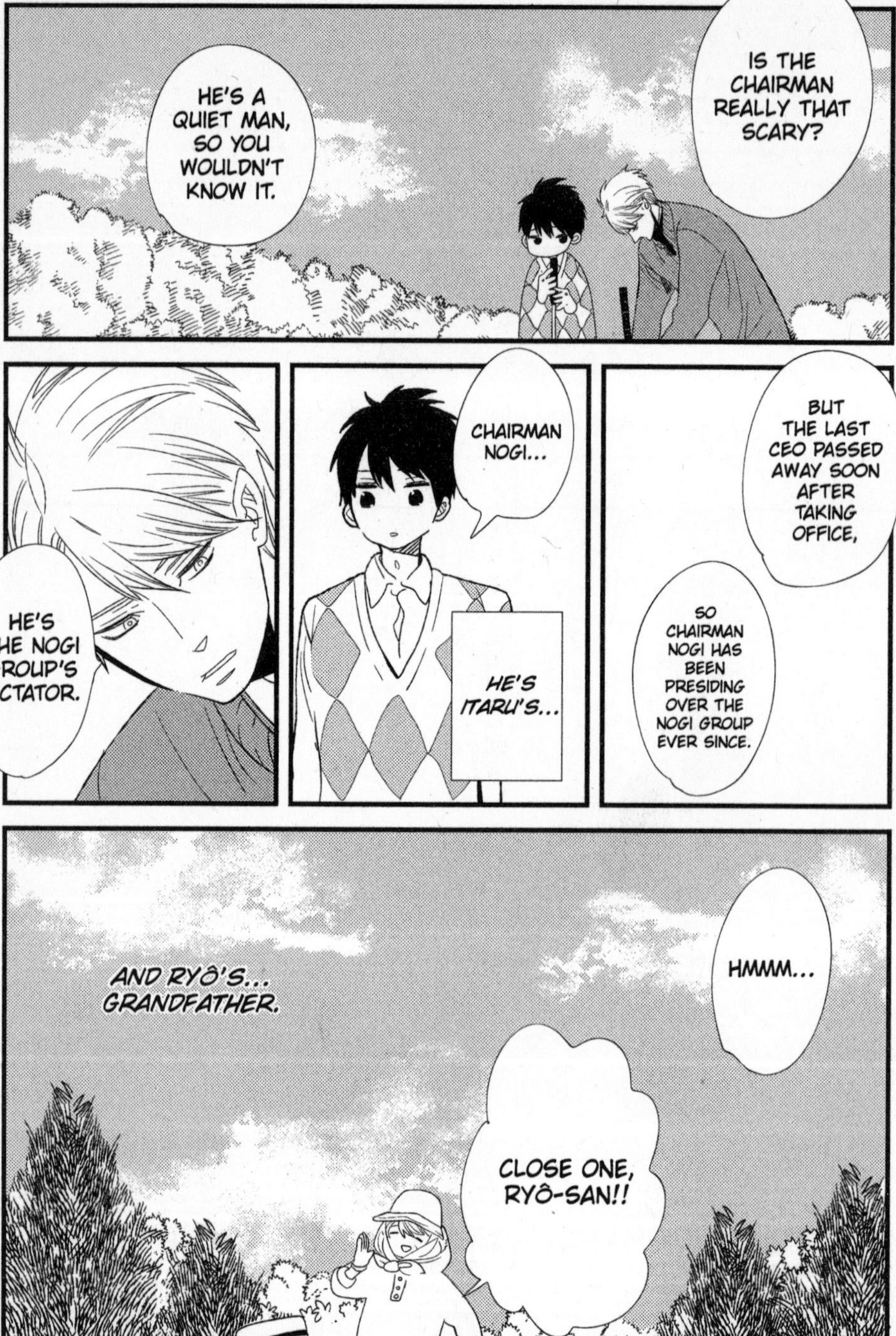
IS THE CHAIRMAN REALLY THAT SCARY?
HE'S A QUIET MAN, SO YOU WOULDN'T KNOW IT.
BUT THE LAST CEO PASSED AWAY SOON AFTER TAKING OFFICE,
SO CHAIRMAN NOGI HAS BEEN PRESIDING OVER THE NOGI GROUP EVER SINCE.
CHAIRMAN NOGI...
HE'S ITARU'S...
HE'S THE NOGI GROUP'S DICTATOR.
HMMM...
AND RYÔ'S... GRANDFATHER.
CLOSE ONE, RYÔ-SAN!!

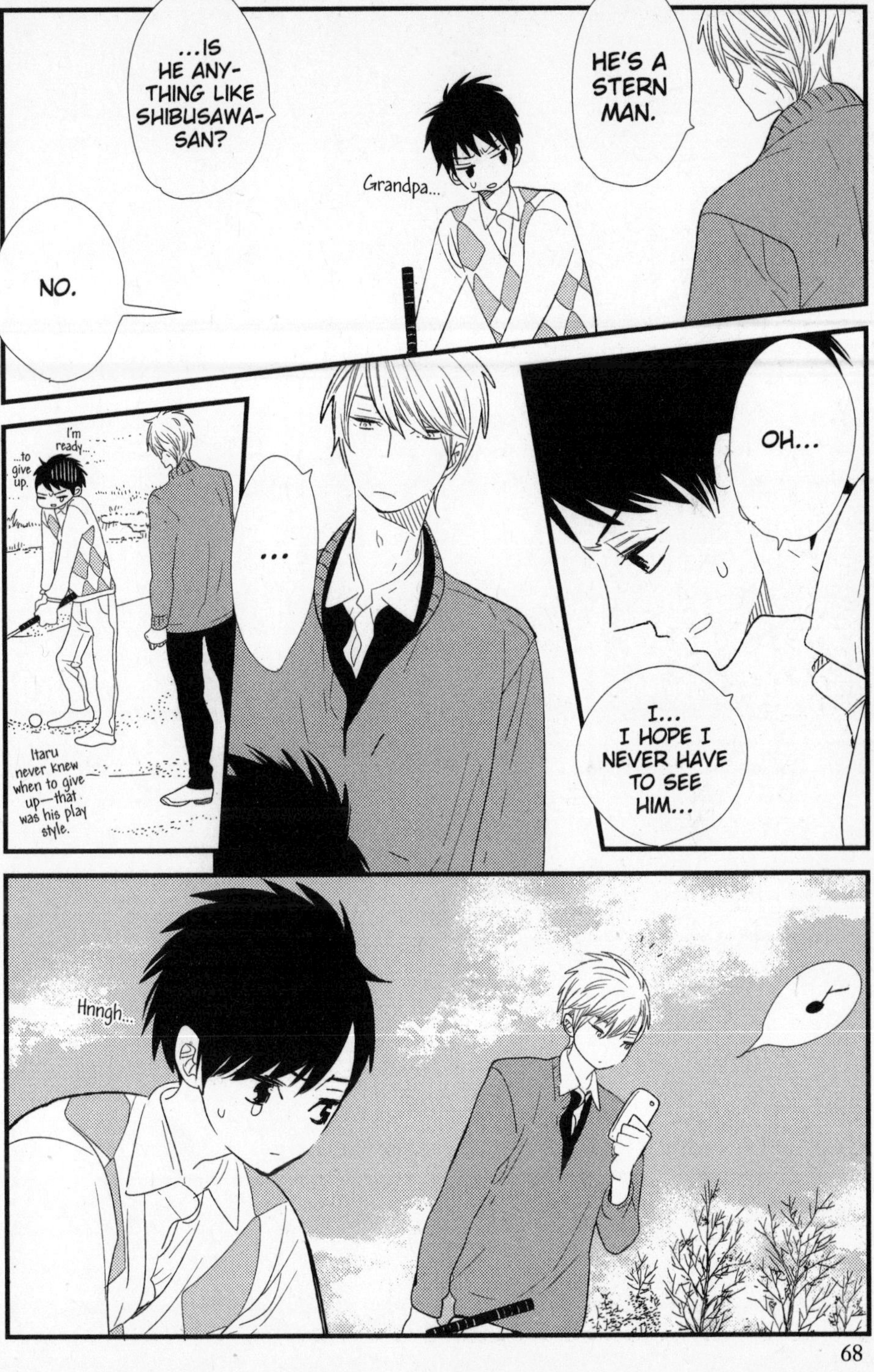
HE'S A STERN MAN.
...IS HE ANY-THING LIKE SHIBUSAWA-SAN?
Grandpa...
NO.
OH...
I... I HOPE I NEVER HAVE TO SEE HIM...
...
I'm ready...
...to give up.
Itaru never knew when to give up—that was his play style.
Hnngh...

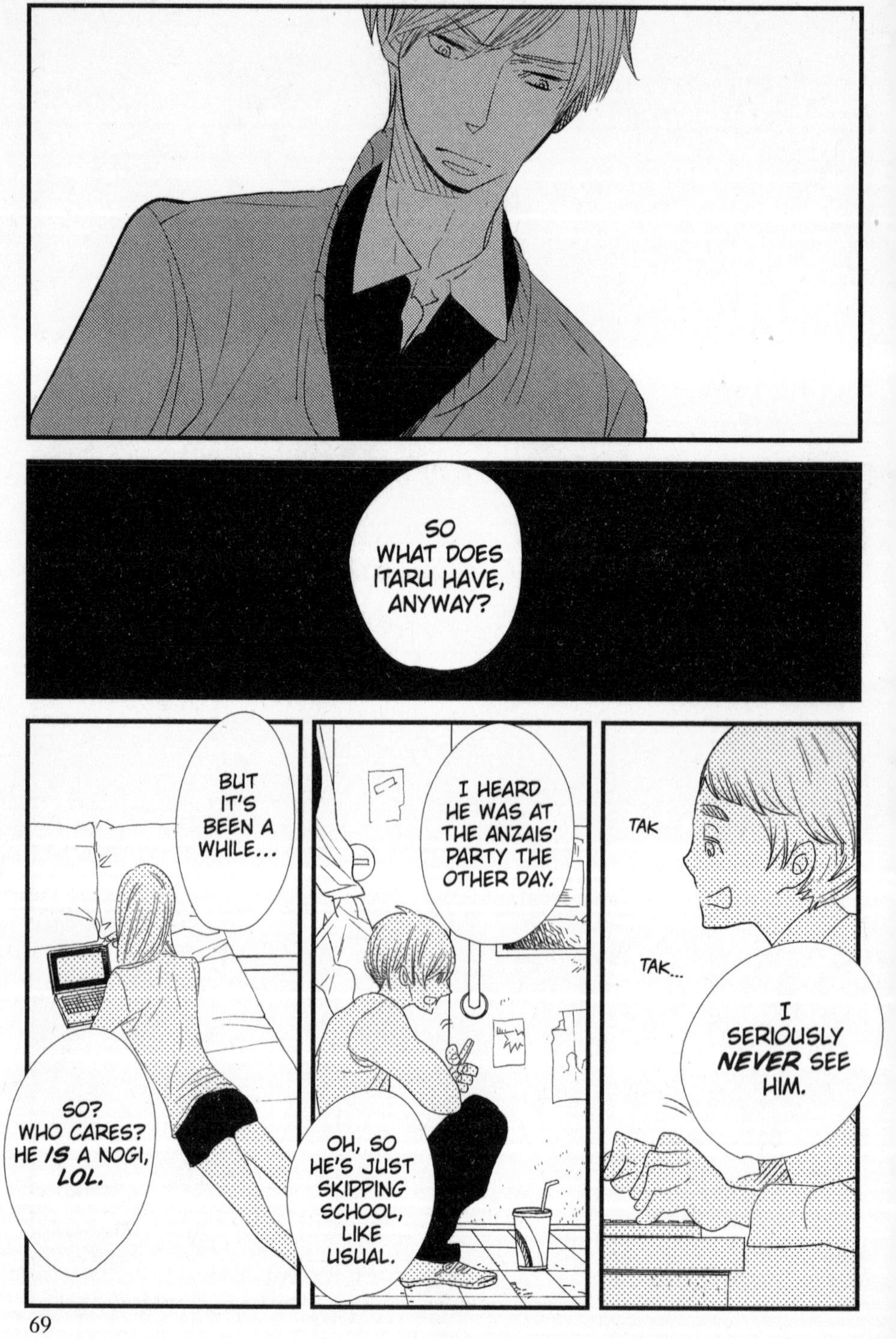
SO WHAT DOES ITARU HAVE, ANYWAY?
TAK
TAK...
I SERIOUSLY NEVER SEE HIM.
I HEARD HE WAS AT THE ANZAIS' PARTY THE OTHER DAY.
OH, SO HE'S JUST SKIPPING SCHOOL, LIKE USUAL.
BUT IT'S BEEN A WHILE...
SO? WHO CARES? HE IS A NOGI, LOL.

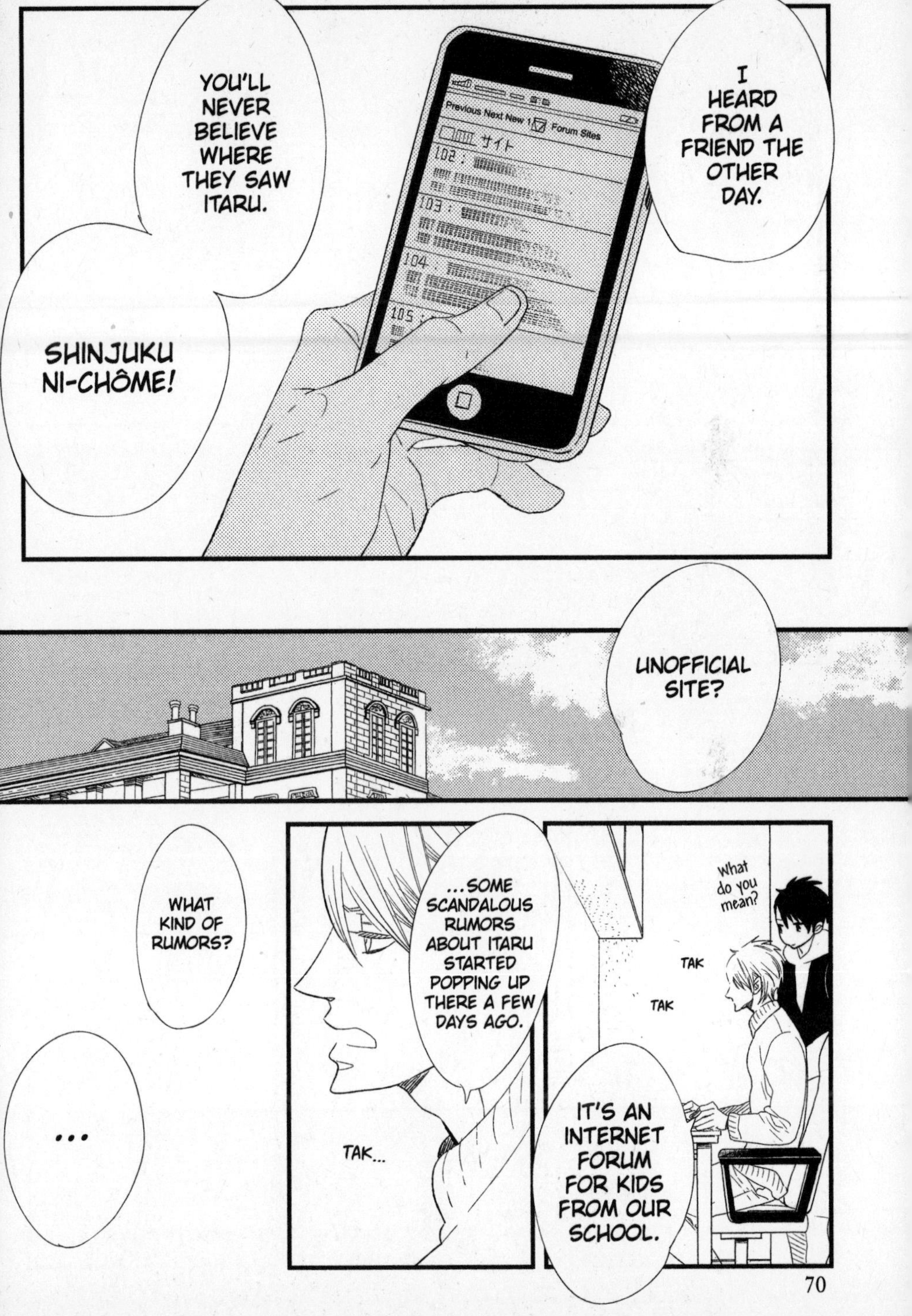
I HEARD FROM A FRIEND THE OTHER DAY.
Previous Next New 1
Forum Sites
サイト
YOU'LL NEVER BELIEVE WHERE THEY SAW ITARU.
SHINJUKU NI-CHÔME!
UNOFFICIAL SITE?
What do you mean?
TAK
TAK
IT'S AN INTERNET FORUM FOR KIDS FROM OUR SCHOOL.
...SOME SCANDALOUS RUMORS ABOUT ITARU STARTED POPPING UP THERE A FEW DAYS AGO.
TAK...
WHAT KIND OF RUMORS?
...

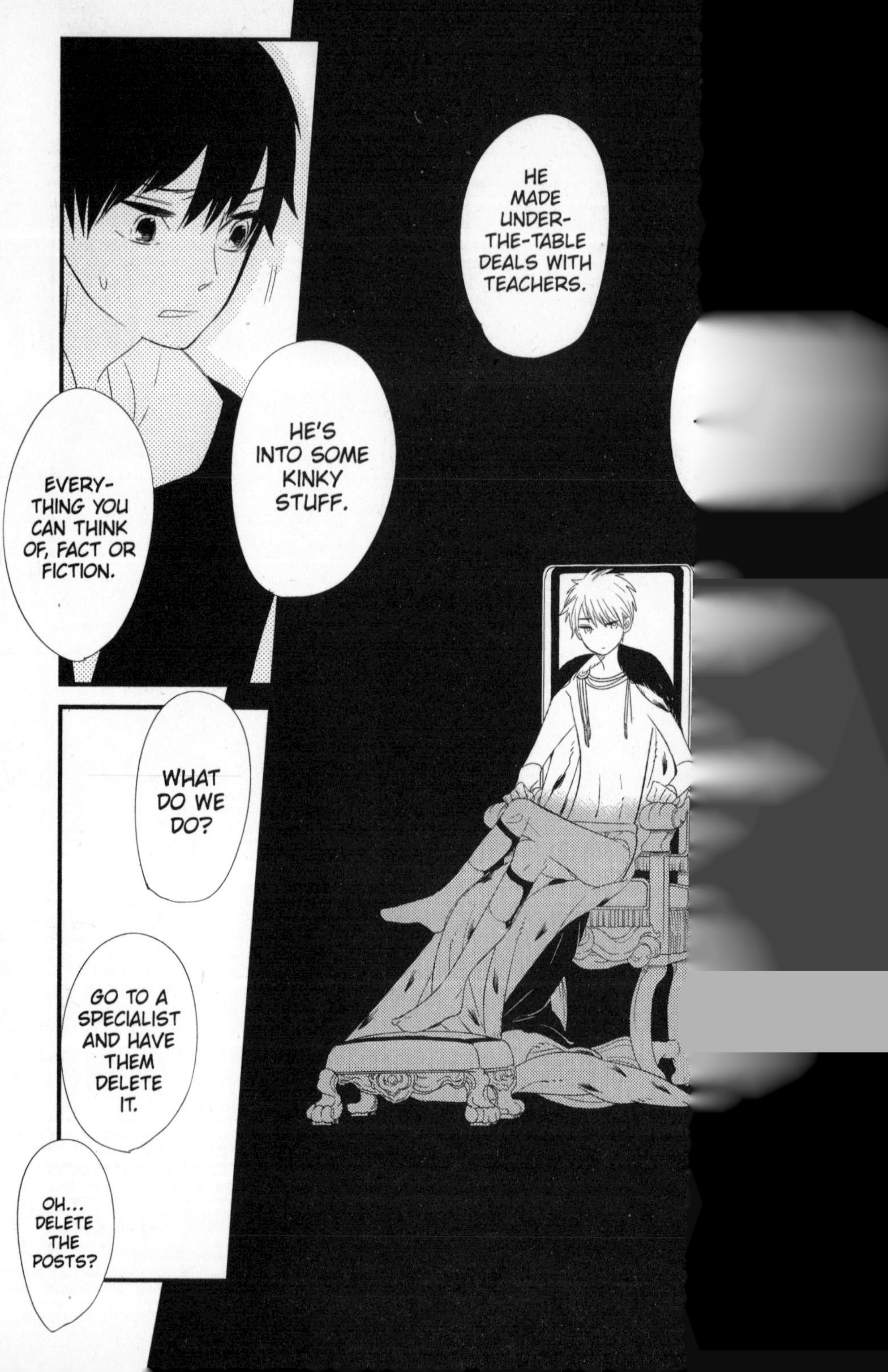
HE MADE UNDER-THE-TABLE DEALS WITH TEACHERS.
HE'S INTO SOME KINKY STUFF.
EVERY-THING YOU CAN THINK OF, FACT OR FICTION.
WHAT DO WE DO?
GO TO A SPECIALIST AND HAVE THEM DELETE IT.
OH... DELETE THE POSTS?

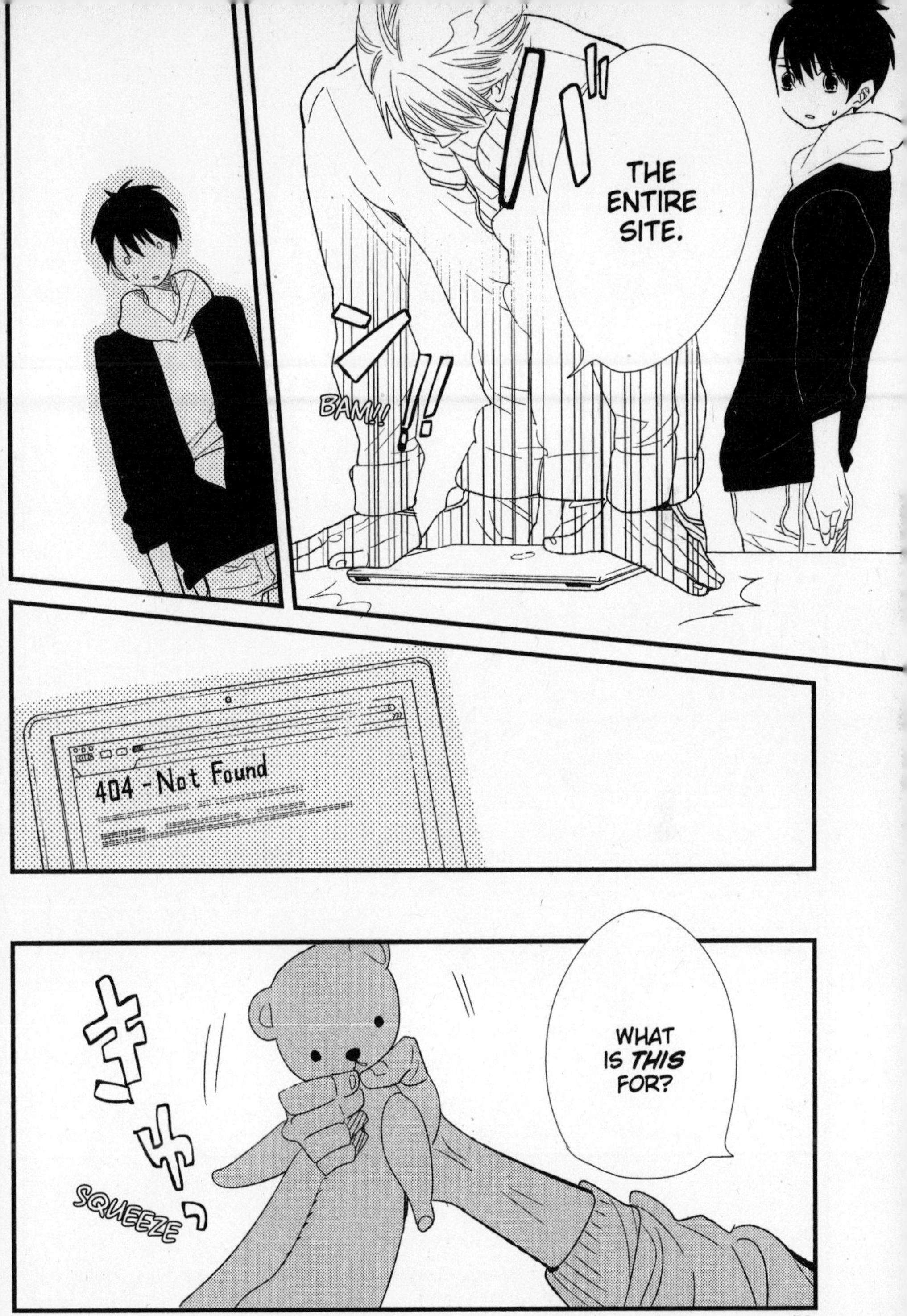
THE ENTIRE SITE.
BAM!!
404 - Not Found
WHAT IS *THIS* FOR?
SQUEEZE

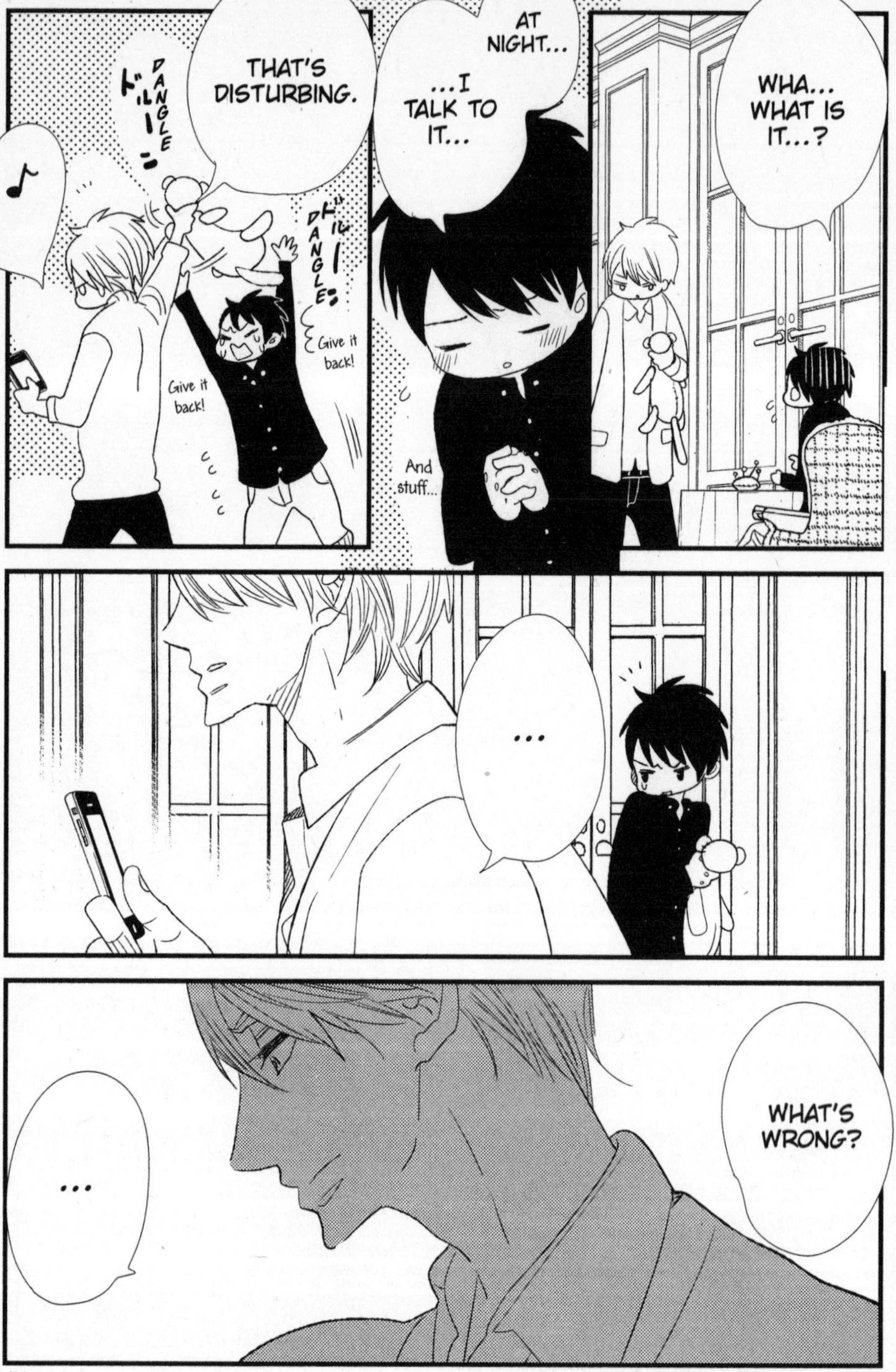
WHA... WHAT IS IT...?
AT NIGHT...
...I TALK TO IT...
And stuff...
THAT'S DISTURBING.
DANGLE
DANGLE
Give it back!
Give it back!
...
WHAT'S WRONG?
...

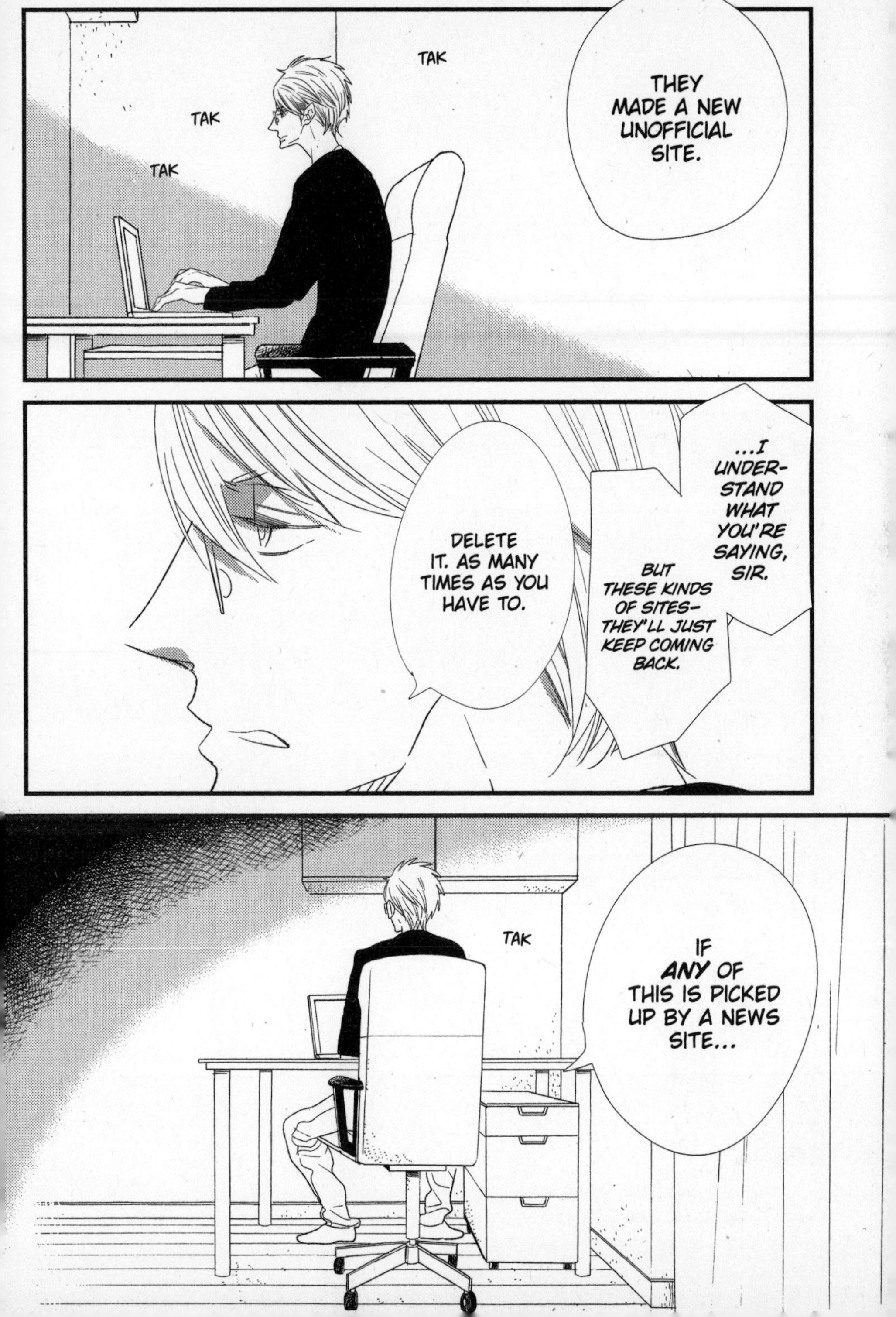
THEY MADE A NEW UNOFFICIAL SITE.
TAK
TAK
TAK
...I UNDER-STAND WHAT YOU'RE SAYING, SIR.
BUT THESE KINDS OF SITES— THEY'LL JUST KEEP COMING BACK.
DELETE IT. AS MANY TIMES AS YOU HAVE TO.
IF ANY OF THIS IS PICKED UP BY A NEWS SITE...
TAK

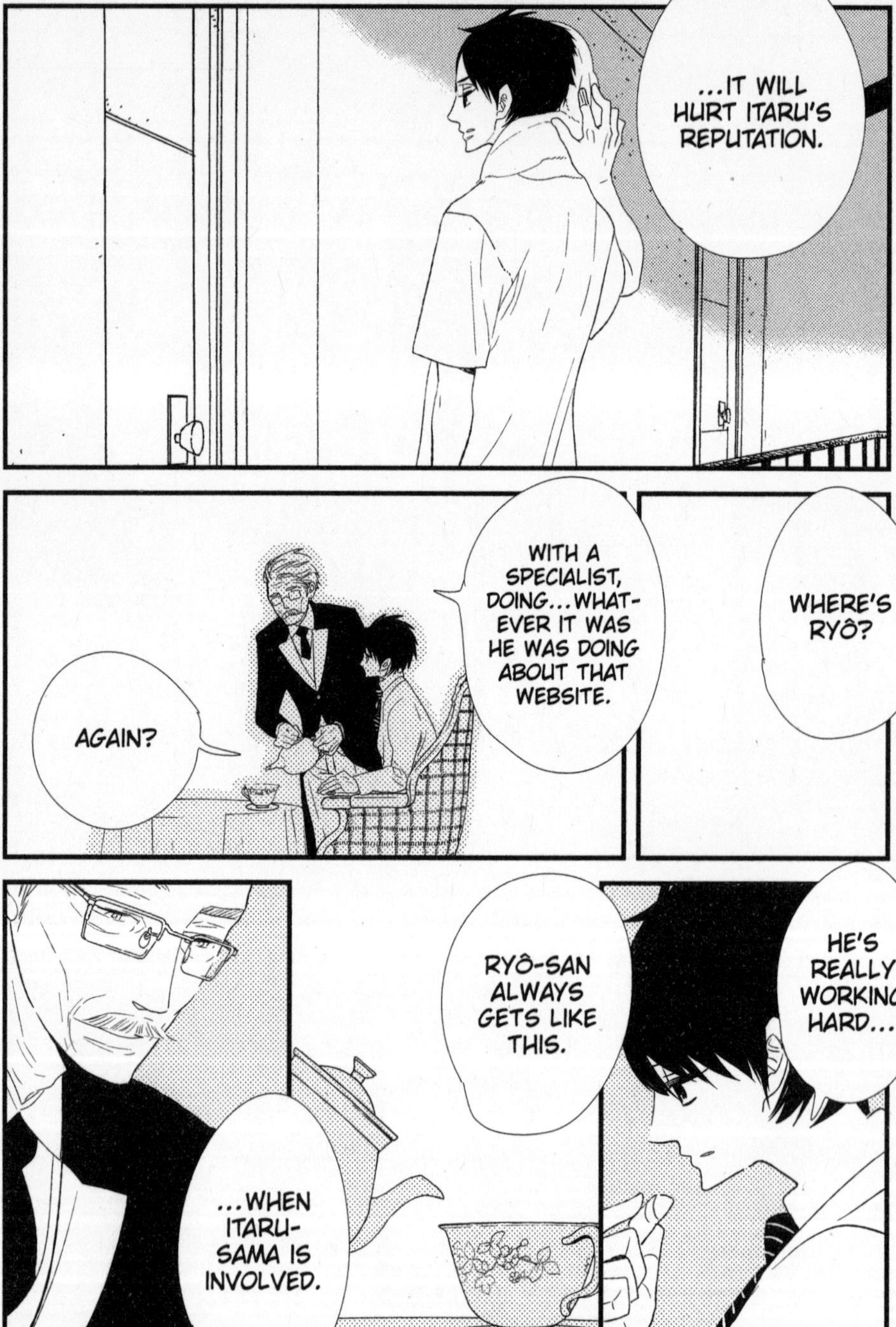
...IT WILL HURT ITARU'S REPUTATION.
WHERE'S RYÔ?
WITH A SPECIALIST, DOING...WHAT-EVER IT WAS HE WAS DOING ABOUT THAT WEBSITE.
AGAIN?
HE'S REALLY WORKING HARD...
RYÔ-SAN ALWAYS GETS LIKE THIS.
...WHEN ITARU-SAMA IS INVOLVED.

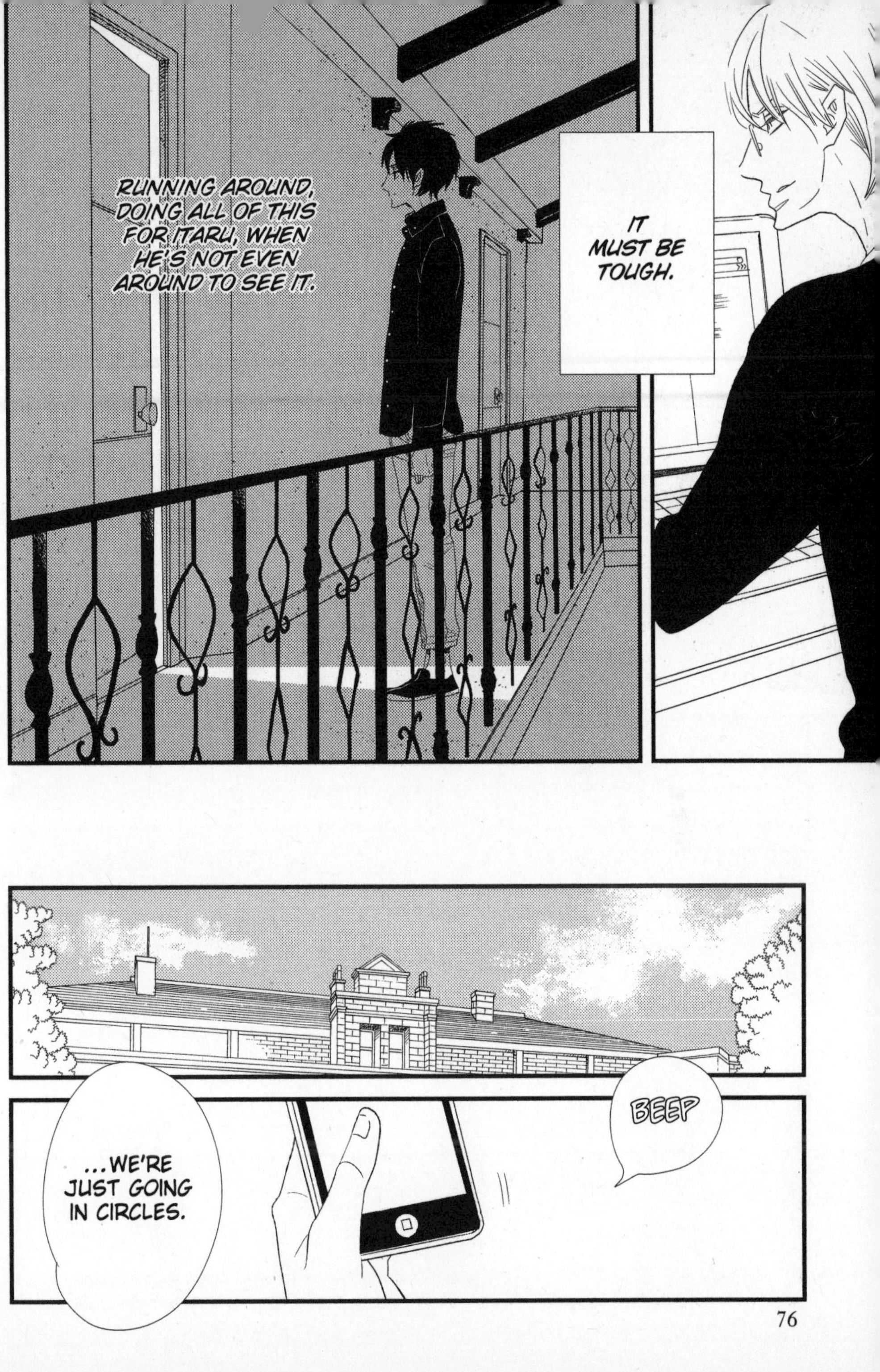
IT MUST BE TOUGH.
RUNNING AROUND, DOING ALL OF THIS FOR ITARU, WHEN HE'S NOT EVEN AROUND TO SEE IT.
BEEP
...WE'RE JUST GOING IN CIRCLES.

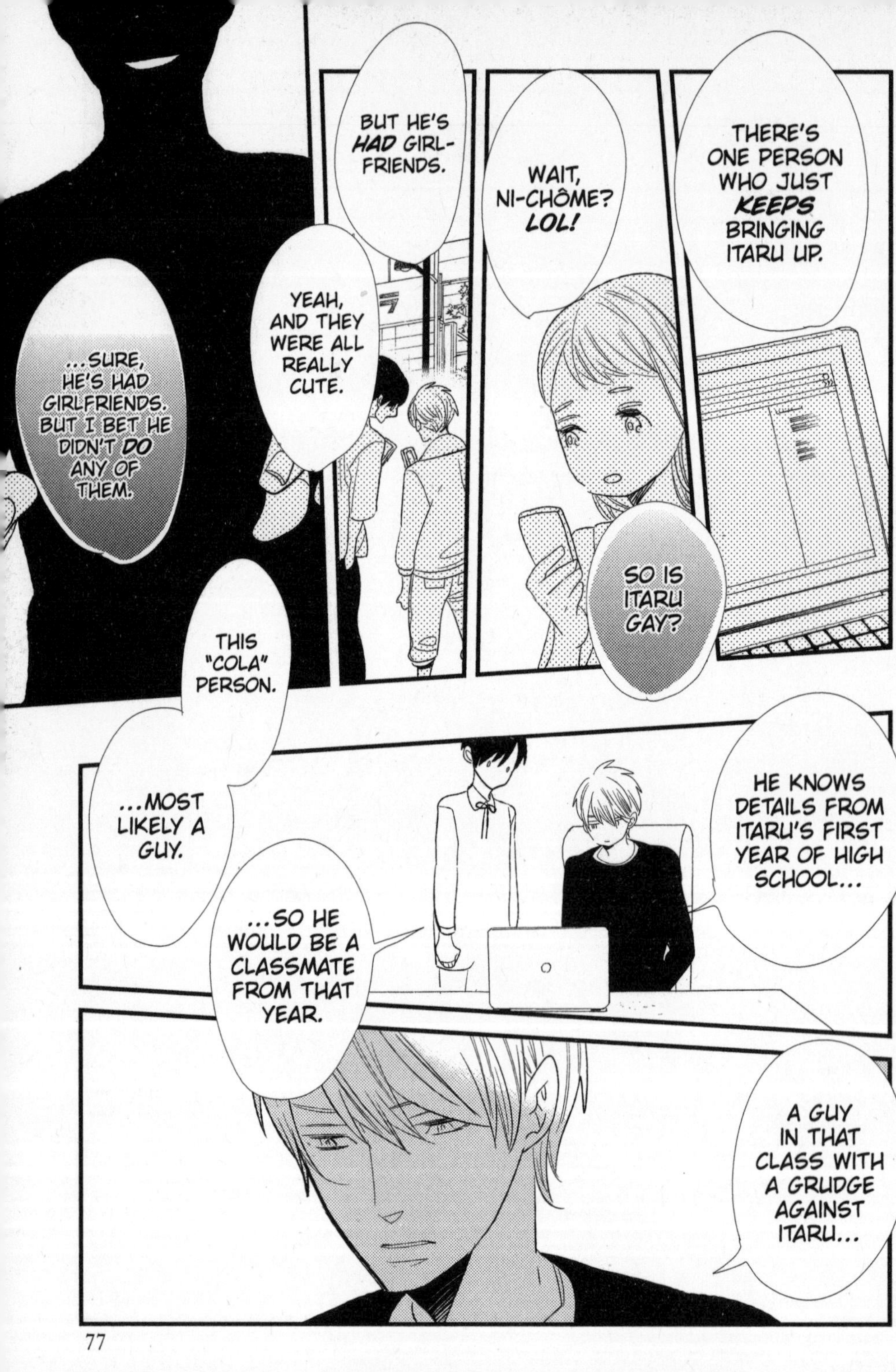
THERE'S ONE PERSON WHO JUST KEEPS BRINGING ITARU UP.
WAIT, NI-CHÔME? LOL!
SO IS ITARU GAY?
BUT HE'S HAD GIRL-FRIENDS.
YEAH, AND THEY WERE ALL REALLY CUTE.
...SURE, HE'S HAD GIRLFRIENDS. BUT I BET HE DIDN'T DO ANY OF THEM.
THIS "COLA" PERSON.
...MOST LIKELY A GUY.
HE KNOWS DETAILS FROM ITARU'S FIRST YEAR OF HIGH SCHOOL...
...SO HE WOULD BE A CLASSMATE FROM THAT YEAR.
A GUY IN THAT CLASS WITH A GRUDGE AGAINST ITARU...

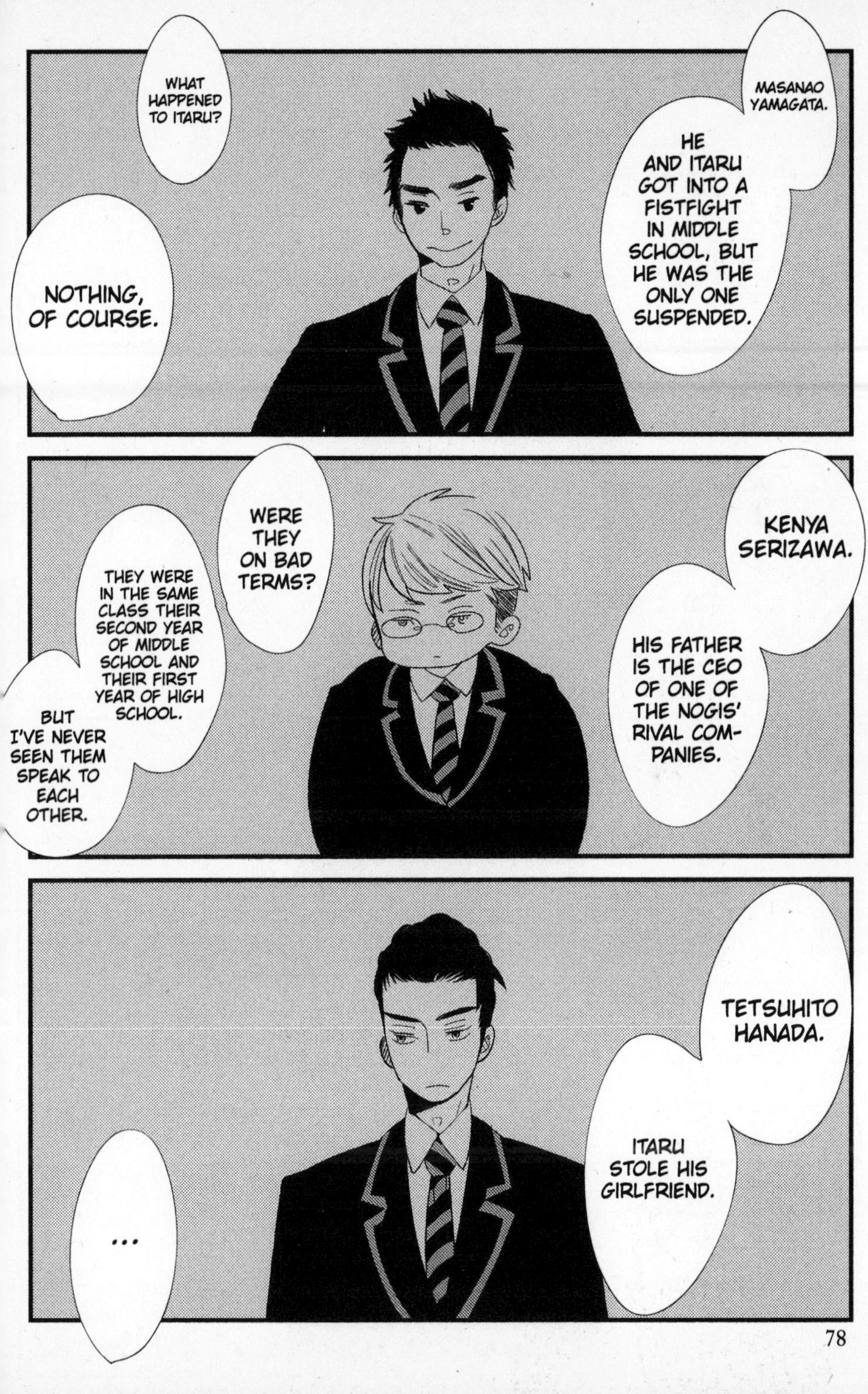
MASANAO YAMAGATA.
HE AND ITARU GOT INTO A FISTFIGHT IN MIDDLE SCHOOL, BUT HE WAS THE ONLY ONE SUSPENDED.
WHAT HAPPENED TO ITARU?
NOTHING, OF COURSE.
KENYA SERIZAWA.
HIS FATHER IS THE CEO OF ONE OF THE NOGIS' RIVAL COM-PANIES.
WERE THEY ON BAD TERMS?
THEY WERE IN THE SAME CLASS THEIR SECOND YEAR OF MIDDLE SCHOOL AND THEIR FIRST YEAR OF HIGH SCHOOL.
BUT I'VE NEVER SEEN THEM SPEAK TO EACH OTHER.
TETSUHITO HANADA.
ITARU STOLE HIS GIRLFRIEND.
...

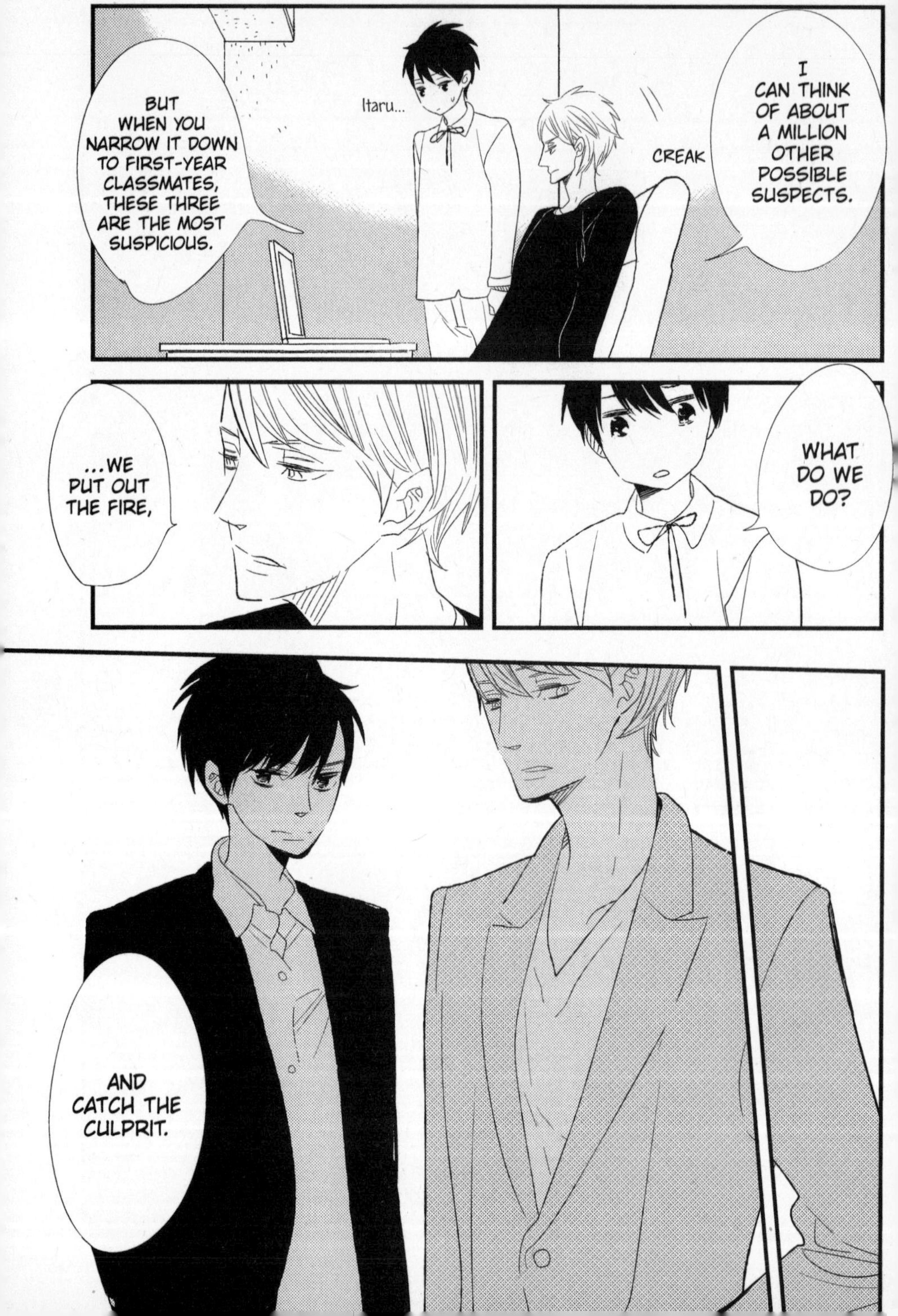
I CAN THINK OF ABOUT A MILLION OTHER POSSIBLE SUSPECTS.
CREAK
Itaru...
BUT WHEN YOU NARROW IT DOWN TO FIRST-YEAR CLASSMATES, THESE THREE ARE THE MOST SUSPICIOUS.
WHAT DO WE DO?
...WE PUT OUT THE FIRE,
AND CATCH THE CULPRIT.

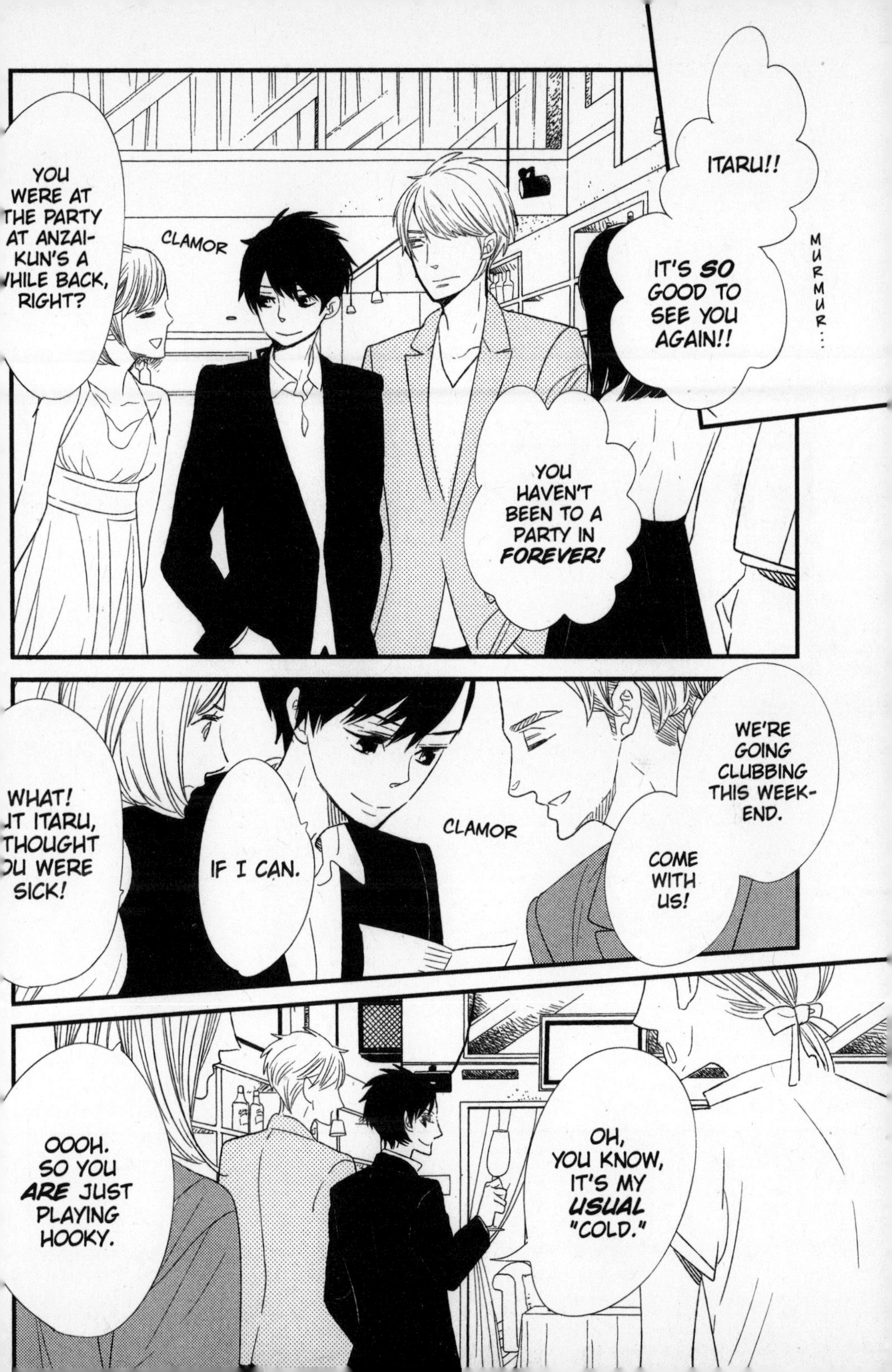
ITARU!!
IT'S SO GOOD TO SEE YOU AGAIN!!
MURMUR...
YOU HAVEN'T BEEN TO A PARTY IN FOREVER!
CLAMOR
YOU WERE AT THE PARTY AT ANZAI-KUN'S A HILE BACK, RIGHT?
WE'RE GOING CLUBBING THIS WEEK-END.
COME WITH US!
CLAMOR
IF I CAN.
WHAT! T ITARU, THOUGHT OU WERE SICK!
OH, YOU KNOW, IT'S MY USUAL "COLD."
OOOH. SO YOU ARE JUST PLAYING HOOKY.

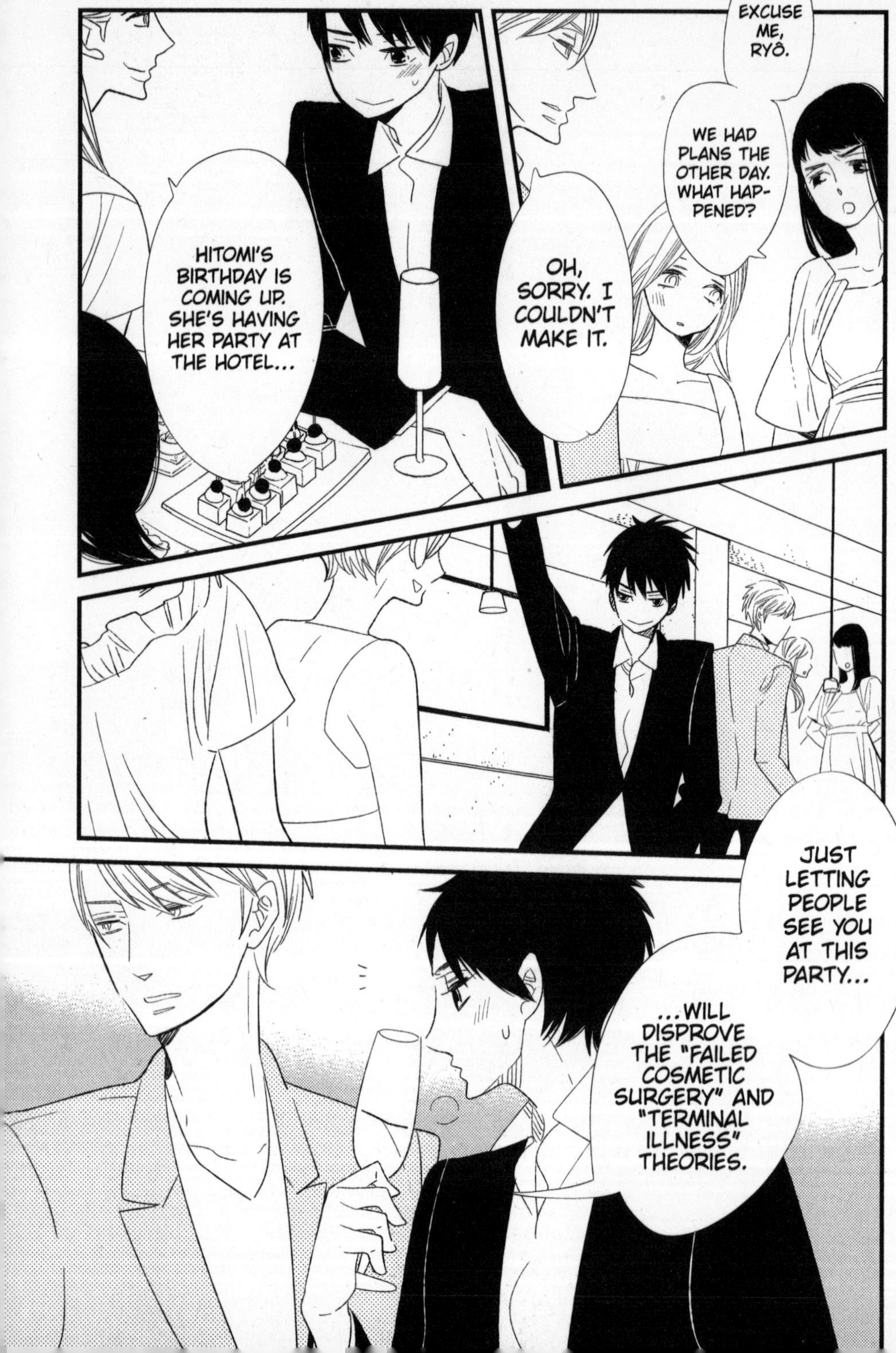
EXCUSE ME, RYÔ.
WE HAD PLANS THE OTHER DAY. WHAT HAP-PENED?
OH, SORRY. I COULDN'T MAKE IT.
HITOMI'S BIRTHDAY IS COMING UP. SHE'S HAVING HER PARTY AT THE HOTEL...
JUST LETTING PEOPLE SEE YOU AT THIS PARTY...
...WILL DISPROVE THE "FAILED COSMETIC SURGERY" AND "TERMINAL ILLNESS" THEORIES.

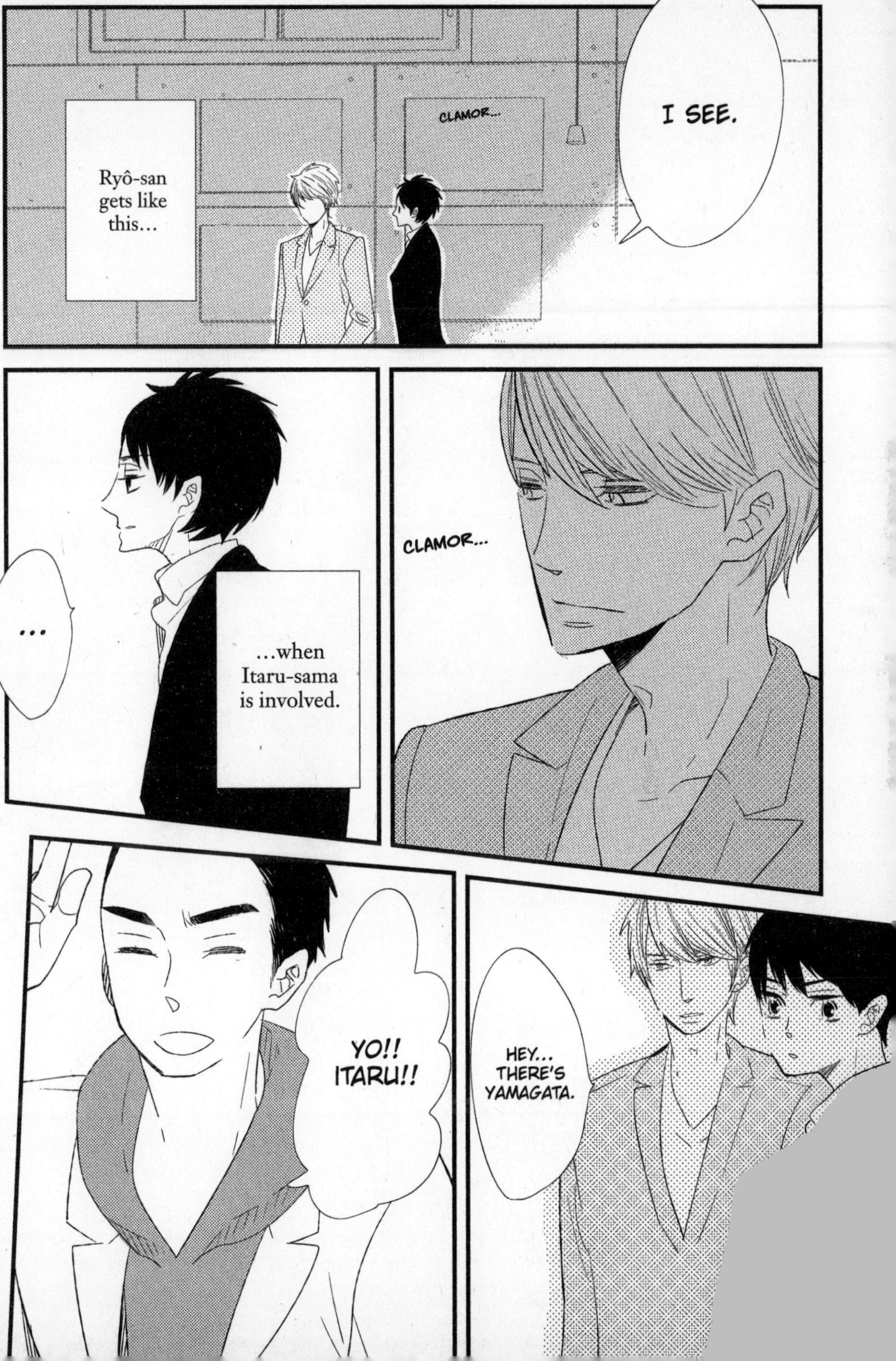
I SEE.
CLAMOR...
Ryô-san gets like this...
CLAMOR...
...when Itaru-sama is involved.
...
HEY... THERE'S YAMAGATA.
YO!! ITARU!!

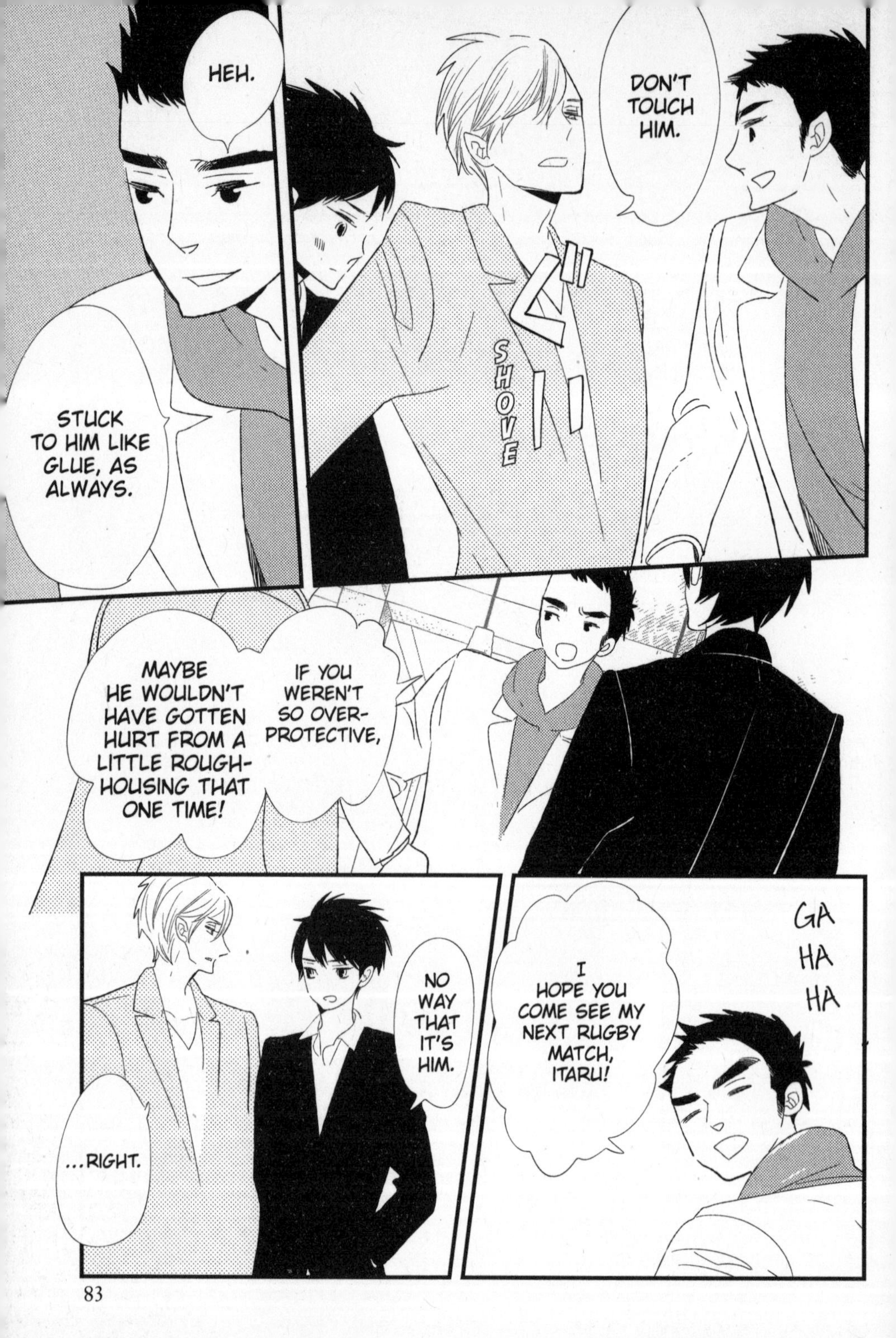
DON'T TOUCH HIM.
SHOVE
HEH.
STUCK TO HIM LIKE GLUE, AS ALWAYS.
IF YOU WEREN'T SO OVER-PROTECTIVE,
MAYBE HE WOULDN'T HAVE GOTTEN HURT FROM A LITTLE ROUGH-HOUSING THAT ONE TIME!
GA HA HA
I HOPE YOU COME SEE MY NEXT RUGBY MATCH, ITARU!
NO WAY THAT IT'S HIM.
...RIGHT.

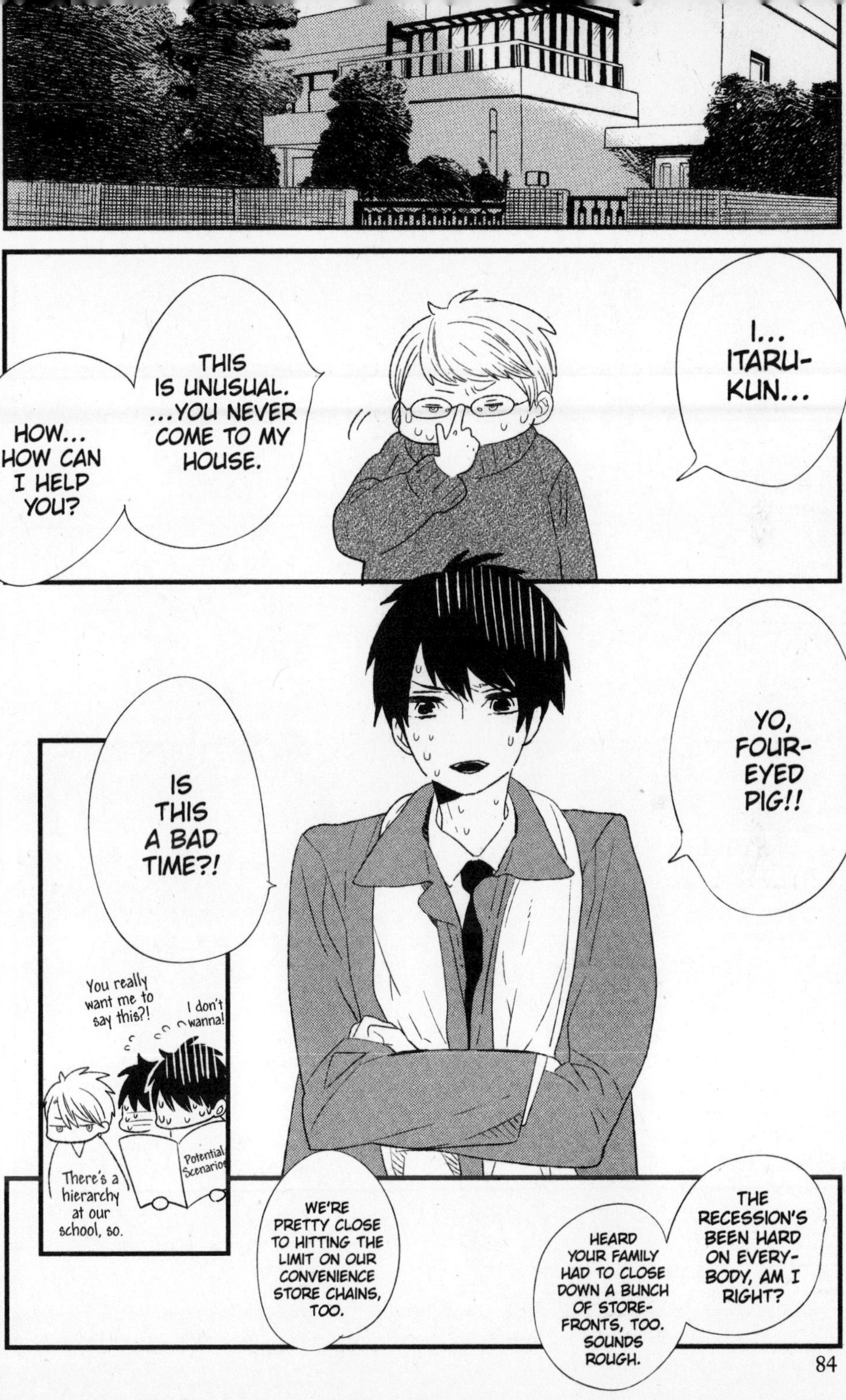
I... ITARU-KUN...
THIS IS UNUSUAL. ...YOU NEVER COME TO MY HOUSE.
HOW... HOW CAN I HELP YOU?
YO, FOUR-EYED PIG!!
IS THIS A BAD TIME?!
You really want me to say this?!
I don't wanna!
Potential Scenarios
There's a hierarchy at our school, so.
THE RECESSION'S BEEN HARD ON EVERY-BODY, AM I RIGHT?
HEARD YOUR FAMILY HAD TO CLOSE DOWN A BUNCH OF STORE-FRONTS, TOO. SOUNDS ROUGH.
WE'RE PRETTY CLOSE TO HITTING THE LIMIT ON OUR CONVENIENCE STORE CHAINS, TOO.

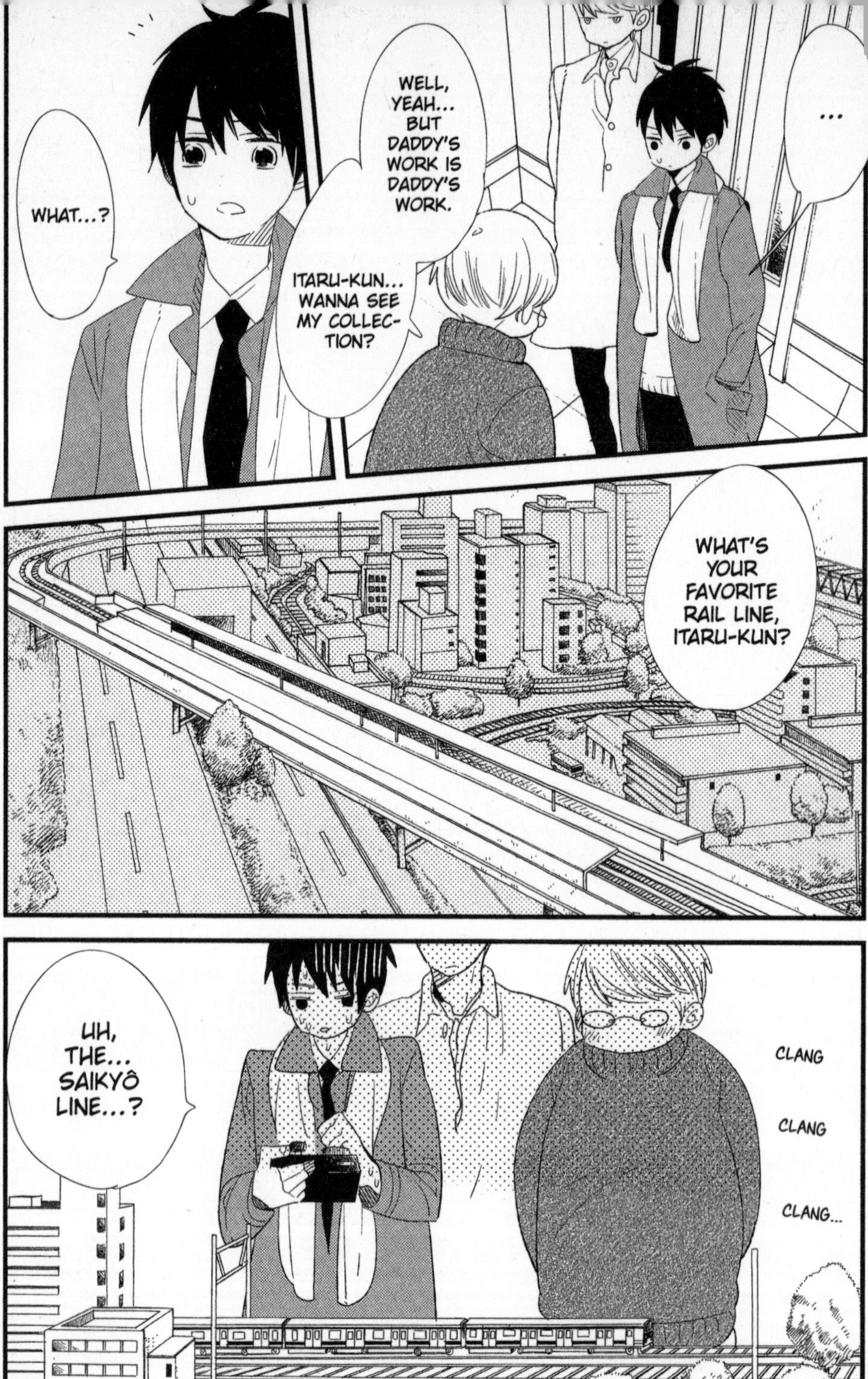
...
WELL, YEAH... BUT DADDY'S WORK IS DADDY'S WORK.
ITARU-KUN... WANNA SEE MY COLLECTION?
WHAT...?
WHAT'S YOUR FAVORITE RAIL LINE, ITARU-KUN?
CLANG
CLANG
CLANG...
UH, THE... SAIKYÔ LINE...?

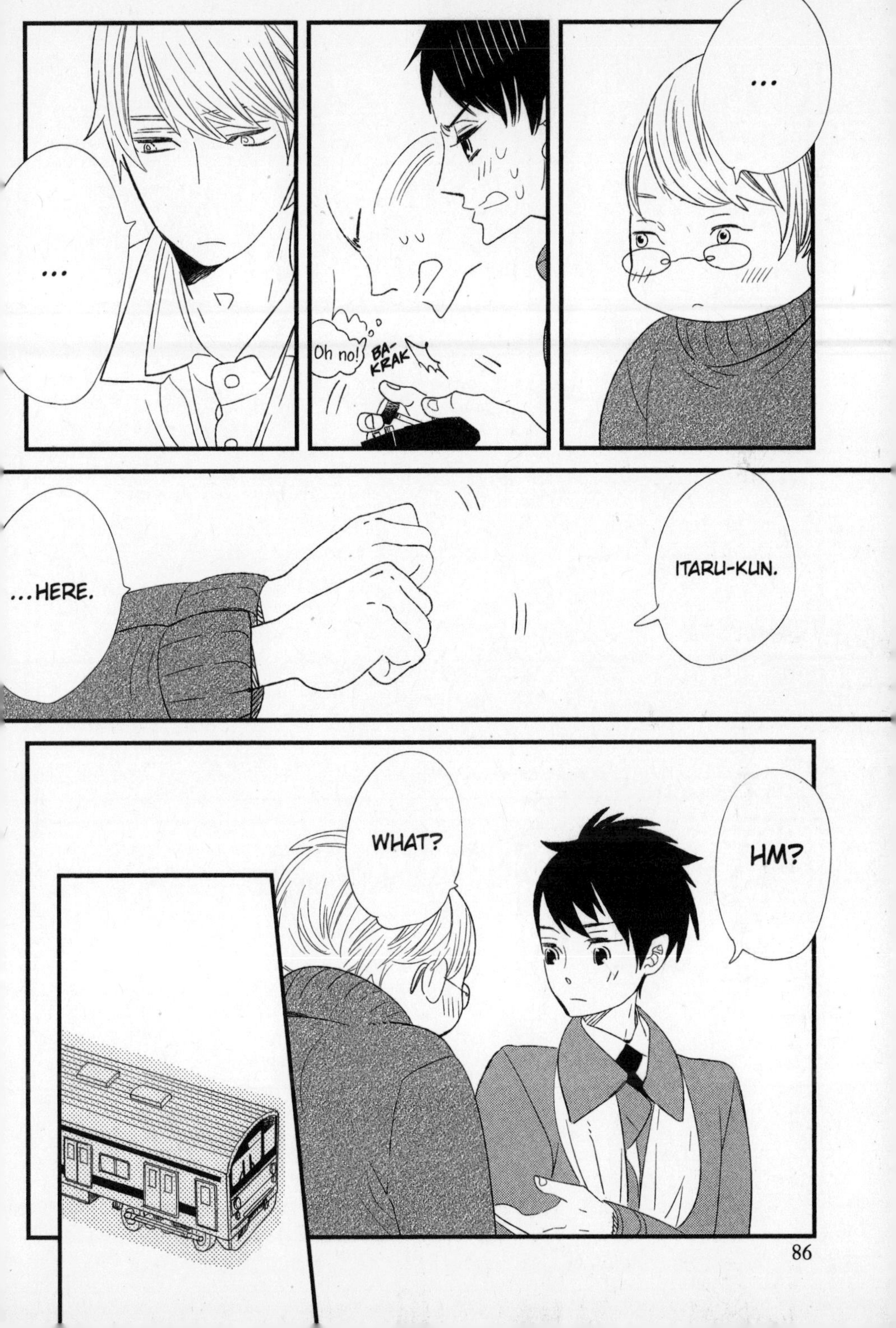
...
Oh no!
BA-KRAK
...
ITARU-KUN.
...HERE.
HM?
WHAT?

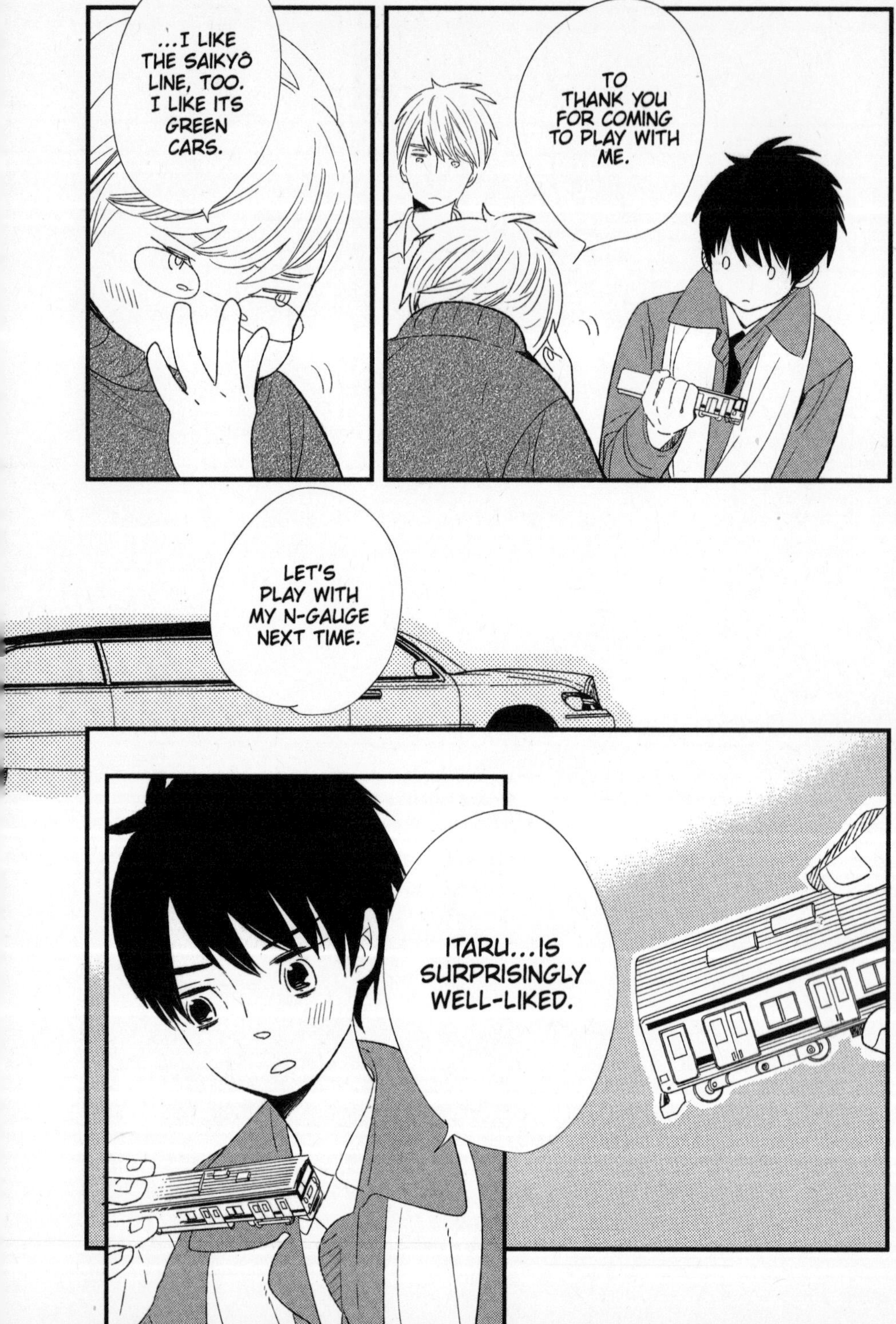
TO THANK YOU FOR COMING TO PLAY WITH ME.
...I LIKE THE SAIKYÔ LINE, TOO. I LIKE ITS GREEN CARS.
LET'S PLAY WITH MY N-GAUGE NEXT TIME.
ITARU...IS SURPRISINGLY WELL-LIKED.

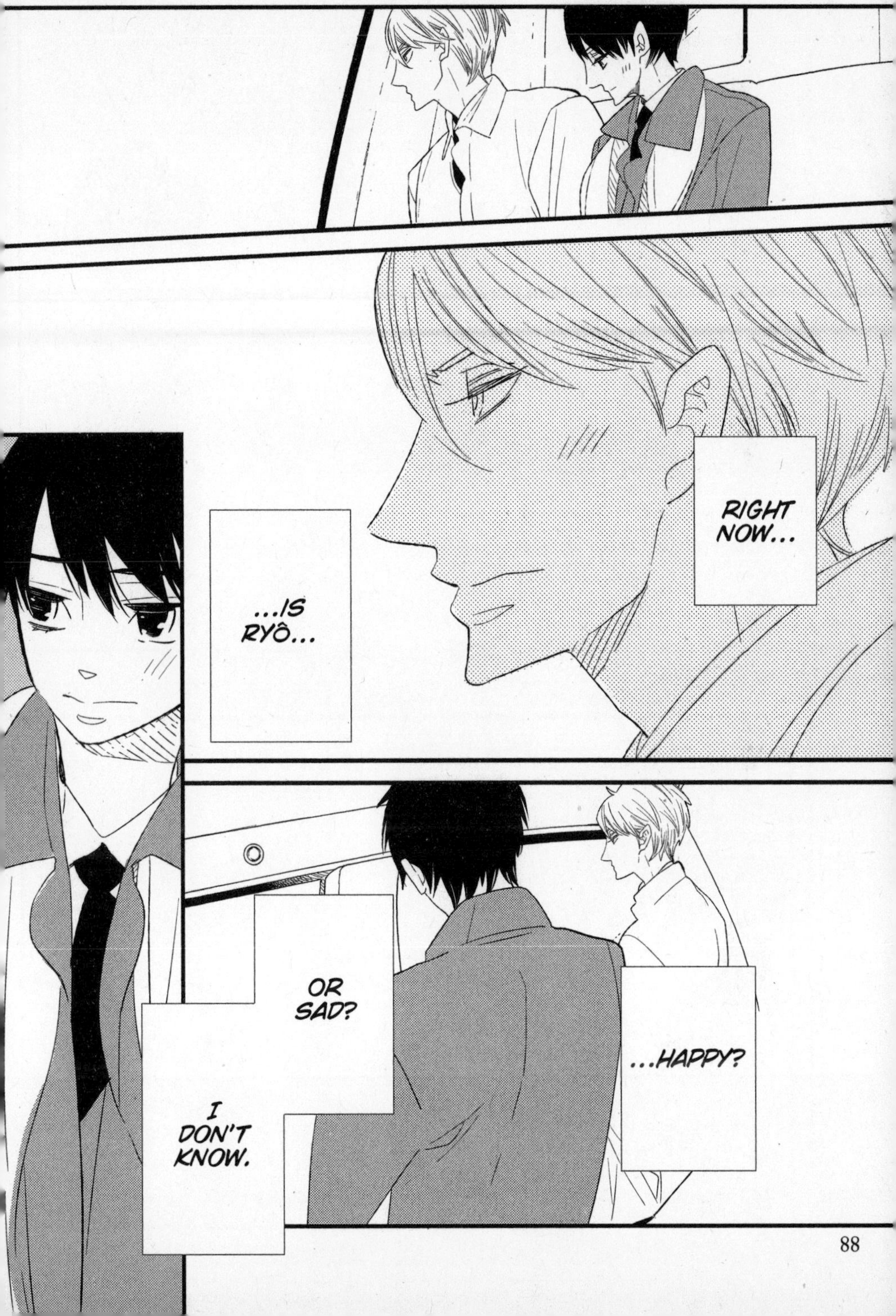
RIGHT NOW...
...IS RYÔ...
...HAPPY?
OR SAD?
I DON'T KNOW.

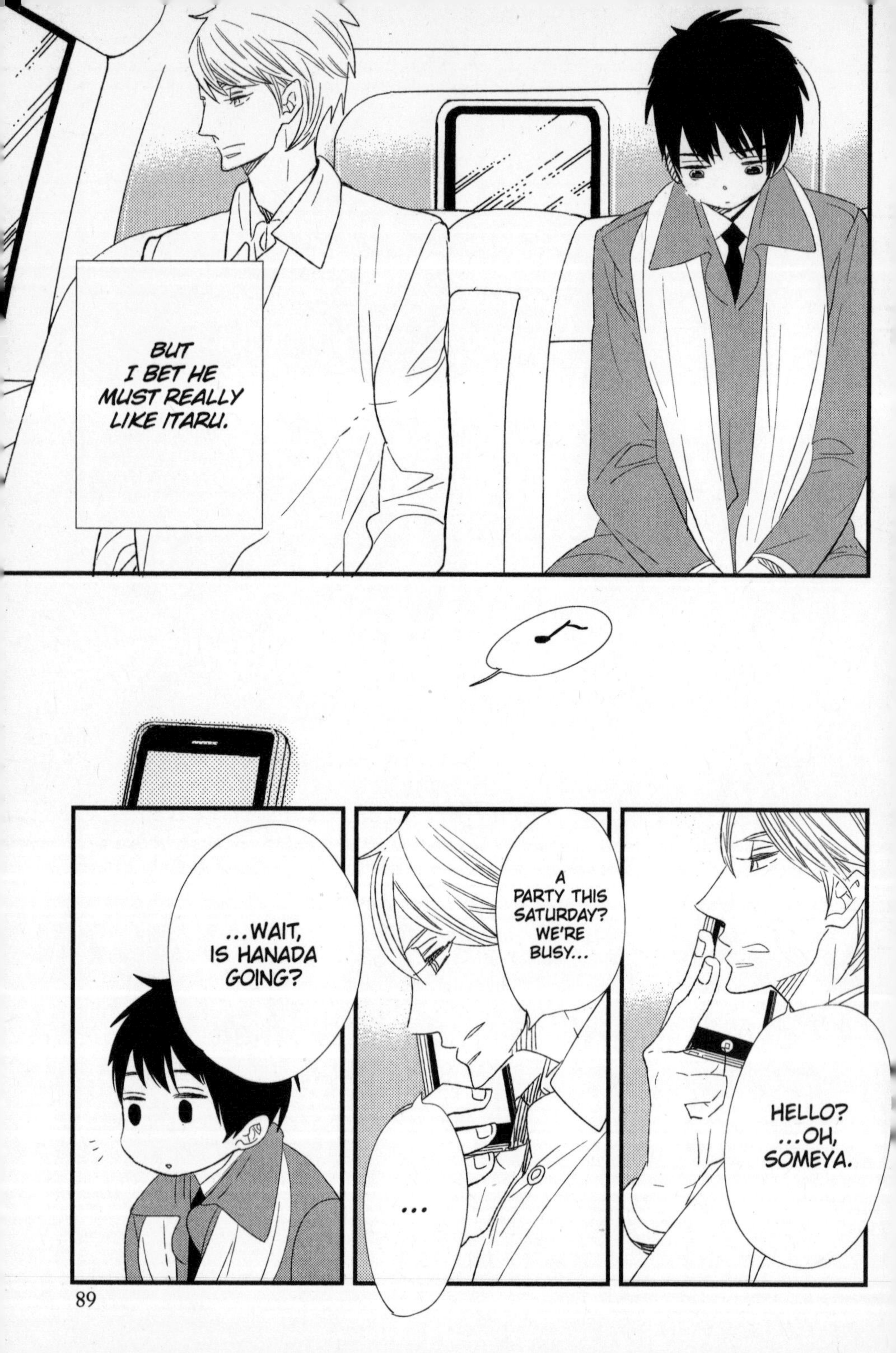
BUT I BET HE MUST REALLY LIKE ITARU.
HELLO? ...OH, SOMEYA.
A PARTY THIS SATURDAY? WE'RE BUSY...
...
...WAIT, IS HANADA GOING?

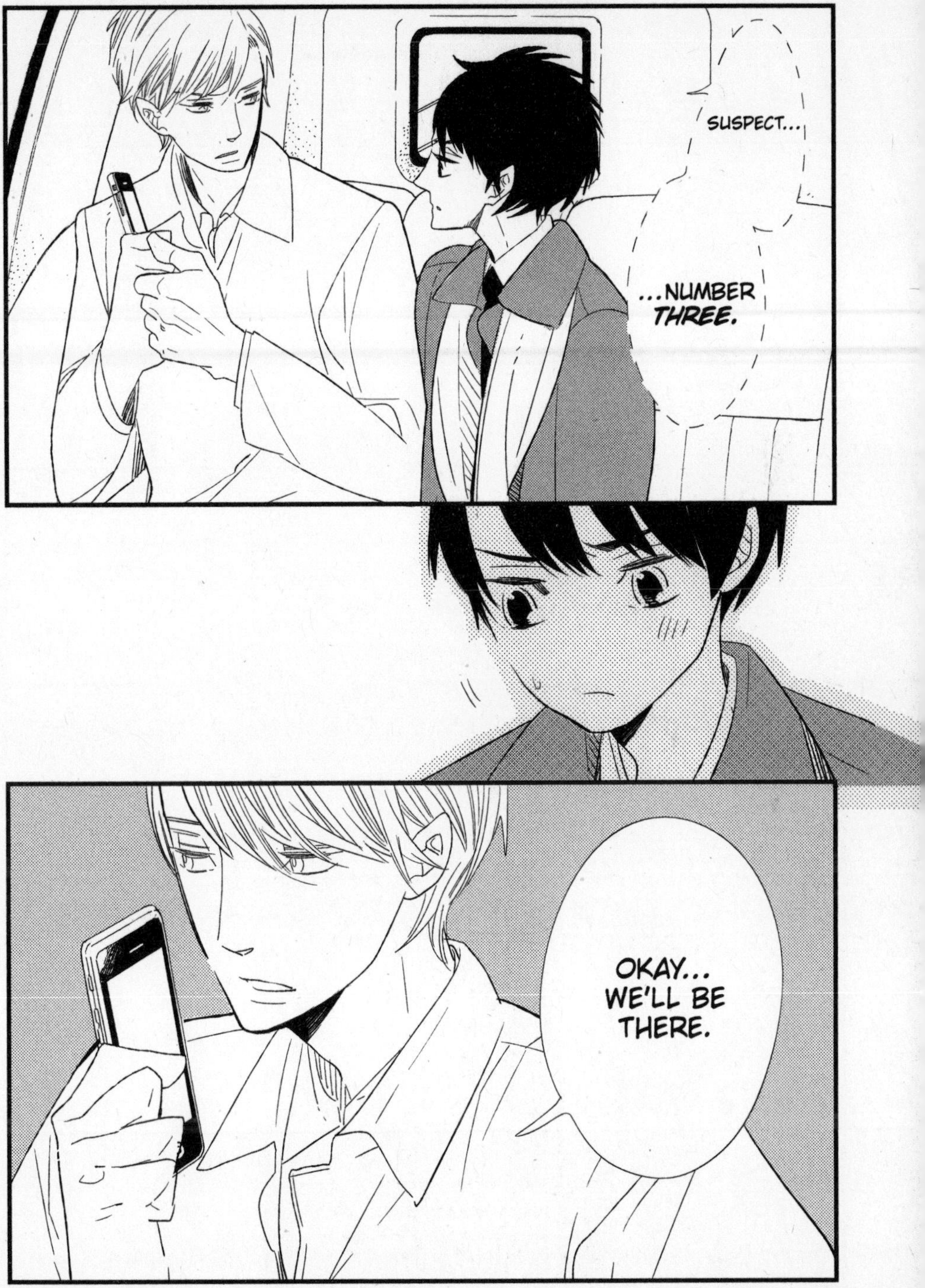
SUSPECT...
...NUMBER THREE.
OKAY... WE'LL BE THERE.

chapter 13

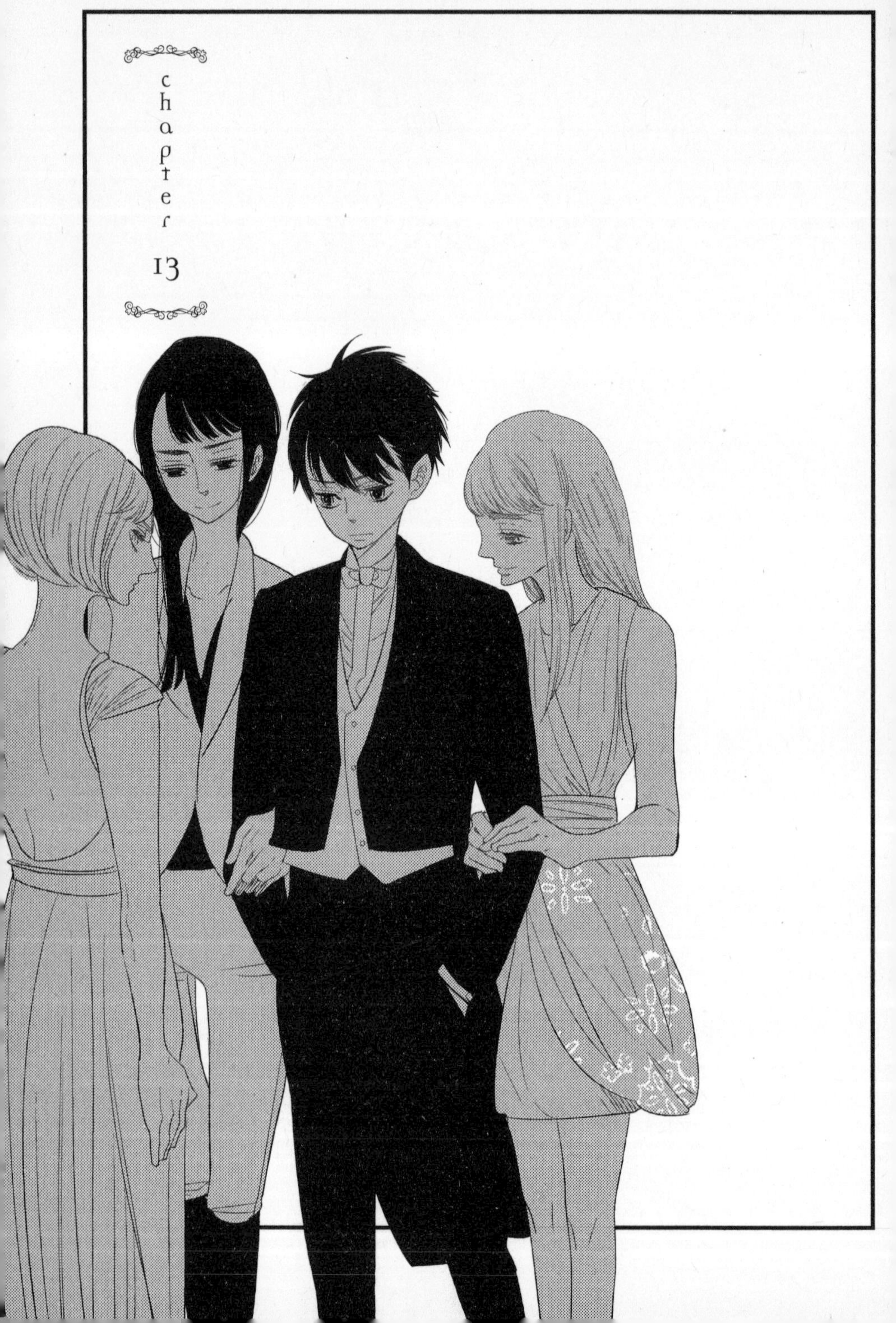

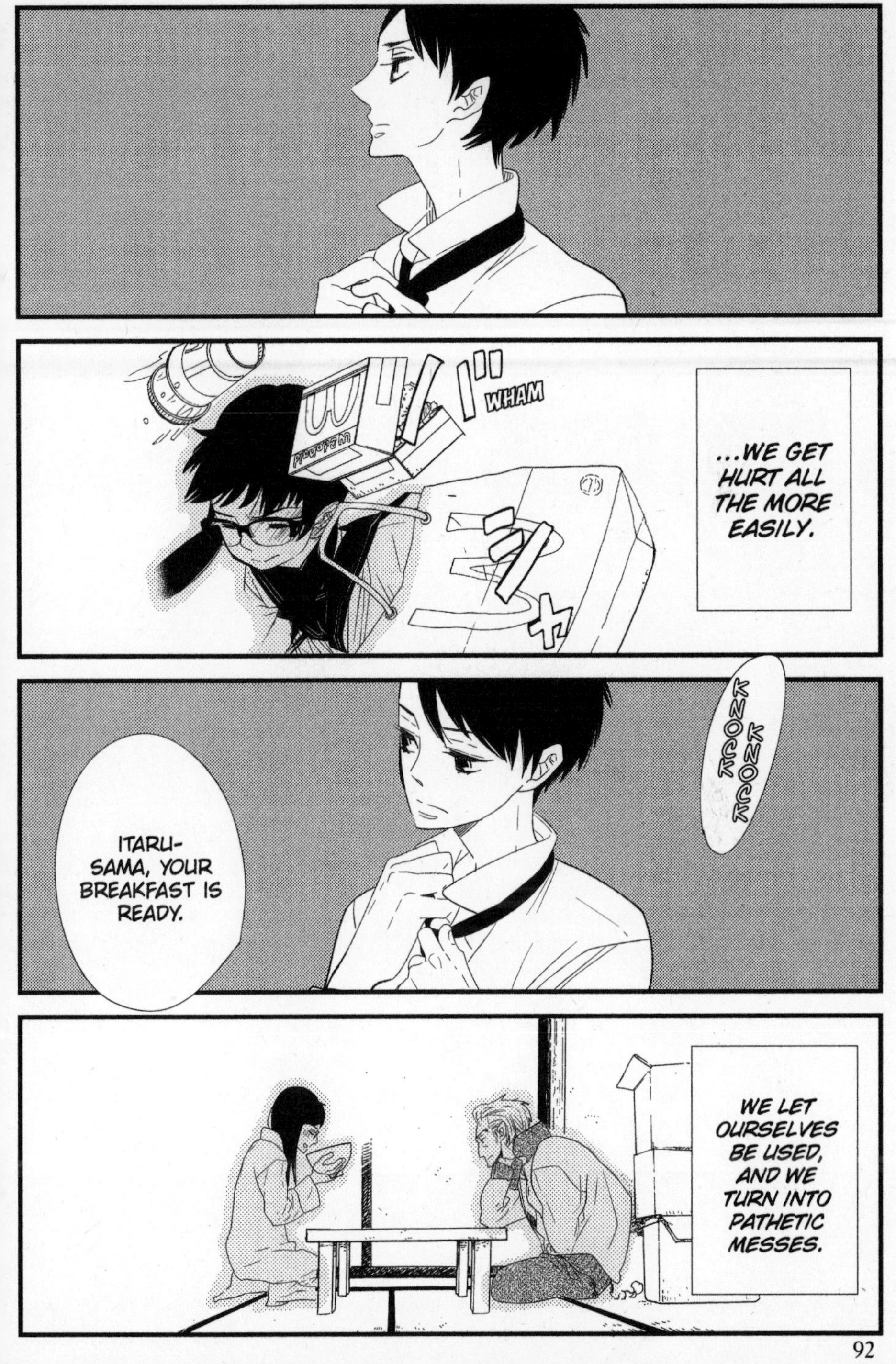
...WE GET HURT ALL THE MORE EASILY.
WHAM
KNOCK KNOCK
ITARU-SAMA, YOUR BREAKFAST IS READY.
WE LET OURSELVES BE USED, AND WE TURN INTO PATHETIC MESSES.

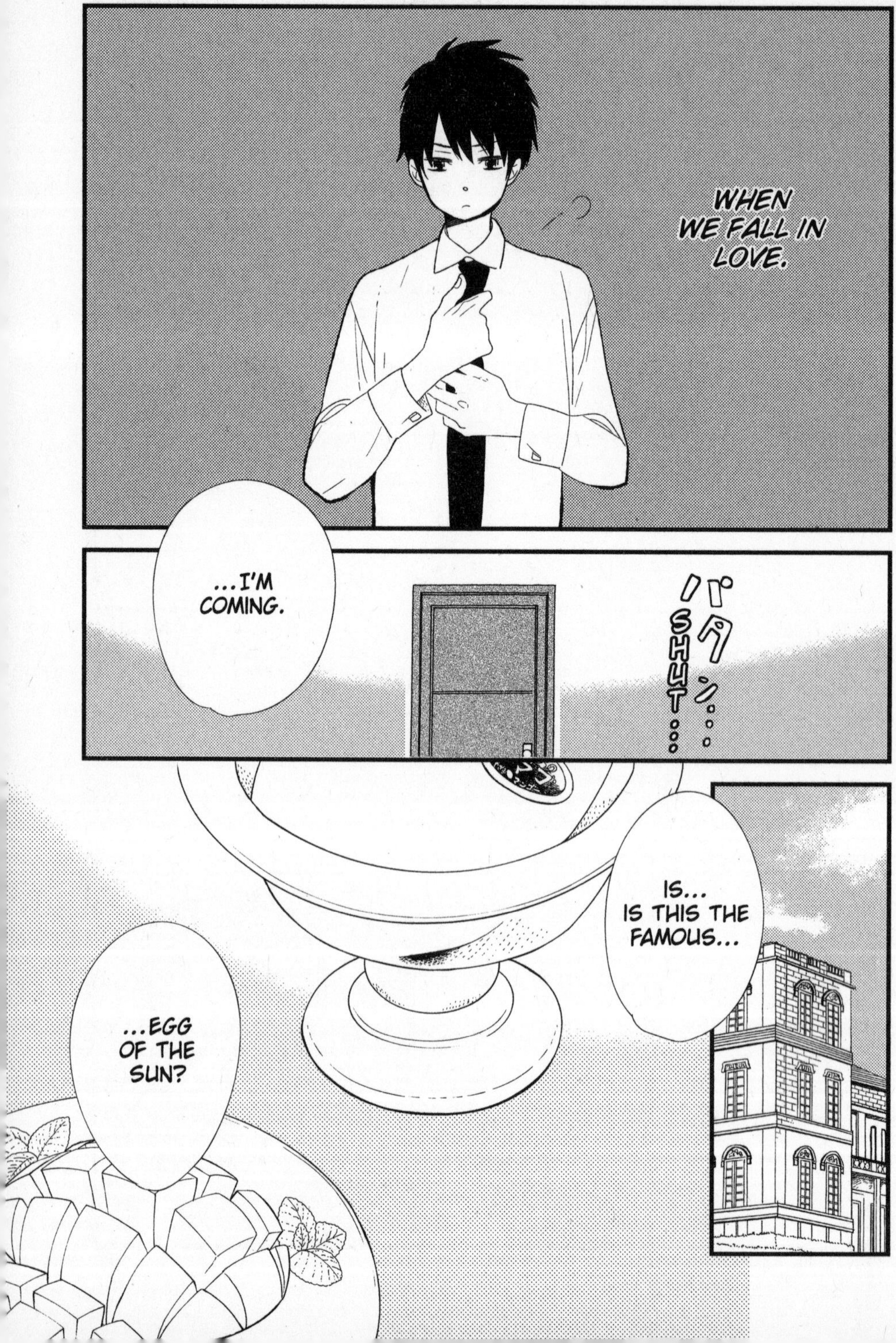
WHEN WE FALL IN LOVE.
パタン…
SHUT…
…I'M COMING.
IS… IS THIS THE FAMOUS…
…EGG OF THE SUN?

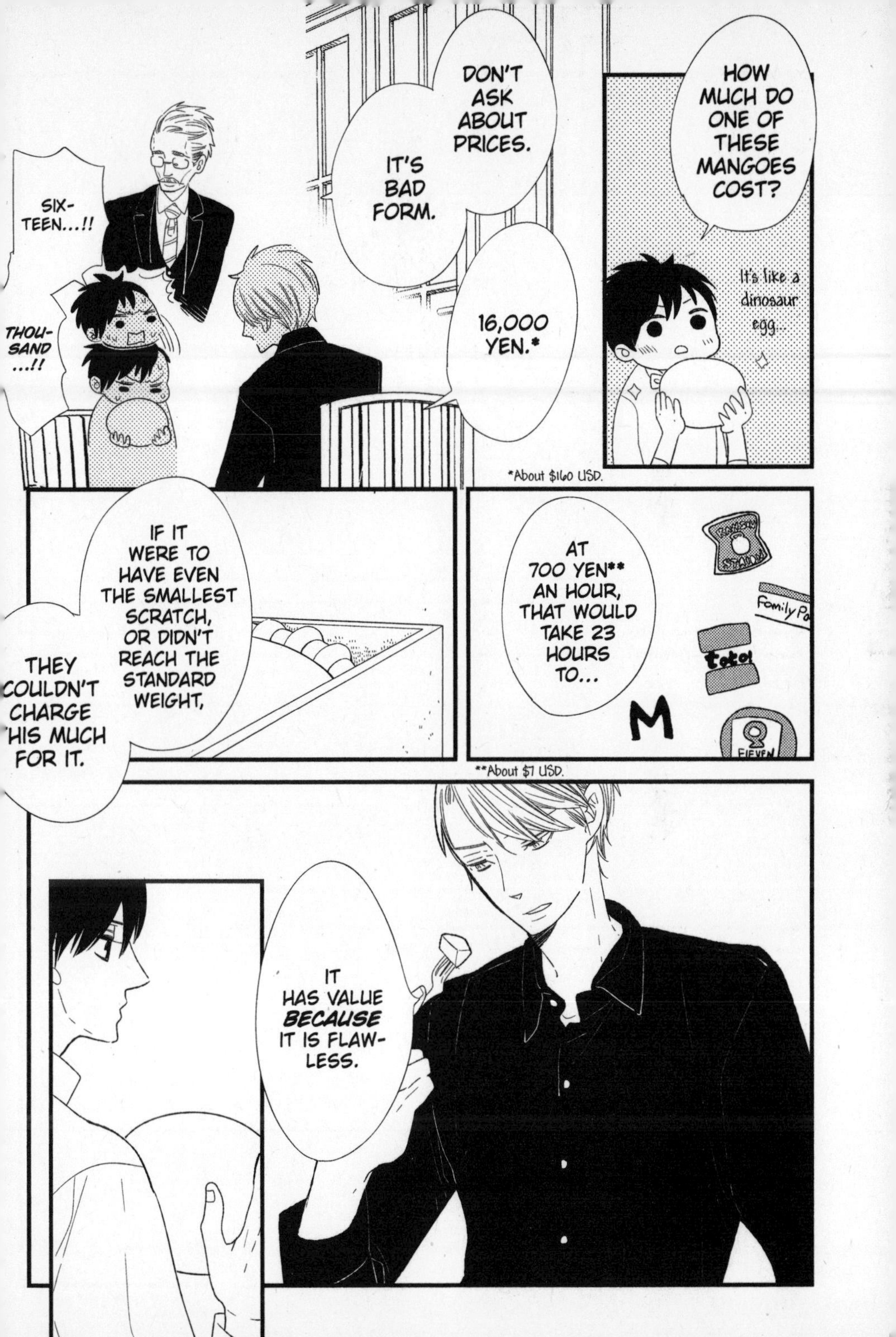
HOW MUCH DO ONE OF THESE MANGOES COST?
It's like a dinosaur egg...
DON'T ASK ABOUT PRICES.
IT'S BAD FORM.
16,000 YEN.*
SIX-TEEN...!!
THOU-SAND...!!
*About $160 USD.
AT 700 YEN** AN HOUR, THAT WOULD TAKE 23 HOURS TO...
Family Po
toko
M
IF IT WERE TO HAVE EVEN THE SMALLEST SCRATCH, OR DIDN'T REACH THE STANDARD WEIGHT,
THEY COULDN'T CHARGE THIS MUCH FOR IT.
**About $7 USD.
IT HAS VALUE BECAUSE IT IS FLAW-LESS.

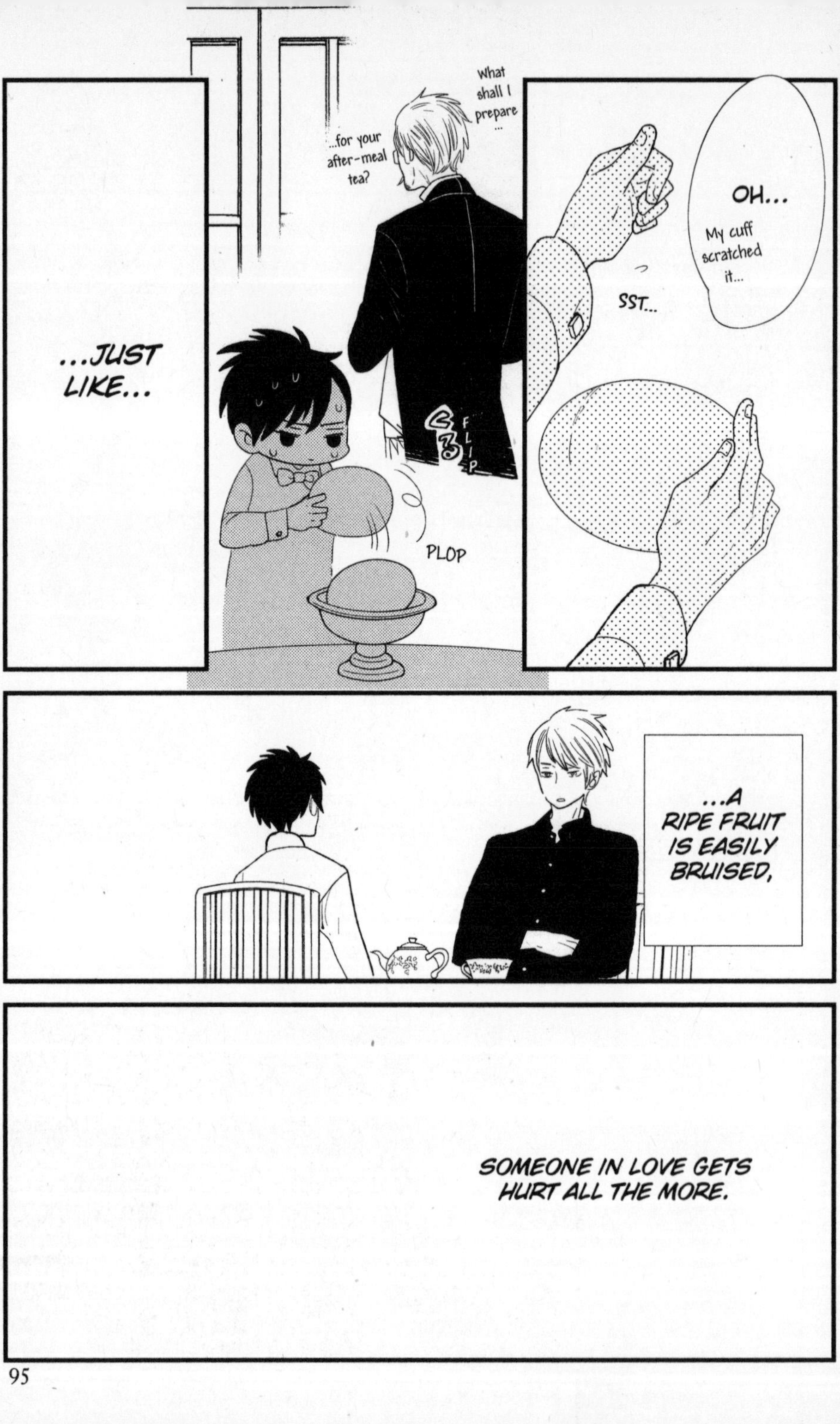

OH...
My cuff scratched it...
SST...
What shall I prepare ...
...for your after-meal tea?
FLIP
PLOP
...JUST LIKE...
...A RIPE FRUIT IS EASILY BRUISED,
SOMEONE IN LOVE GETS HURT ALL THE MORE.

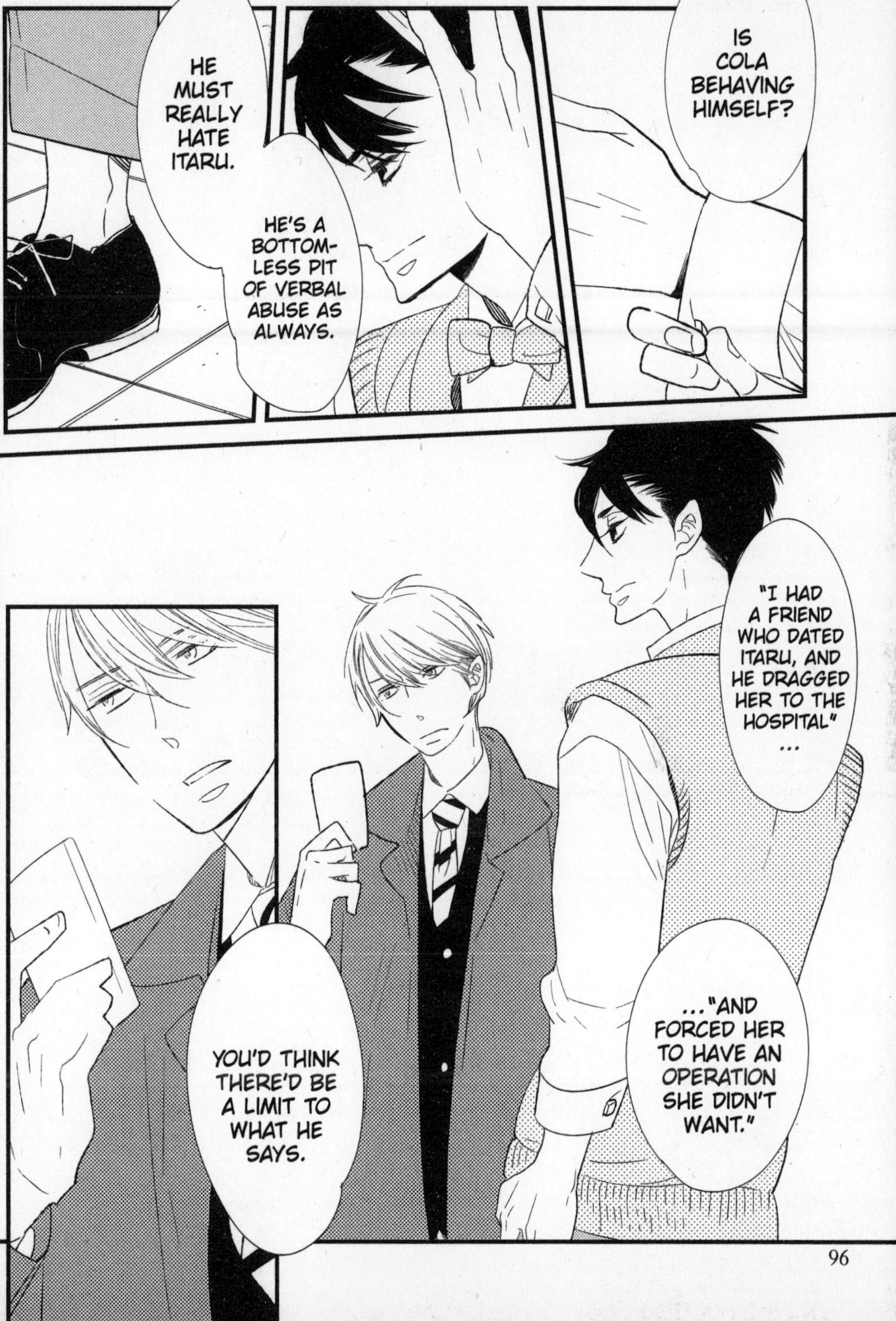
IS COLA BEHAVING HIMSELF?
HE MUST REALLY HATE ITARU.
HE'S A BOTTOMLESS PIT OF VERBAL ABUSE AS ALWAYS.
"I HAD A FRIEND WHO DATED ITARU, AND HE DRAGGED HER TO THE HOSPITAL" ...
..."AND FORCED HER TO HAVE AN OPERATION SHE DIDN'T WANT."
YOU'D THINK THERE'D BE A LIMIT TO WHAT HE SAYS.

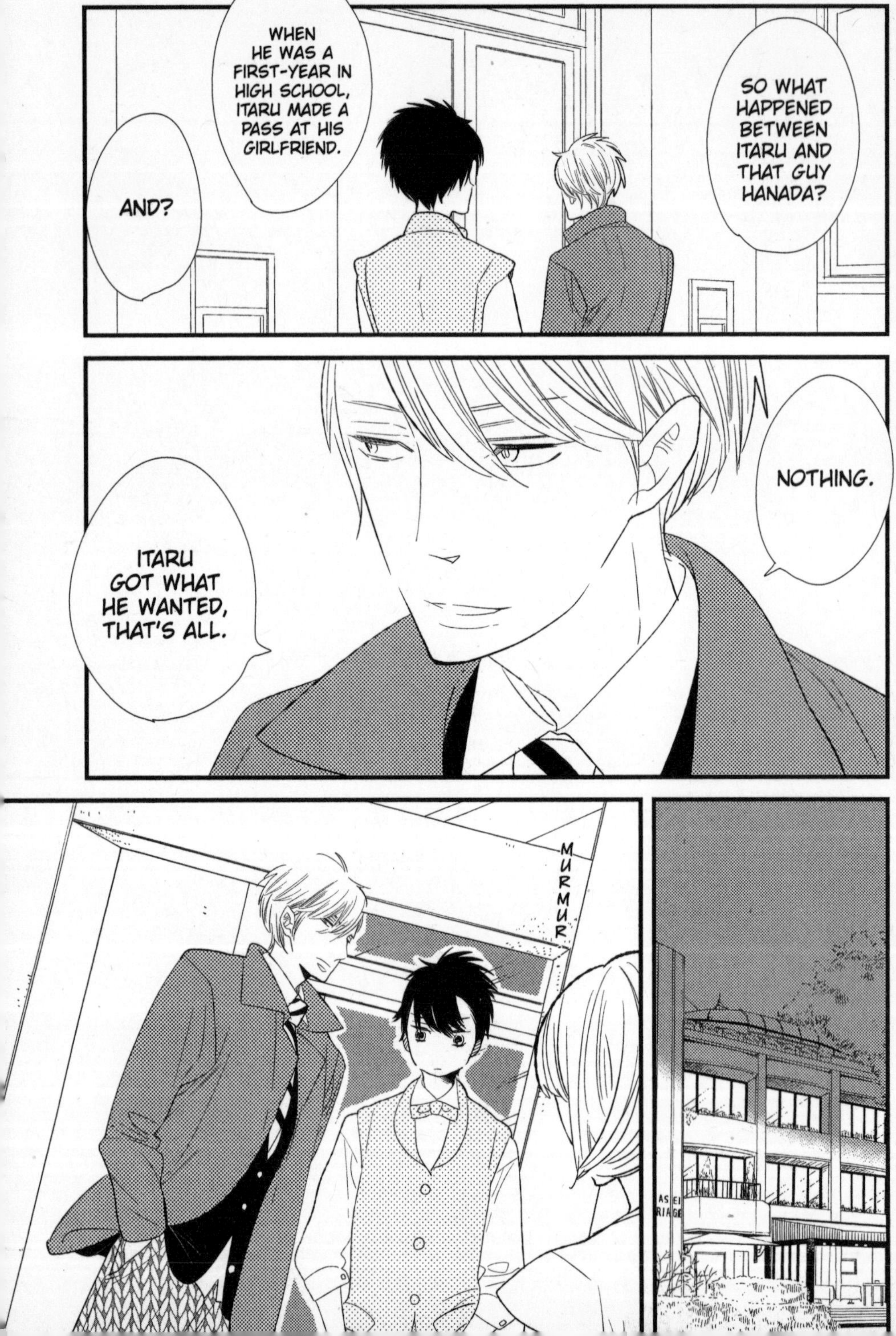
SO WHAT HAPPENED BETWEEN ITARU AND THAT GUY HANADA?
WHEN HE WAS A FIRST-YEAR IN HIGH SCHOOL, ITARU MADE A PASS AT HIS GIRLFRIEND.
AND?
NOTHING.
ITARU GOT WHAT HE WANTED, THAT'S ALL.
MURMUR

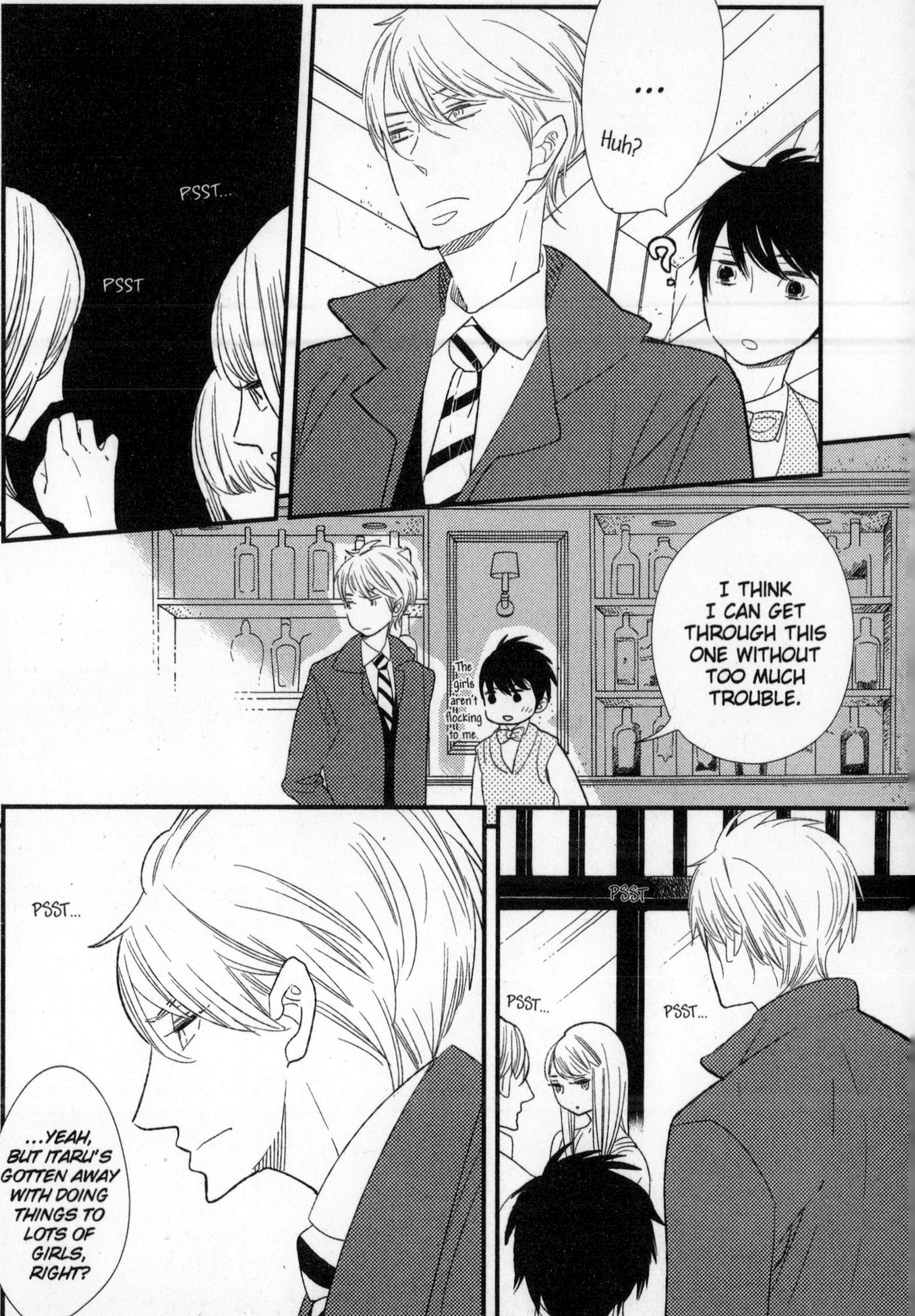
...
Huh?
PSST...
PSST
I THINK I CAN GET THROUGH THIS ONE WITHOUT TOO MUCH TROUBLE.
The girls aren't flocking to me.
PSST
PSST...
PSST...
PSST...
...YEAH, BUT ITARU'S GOTTEN AWAY WITH DOING THINGS TO LOTS OF GIRLS, RIGHT?

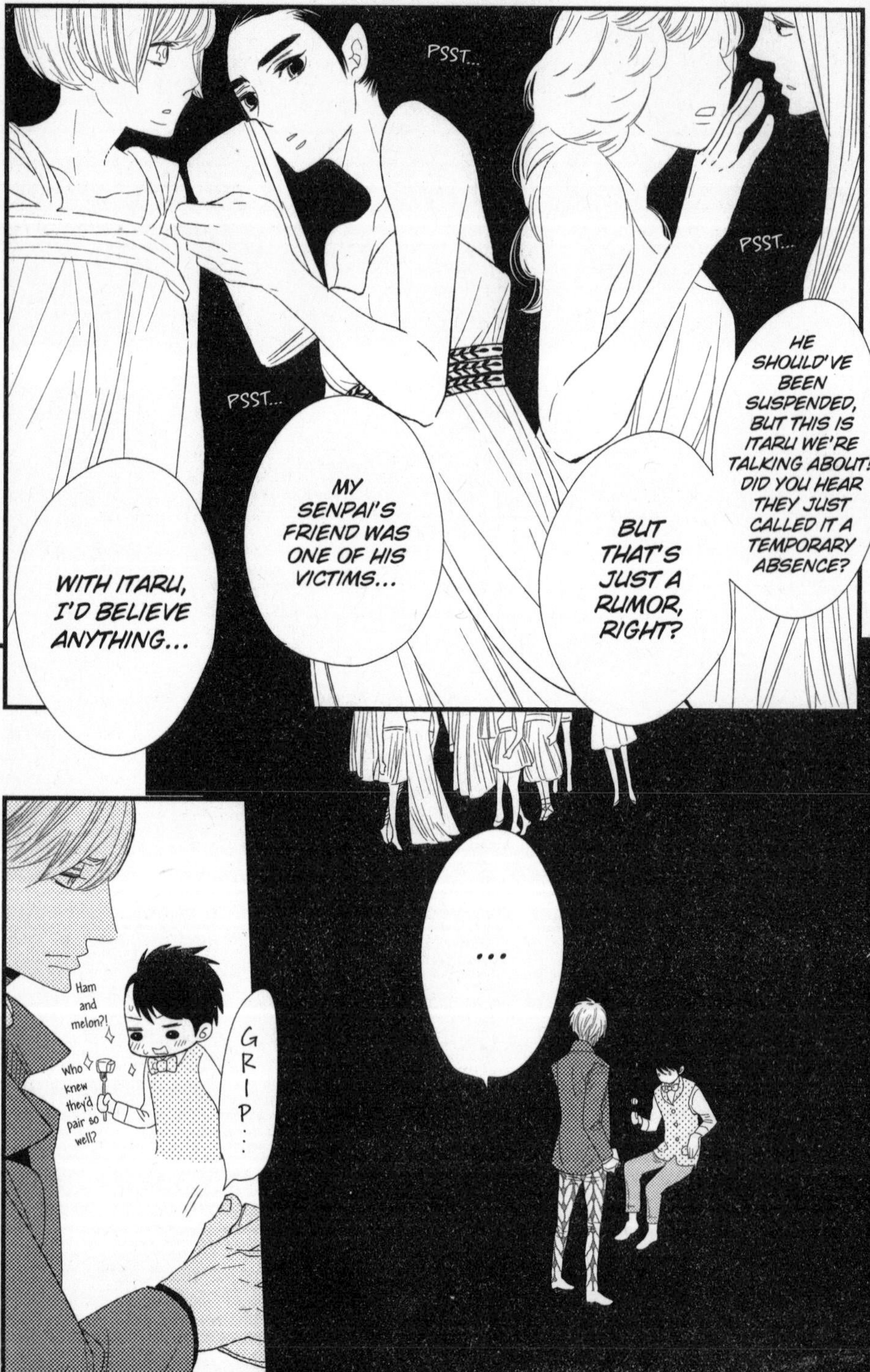
PSST...
HE SHOULD'VE BEEN SUSPENDED, BUT THIS IS ITARU WE'RE TALKING ABOUT! DID YOU HEAR THEY JUST CALLED IT A TEMPORARY ABSENCE?
BUT THAT'S JUST A RUMOR, RIGHT?
PSST...
MY SENPAI'S FRIEND WAS ONE OF HIS VICTIMS...
PSST...
WITH ITARU, I'D BELIEVE ANYTHING...
...
GRIP...
Ham and melon?!
Who knew they'd pair so well?

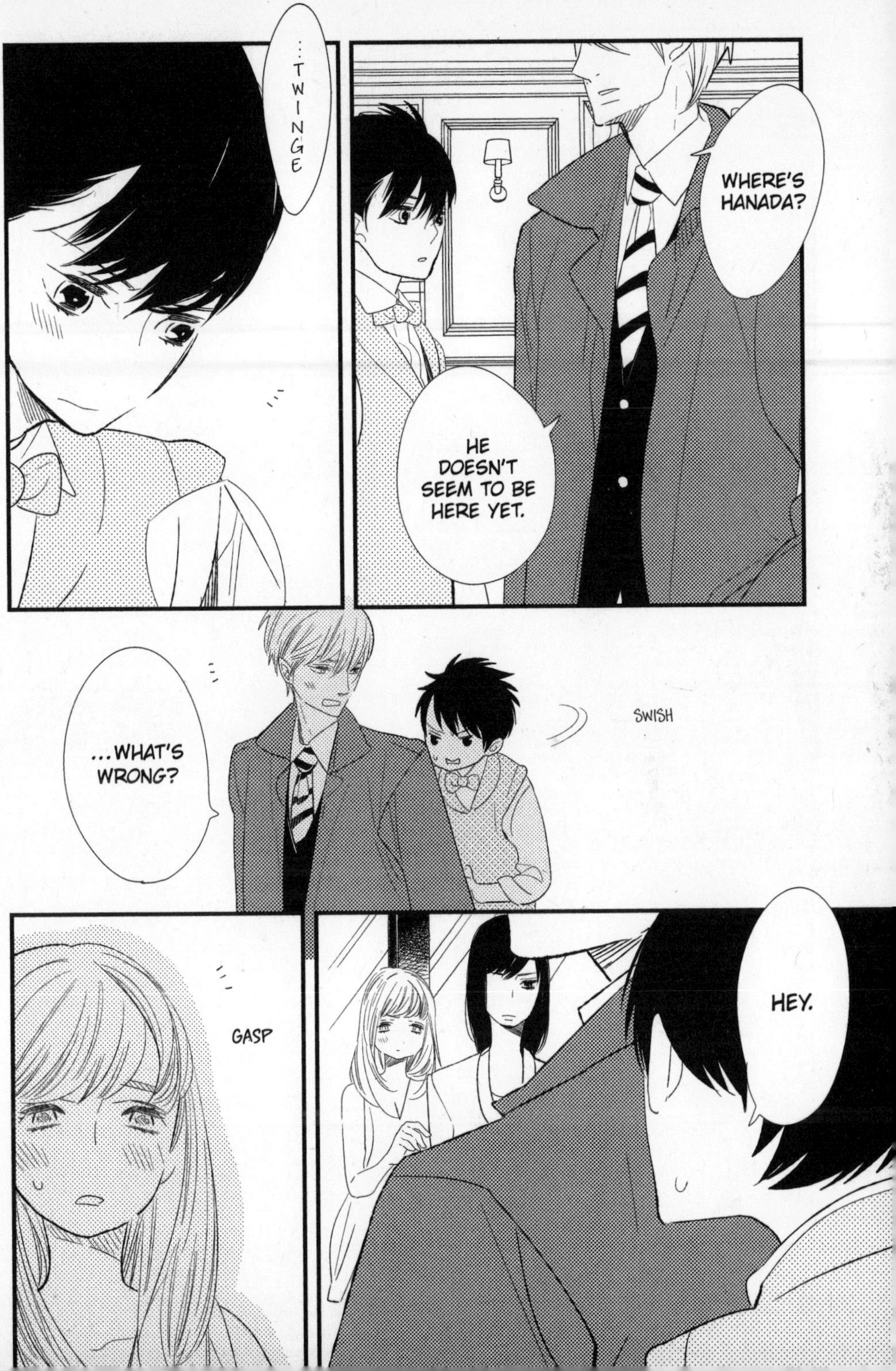
WHERE'S HANADA?
HE DOESN'T SEEM TO BE HERE YET.
...TWINGE
SWISH
...WHAT'S WRONG?
HEY.
GASP

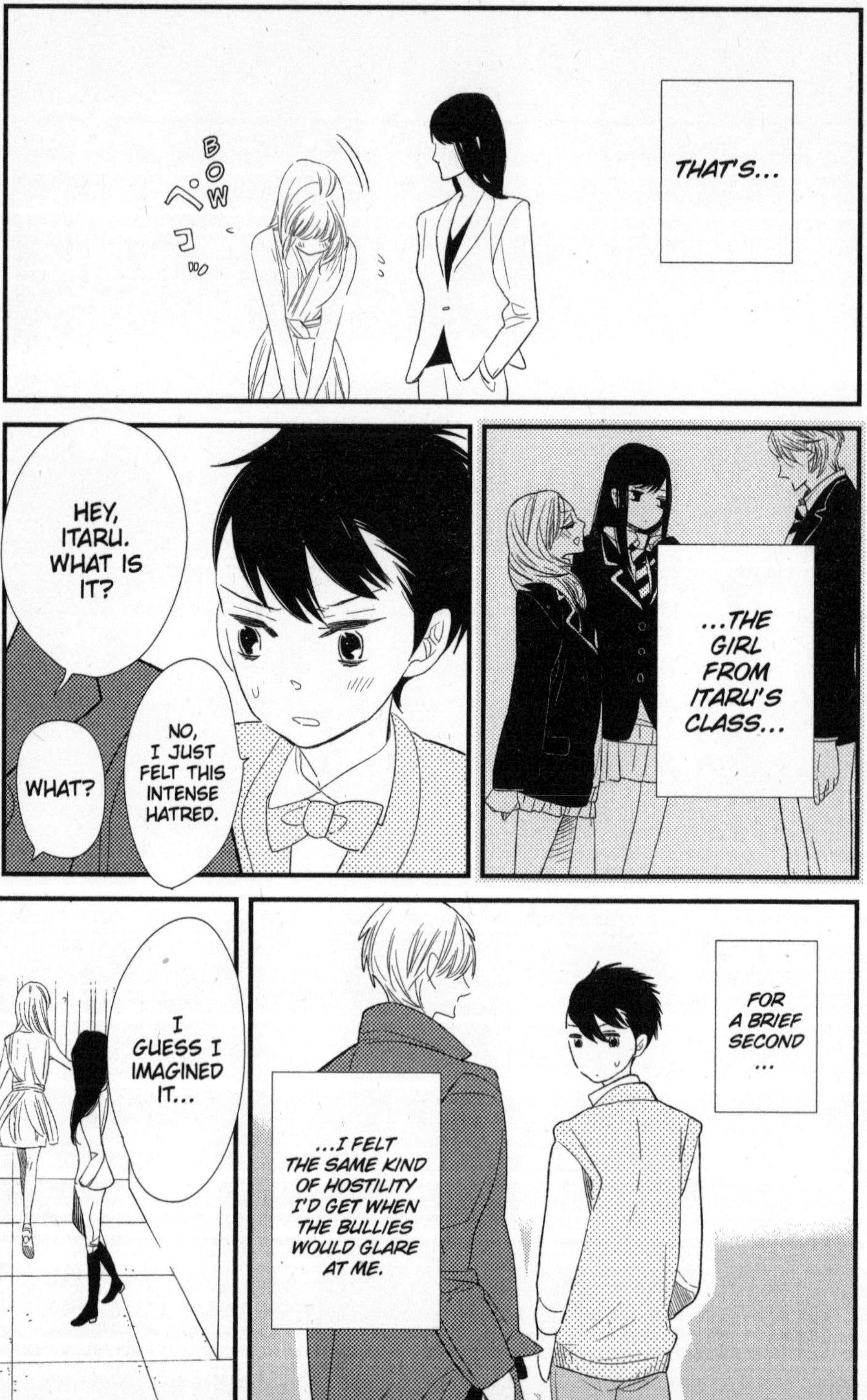
THAT'S...
BOW
...THE GIRL FROM ITARU'S CLASS...
HEY, ITARU. WHAT IS IT?
NO, I JUST FELT THIS INTENSE HATRED.
WHAT?
FOR A BRIEF SECOND...
...I FELT THE SAME KIND OF HOSTILITY I'D GET WHEN THE BULLIES WOULD GLARE AT ME.
I GUESS I IMAGINED IT...

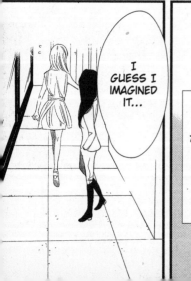

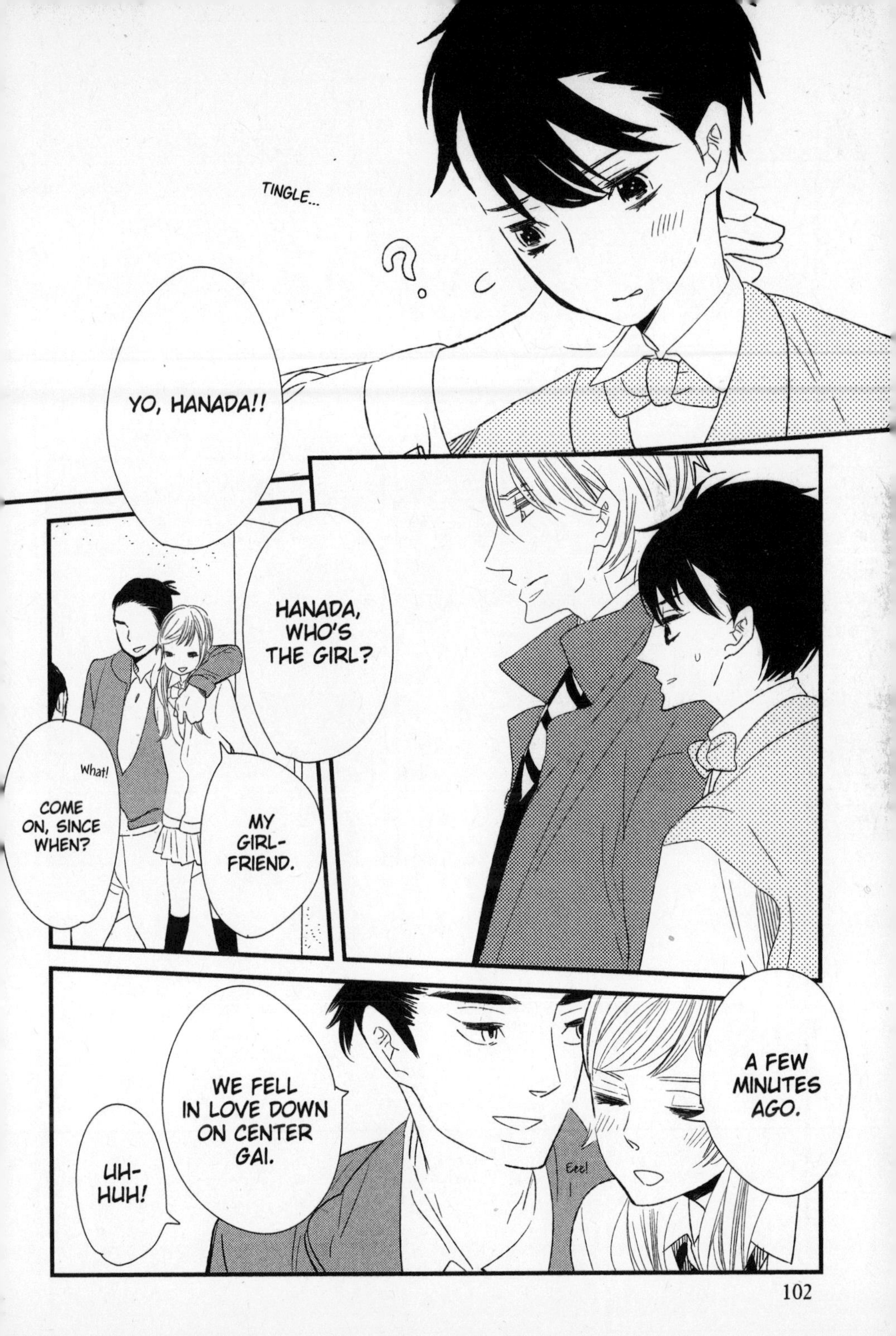
TINGLE...
YO, HANADA!!
HANADA, WHO'S THE GIRL?
MY GIRL-FRIEND.
What!
COME ON, SINCE WHEN?
A FEW MINUTES AGO.
Eee!
WE FELL IN LOVE DOWN ON CENTER GAI.
UH-HUH!

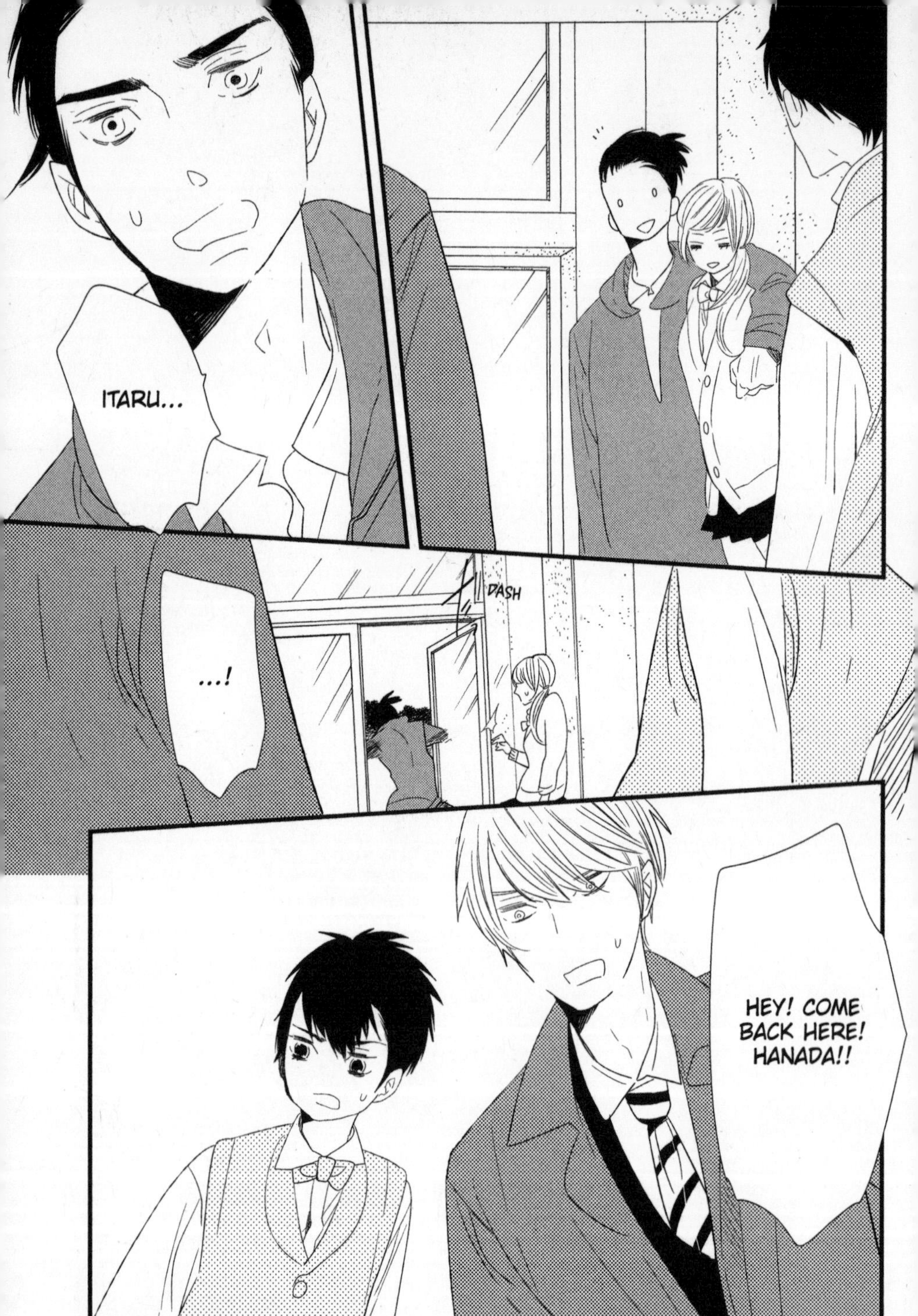
ITARU...
DASH
...!
HEY! COME BACK HERE! HANADA!!

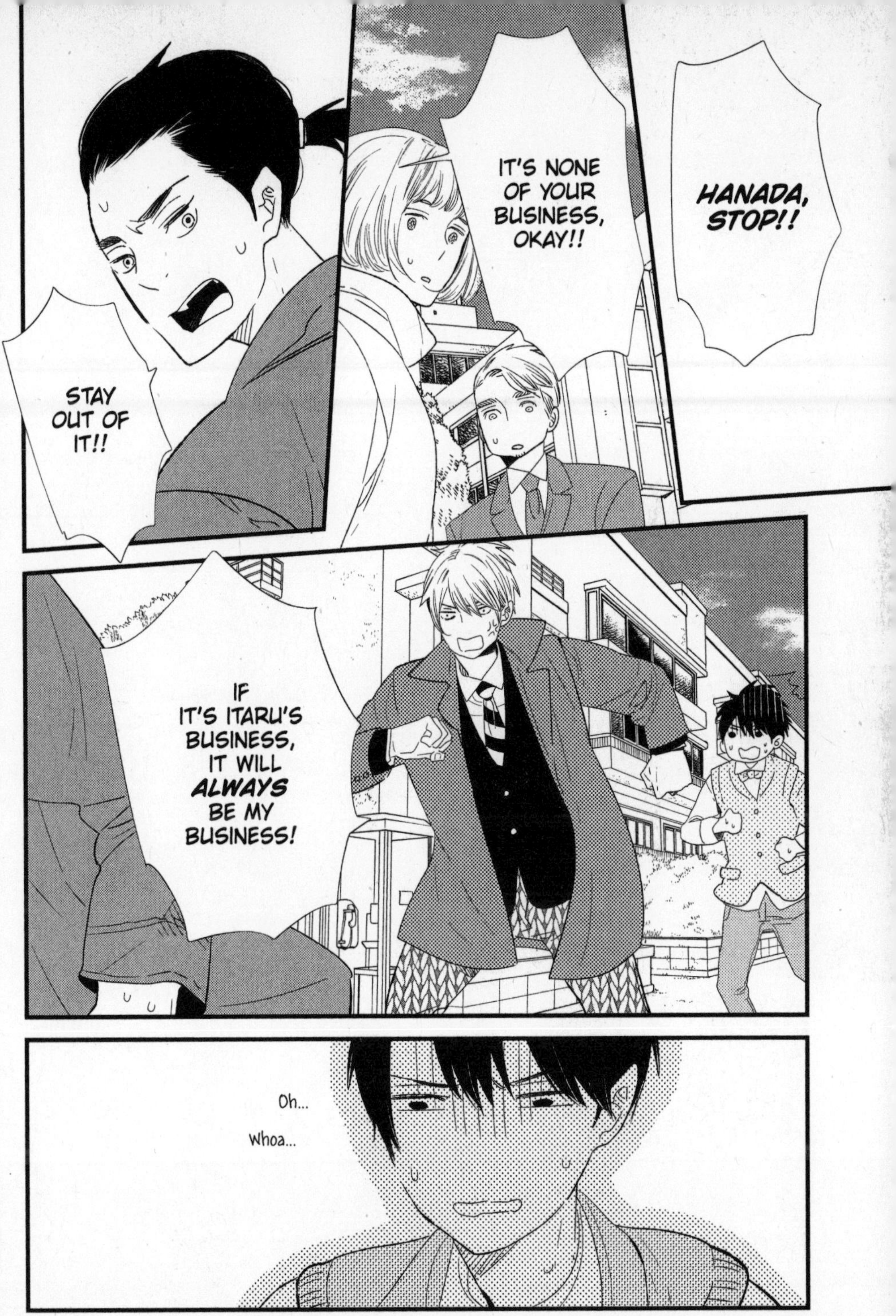
HANADA, STOP!!
IT'S NONE OF YOUR BUSINESS, OKAY!!
STAY OUT OF IT!!
IF IT'S ITARU'S BUSINESS, IT WILL ALWAYS BE MY BUSINESS!
Oh...
Whoa...

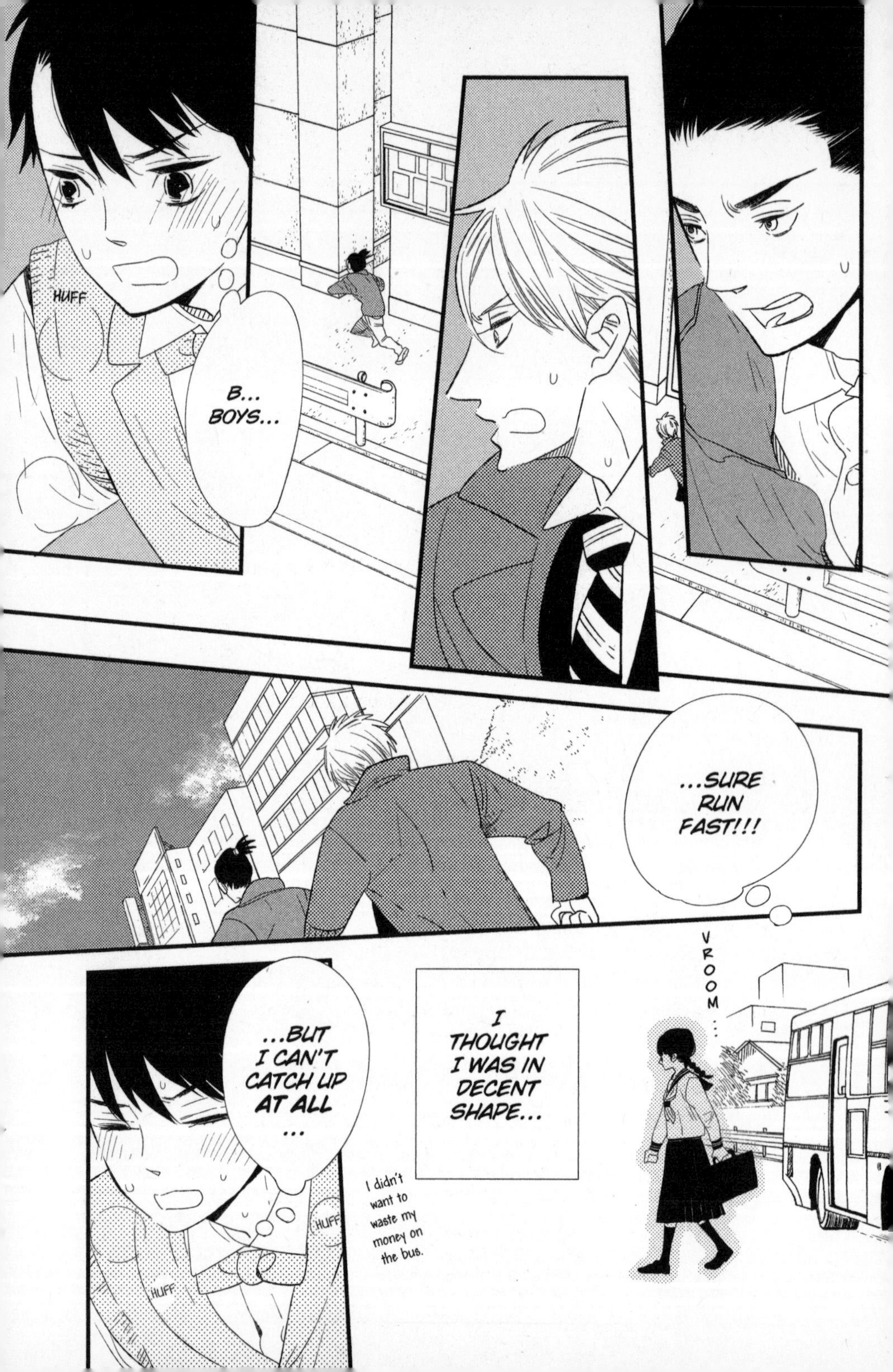
HUFF
B... BOYS...
...SURE RUN FAST!!!
VROOM...
I didn't want to waste my money on the bus.
I THOUGHT I WAS IN DECENT SHAPE...
...BUT I CAN'T CATCH UP AT ALL...
HUFF
HUFF

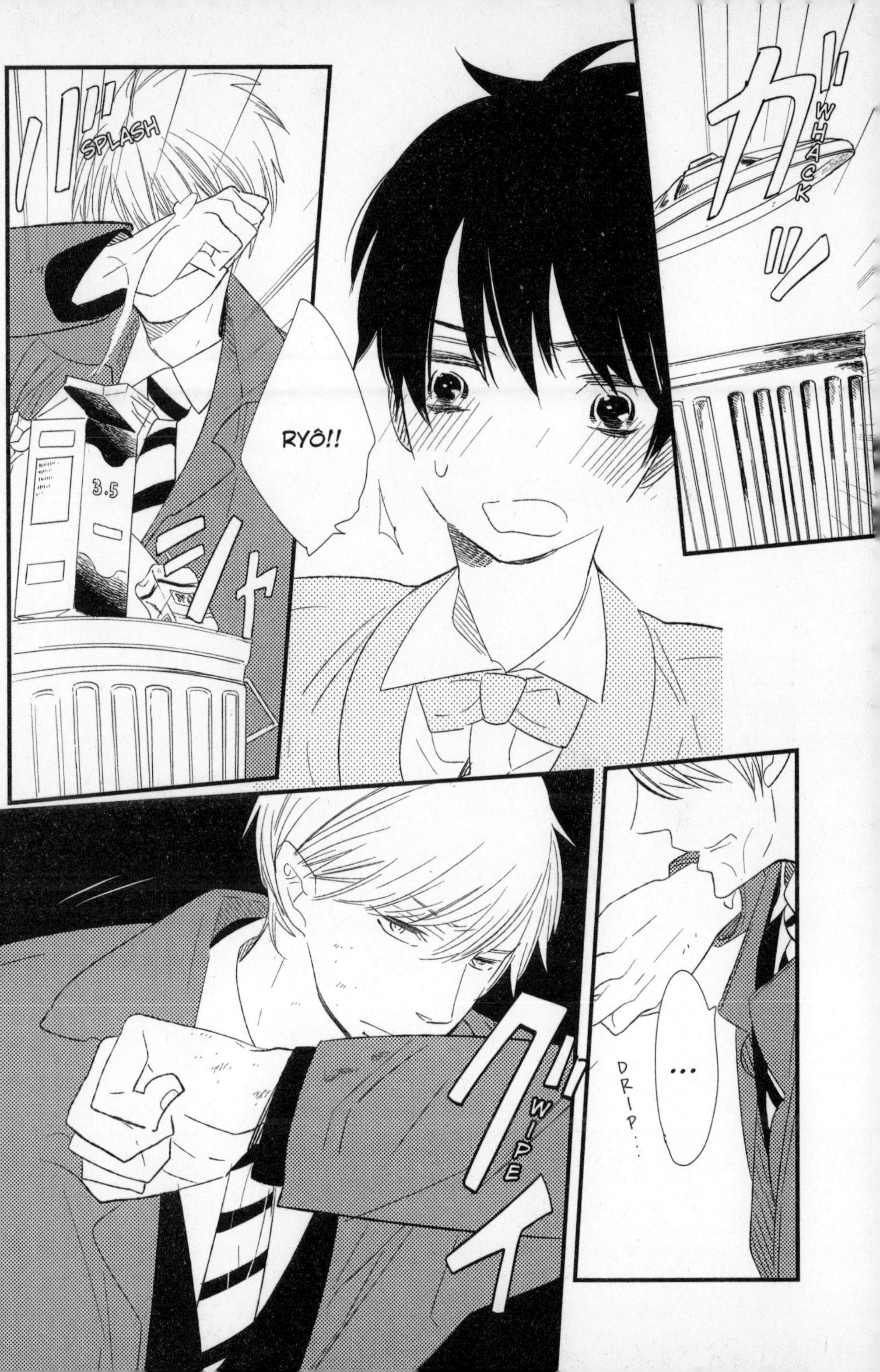
WHACK
RYÔ!!
SPLASH
DRIP...
...
WIPE

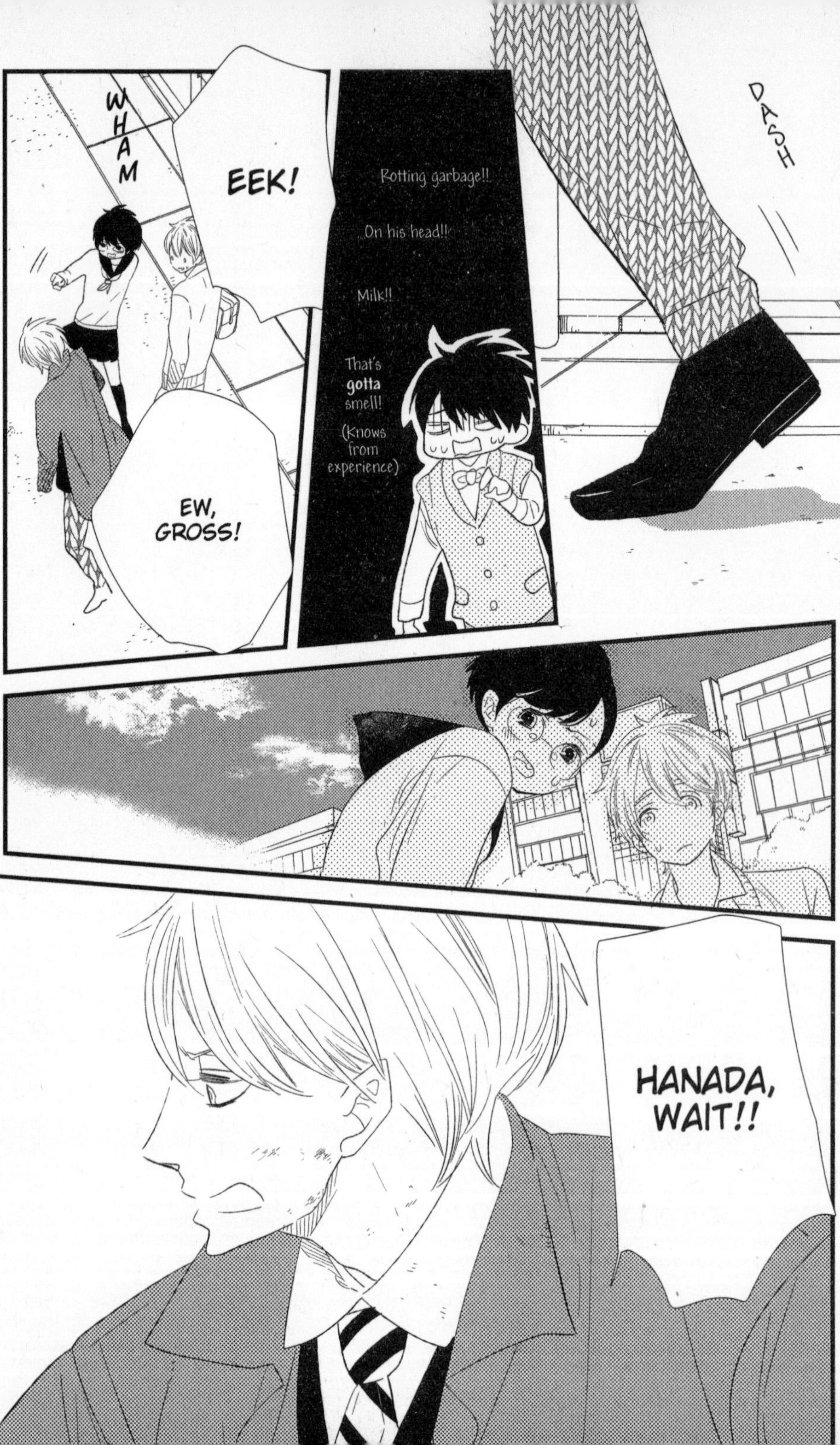
DASH
Rotting garbage!!
On his head!!
Milk!!
That's gotta smell!
(Knows from experience)
WHAM
EEK!
EW, GROSS!
HANADA, WAIT!!

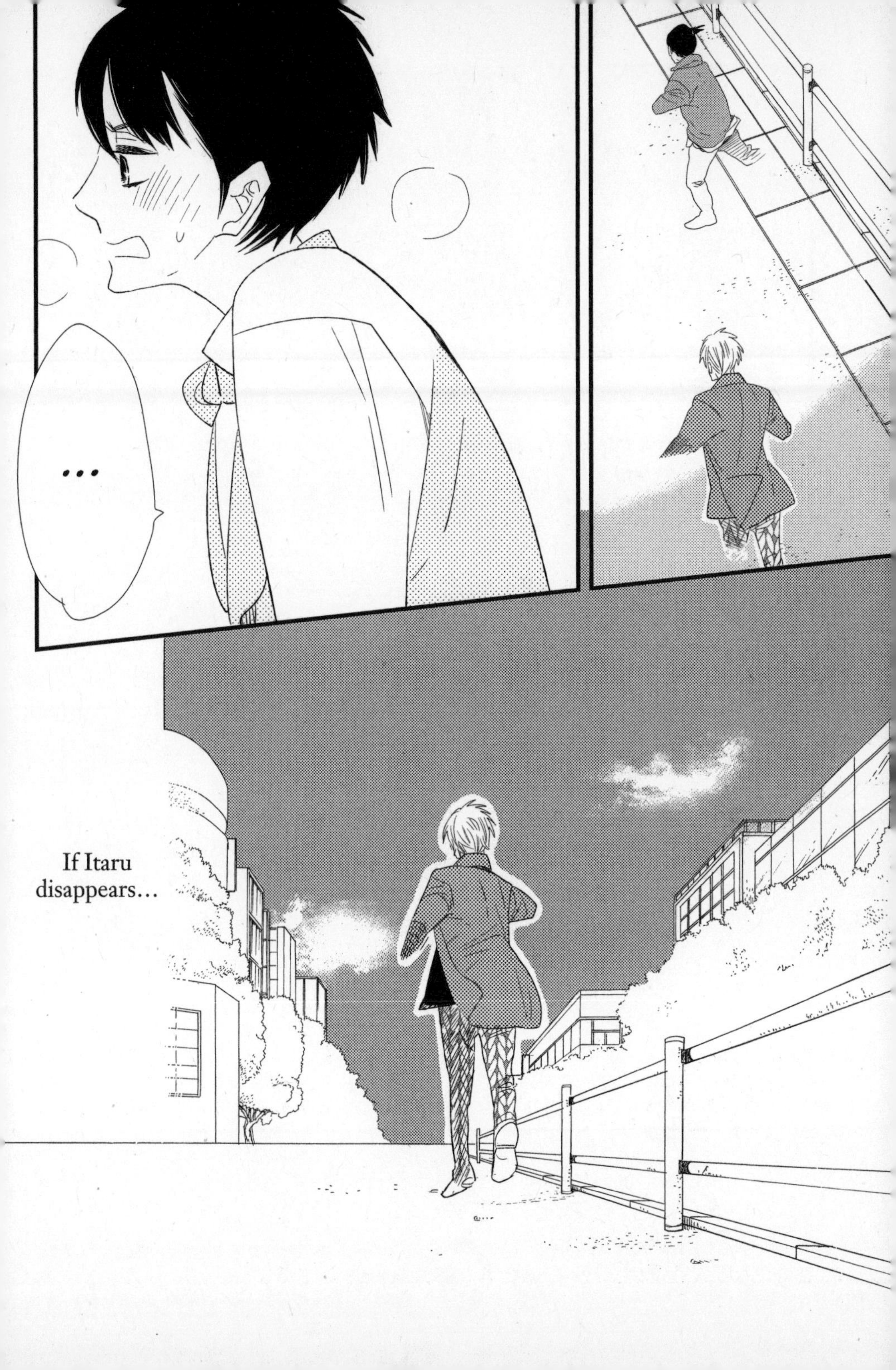
...
If Itaru disappears...

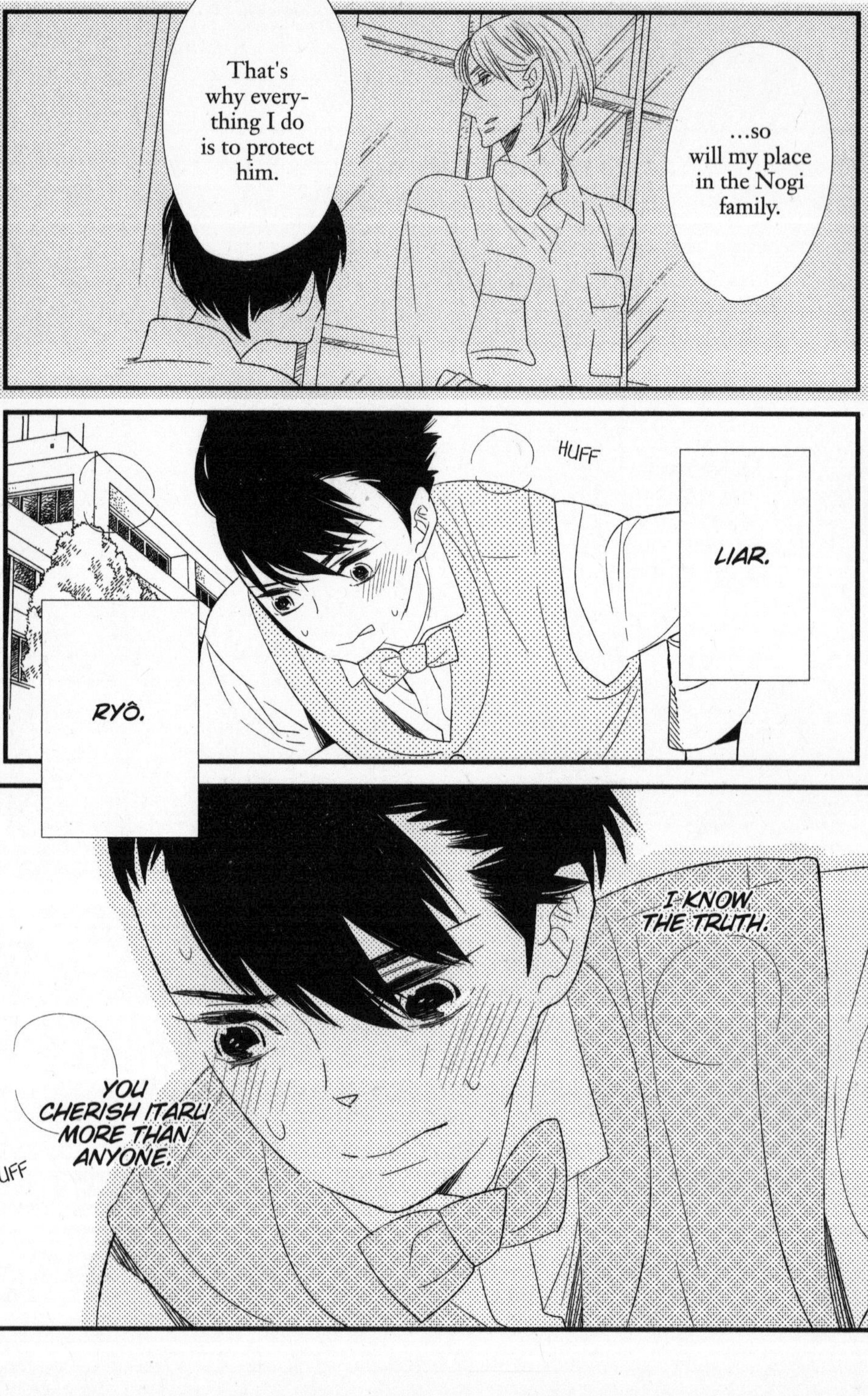
…so will my place in the Nogi family.
That's why every-thing I do is to protect him.
HUFF
LIAR.
RYÔ.
I KNOW THE TRUTH.
YOU CHERISH ITARU MORE THAN ANYONE.
HUFF

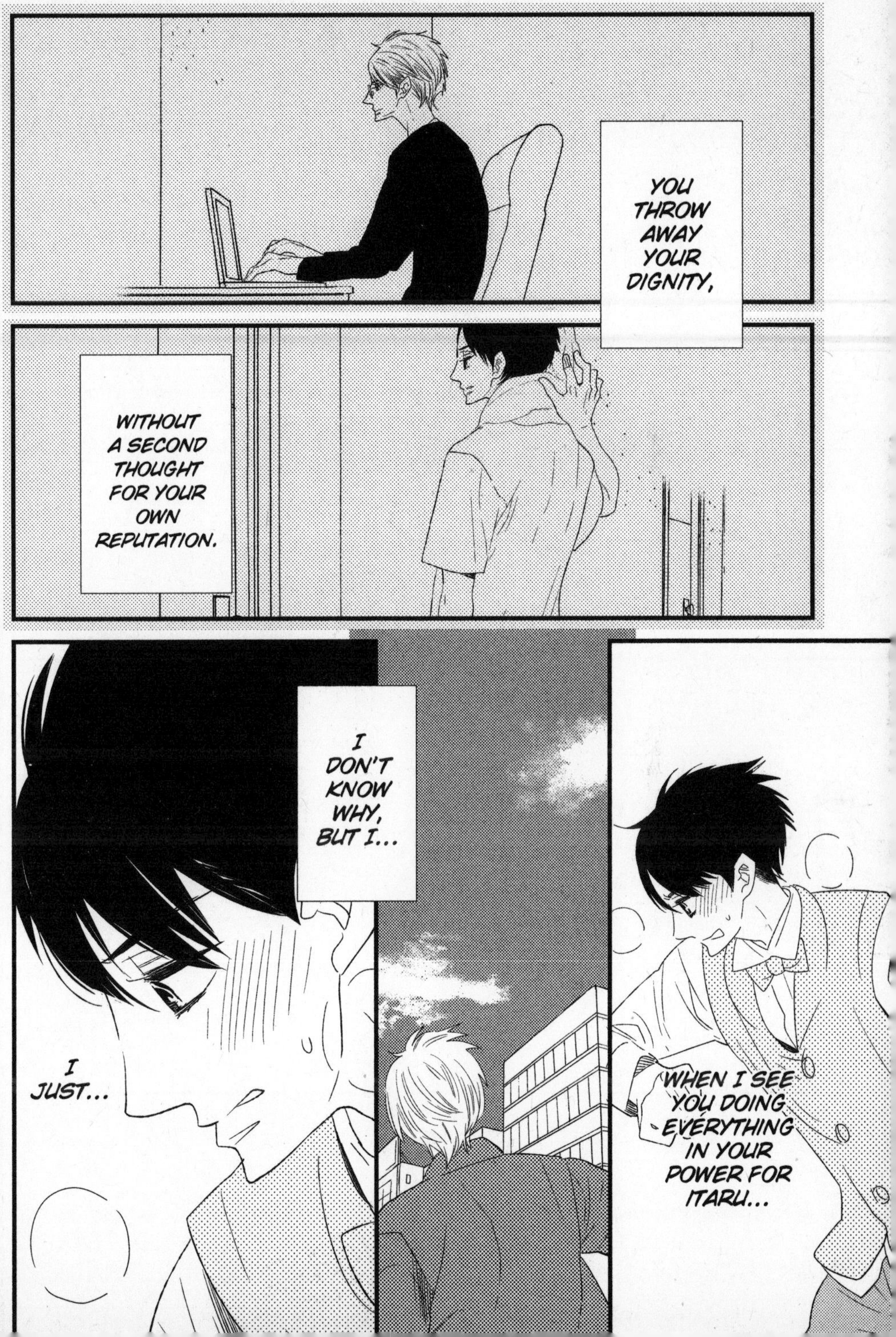
YOU THROW AWAY YOUR DIGNITY,
WITHOUT A SECOND THOUGHT FOR YOUR OWN REPUTATION.
WHEN I SEE YOU DOING EVERYTHING IN YOUR POWER FOR ITARU...
I DON'T KNOW WHY, BUT I...
I JUST...

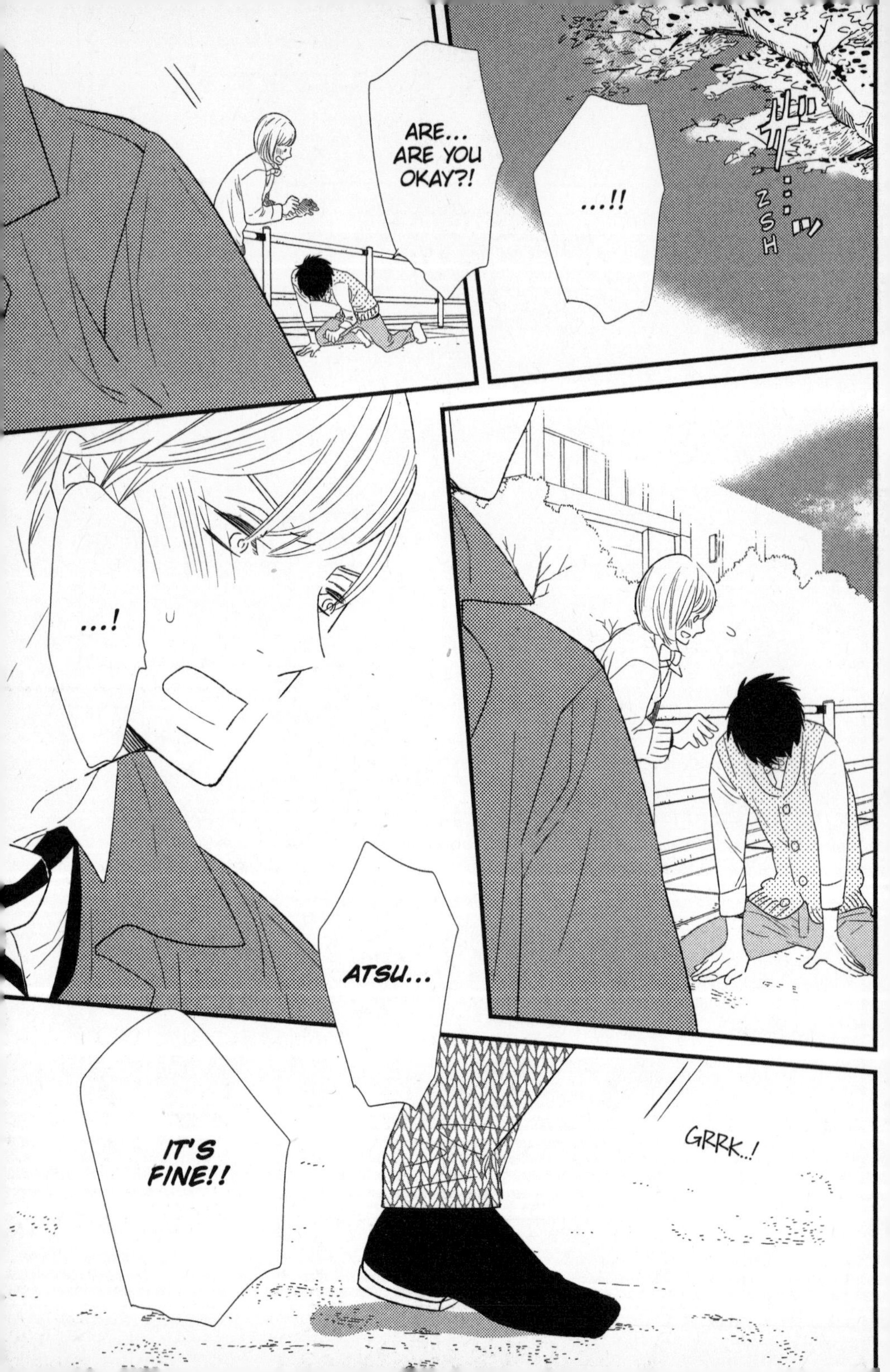

...!!
ZSH
ARE... ARE YOU OKAY?!
...!
ATSU...
GRRK..!
IT'S FINE!!

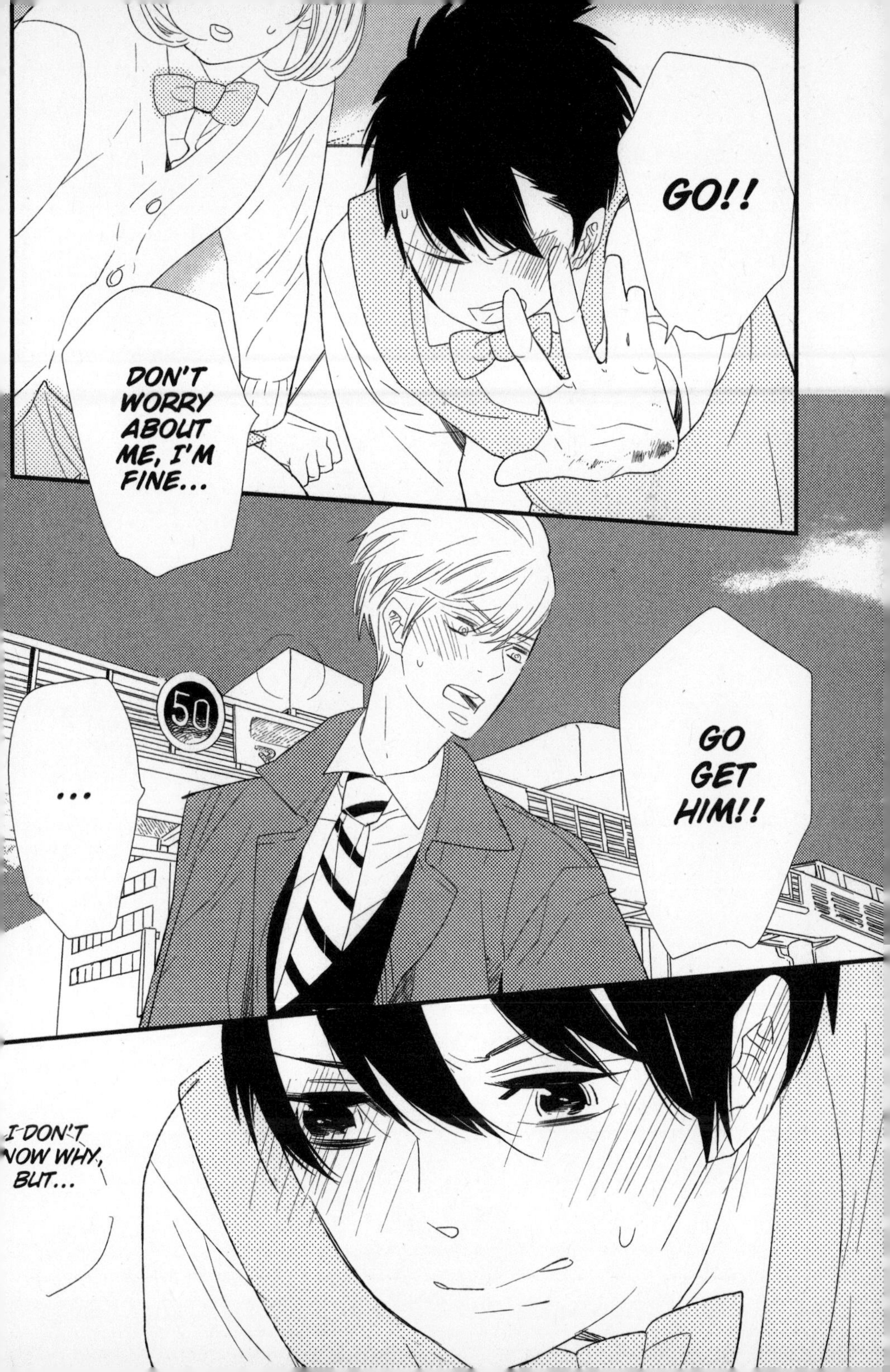
GO!!
DON'T WORRY ABOUT ME, I'M FINE...
GO GET HIM!!
...
I DON'T NOW WHY, BUT...

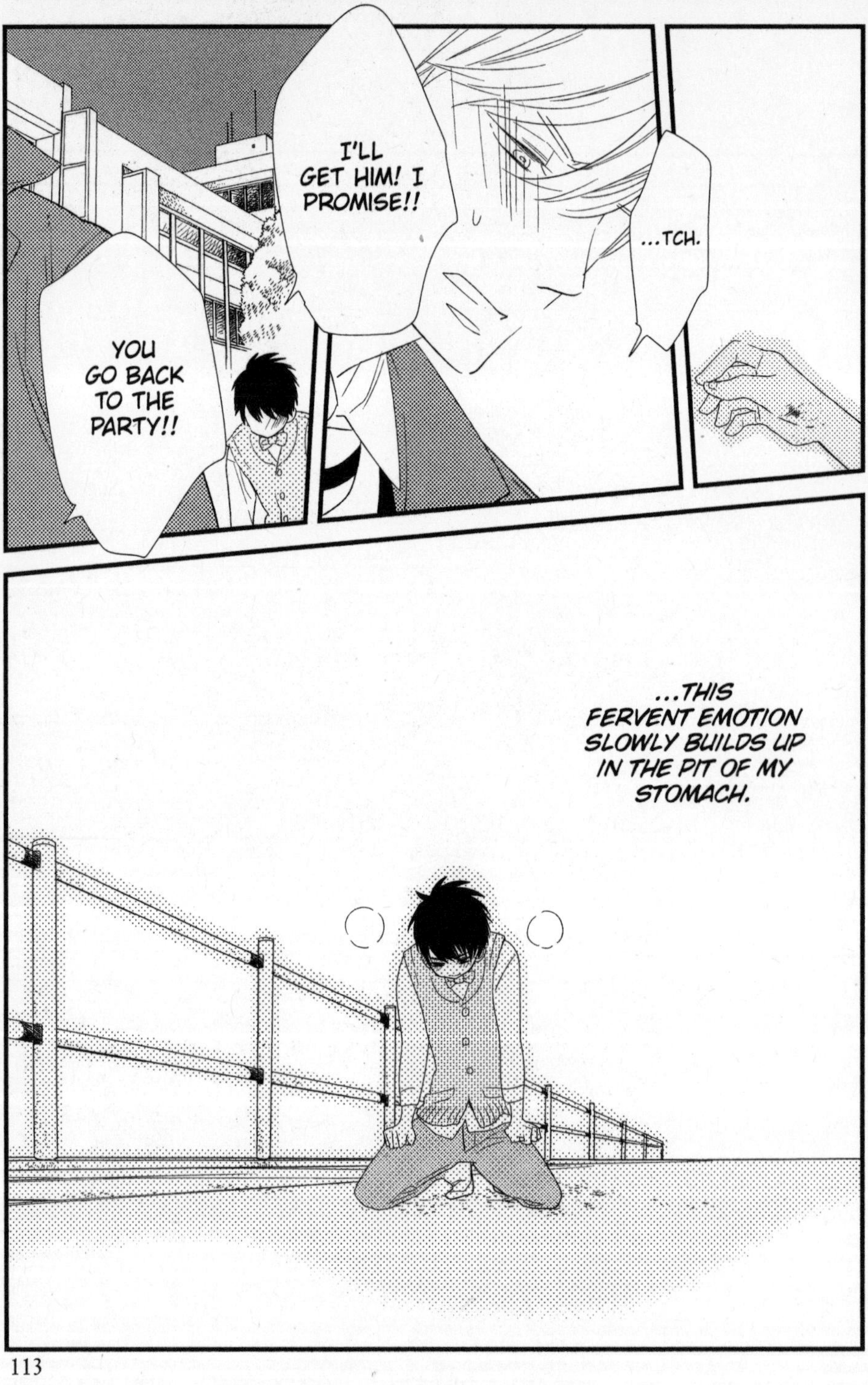
...TCH.
I'LL GET HIM! I PROMISE!!
YOU GO BACK TO THE PARTY!!
...THIS FERVENT EMOTION SLOWLY BUILDS UP IN THE PIT OF MY STOMACH.

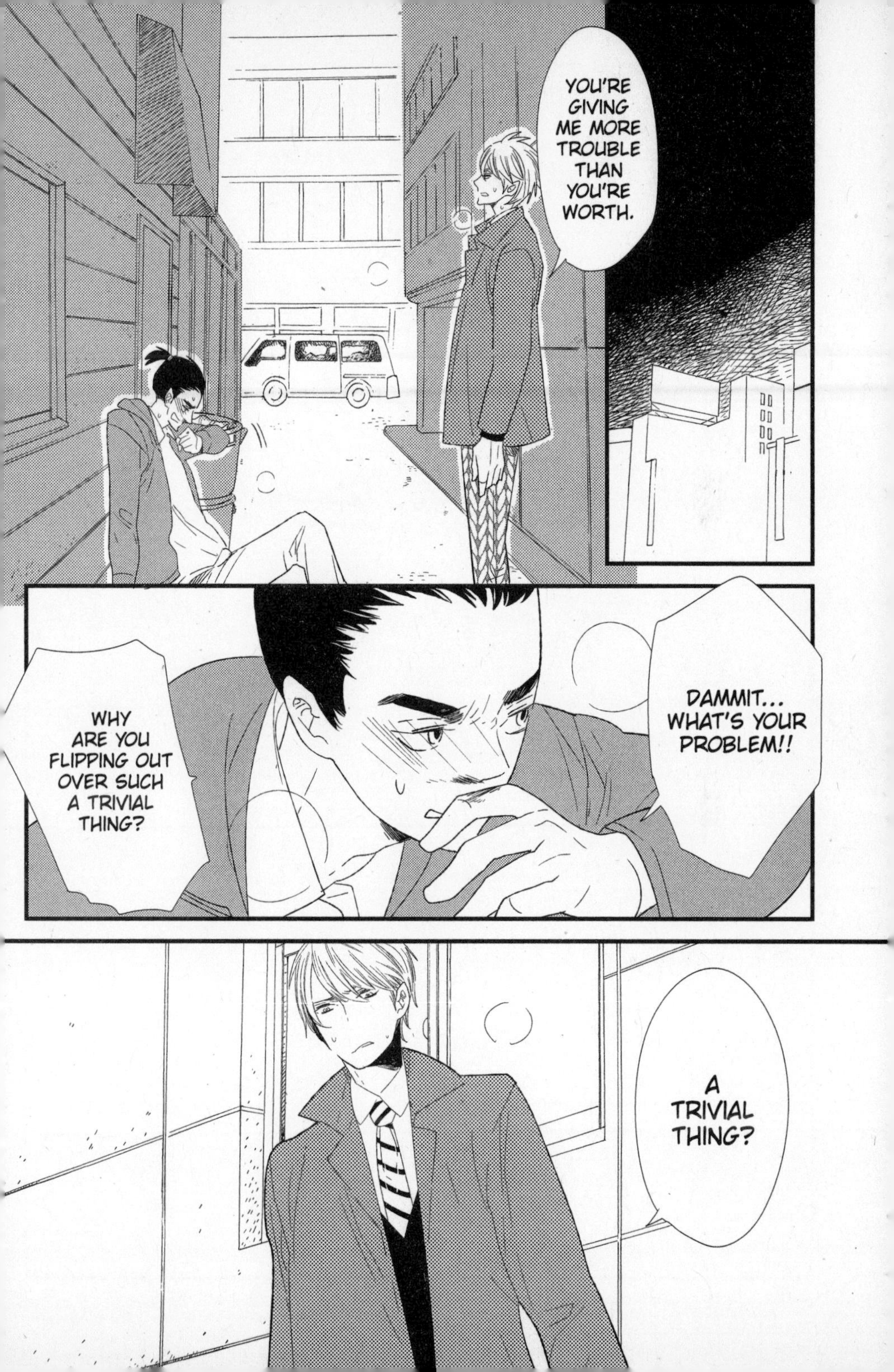
YOU'RE GIVING ME MORE TROUBLE THAN YOU'RE WORTH.
DAMMIT... WHAT'S YOUR PROBLEM!!
WHY ARE YOU FLIPPING OUT OVER SUCH A TRIVIAL THING?
A TRIVIAL THING?

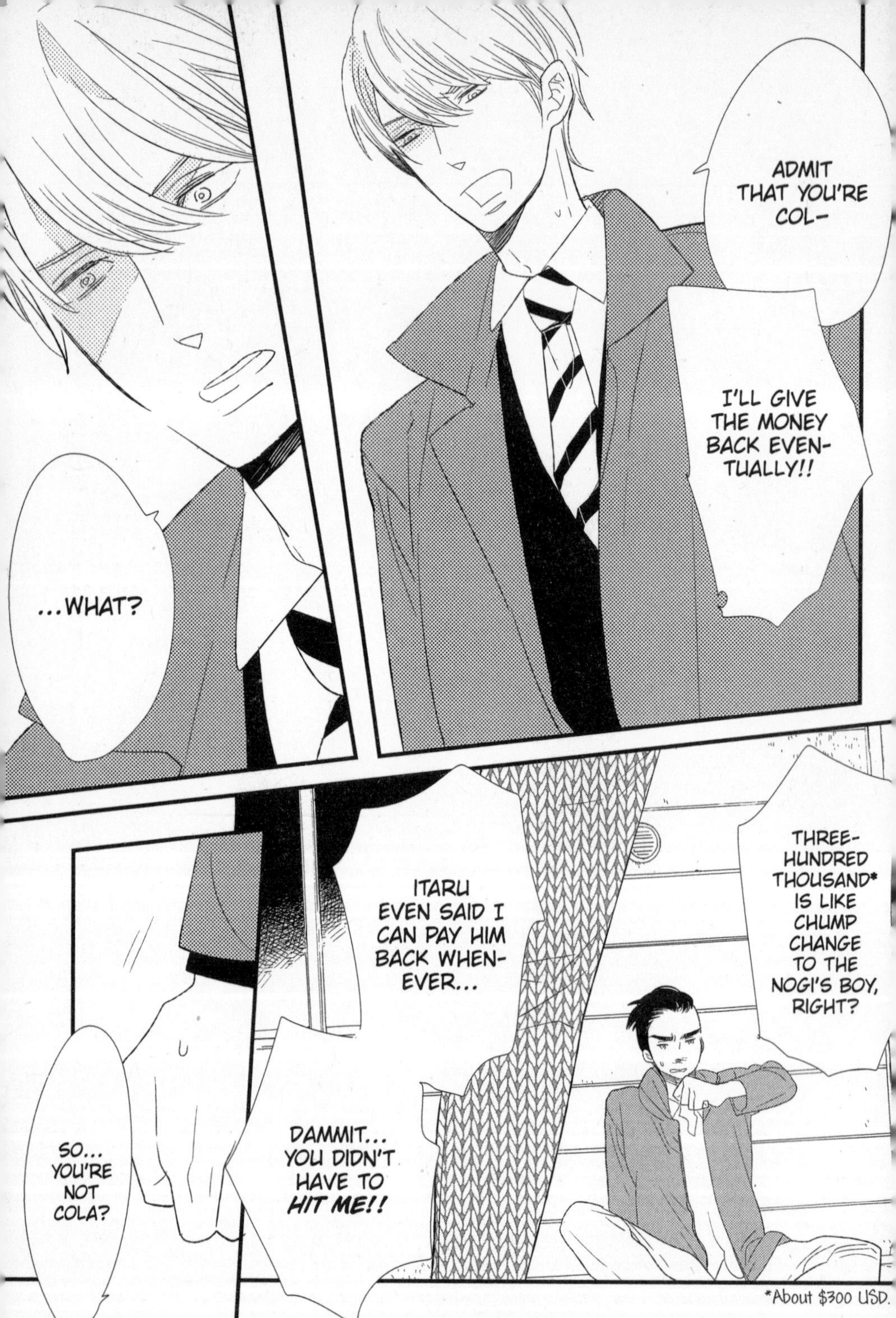
ADMIT THAT YOU'RE COL–
I'LL GIVE THE MONEY BACK EVEN-TUALLY!!
...WHAT?
THREE-HUNDRED THOUSAND* IS LIKE CHUMP CHANGE TO THE NOGI'S BOY, RIGHT?
ITARU EVEN SAID I CAN PAY HIM BACK WHEN-EVER...
DAMMIT... YOU DIDN'T HAVE TO *HIT ME!!*
SO... YOU'RE NOT COLA?

*About $300 USD.

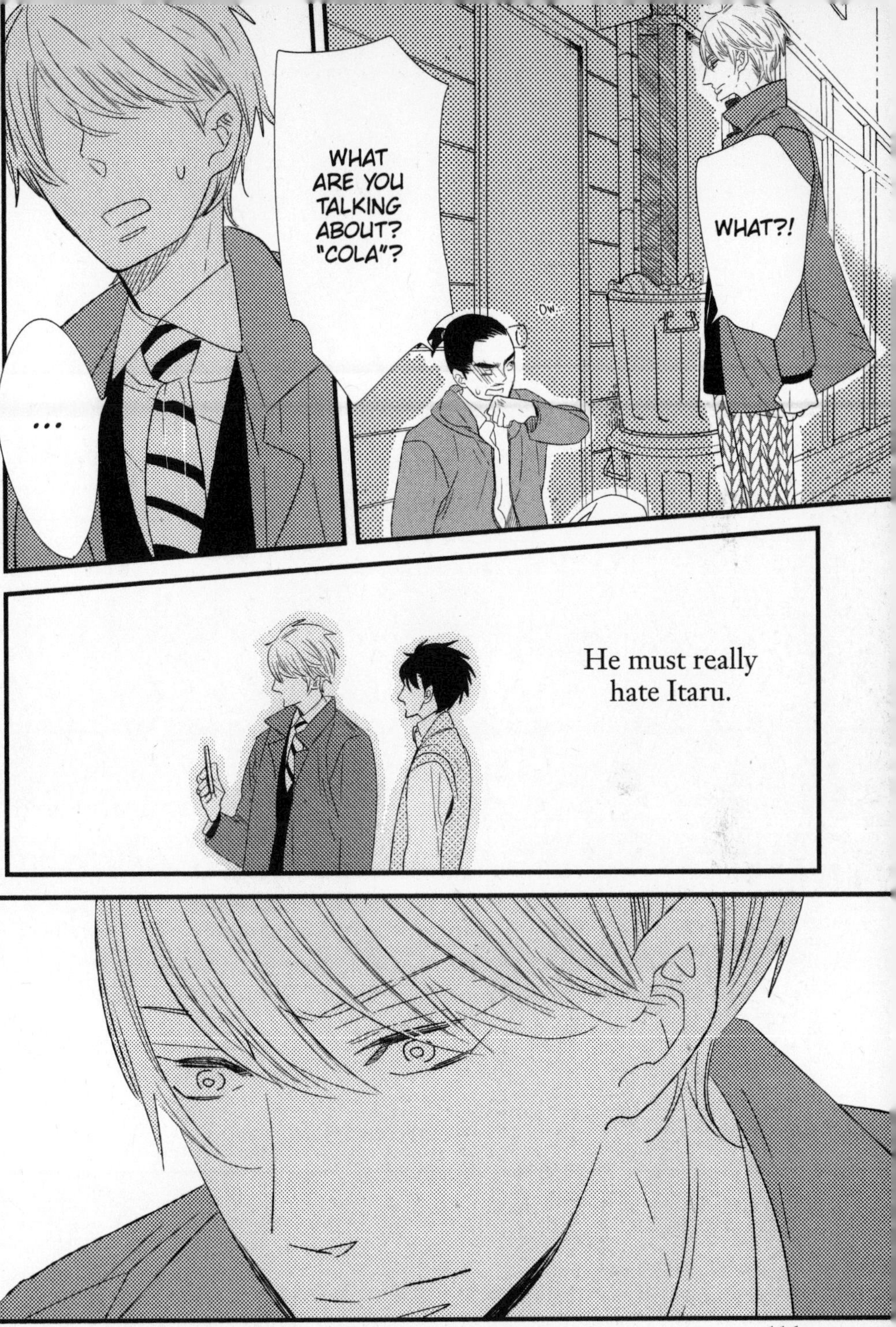
WHAT?!
WHAT ARE YOU TALKING ABOUT? "COLA"?
OW
...
He must really hate Itaru.

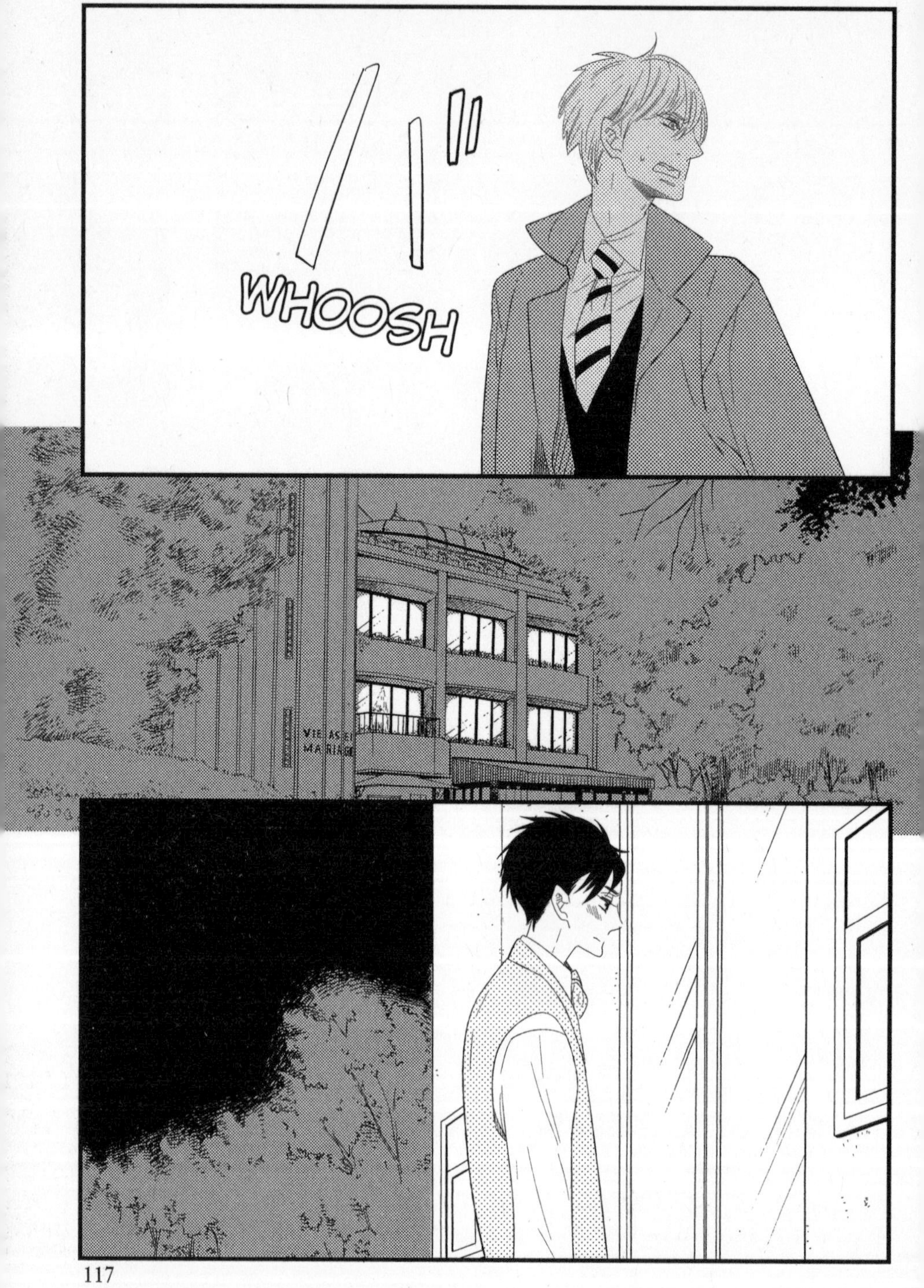
WHOOSH

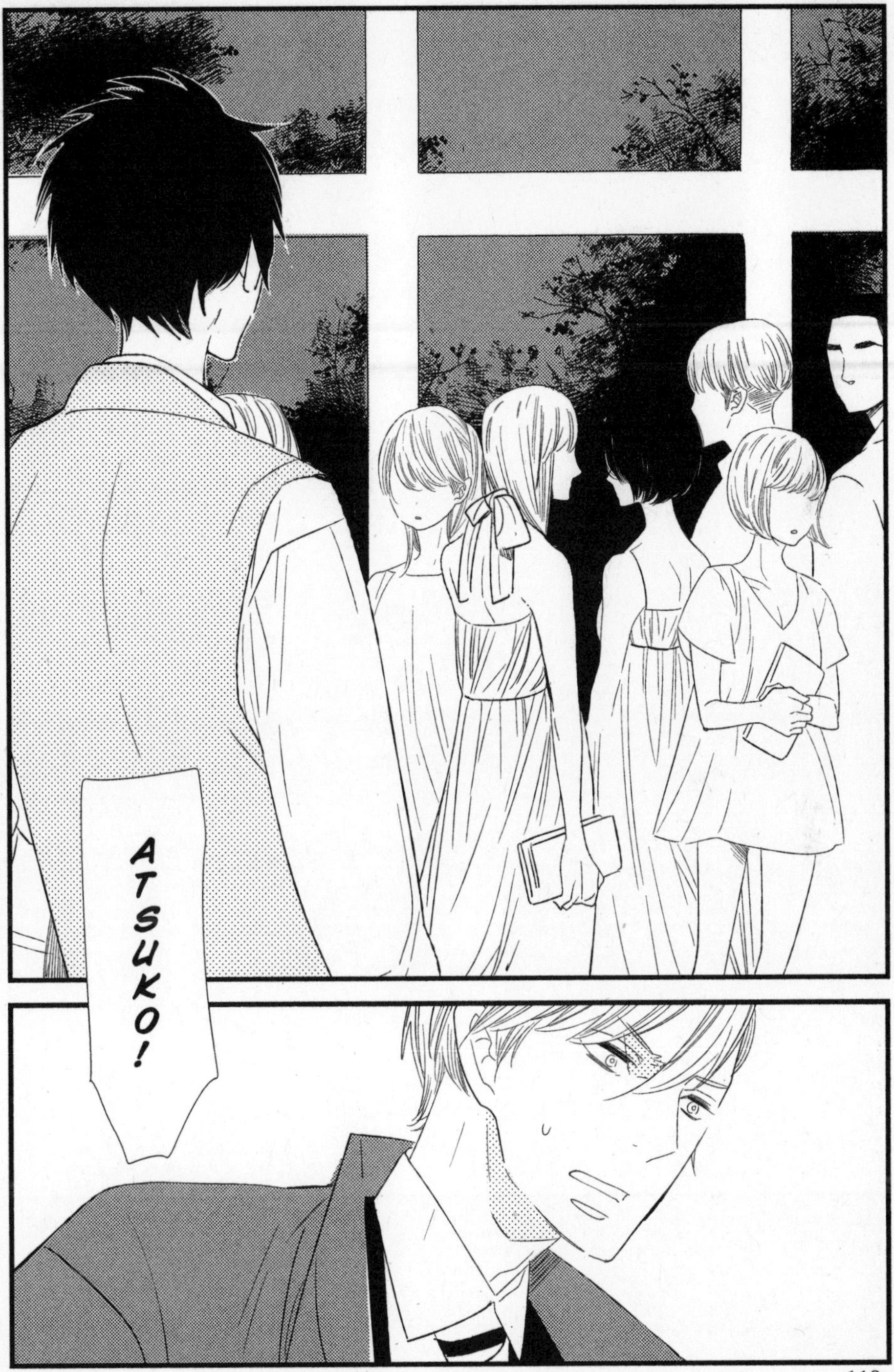
ATSUKO!

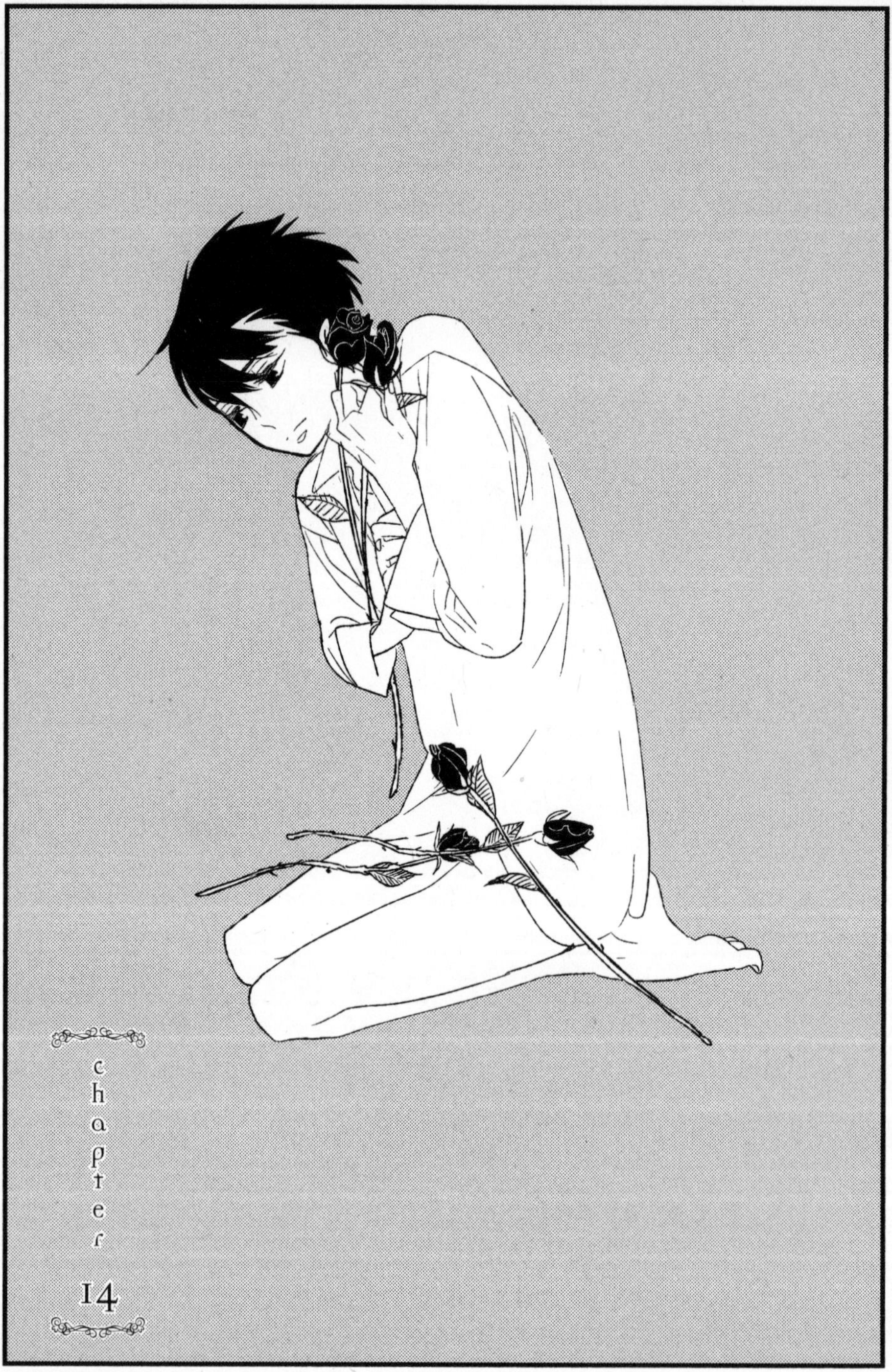
chapter
14

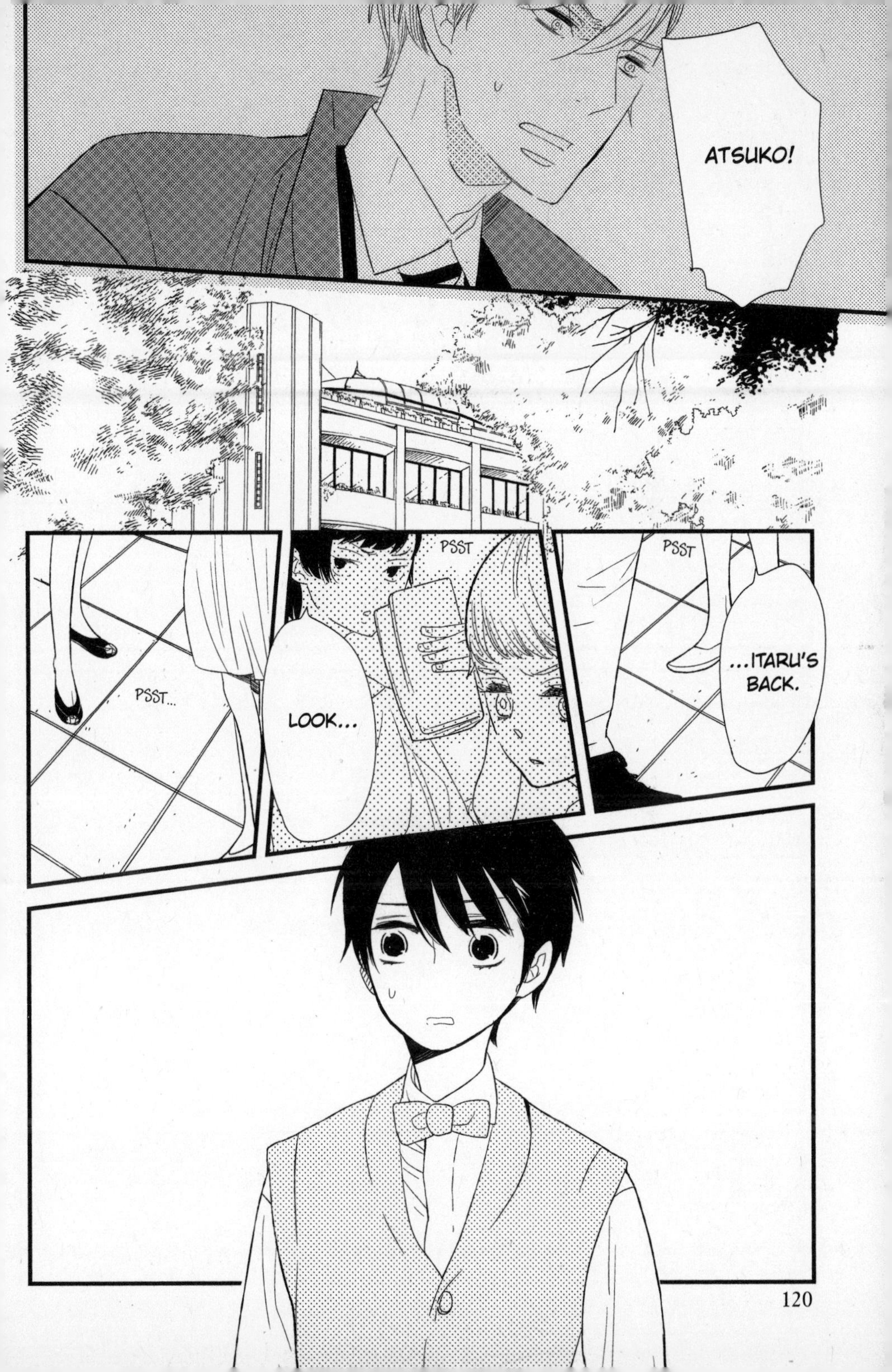
ATSUKO!
PSST
...ITARU'S BACK.
PSST
LOOK...
PSST...

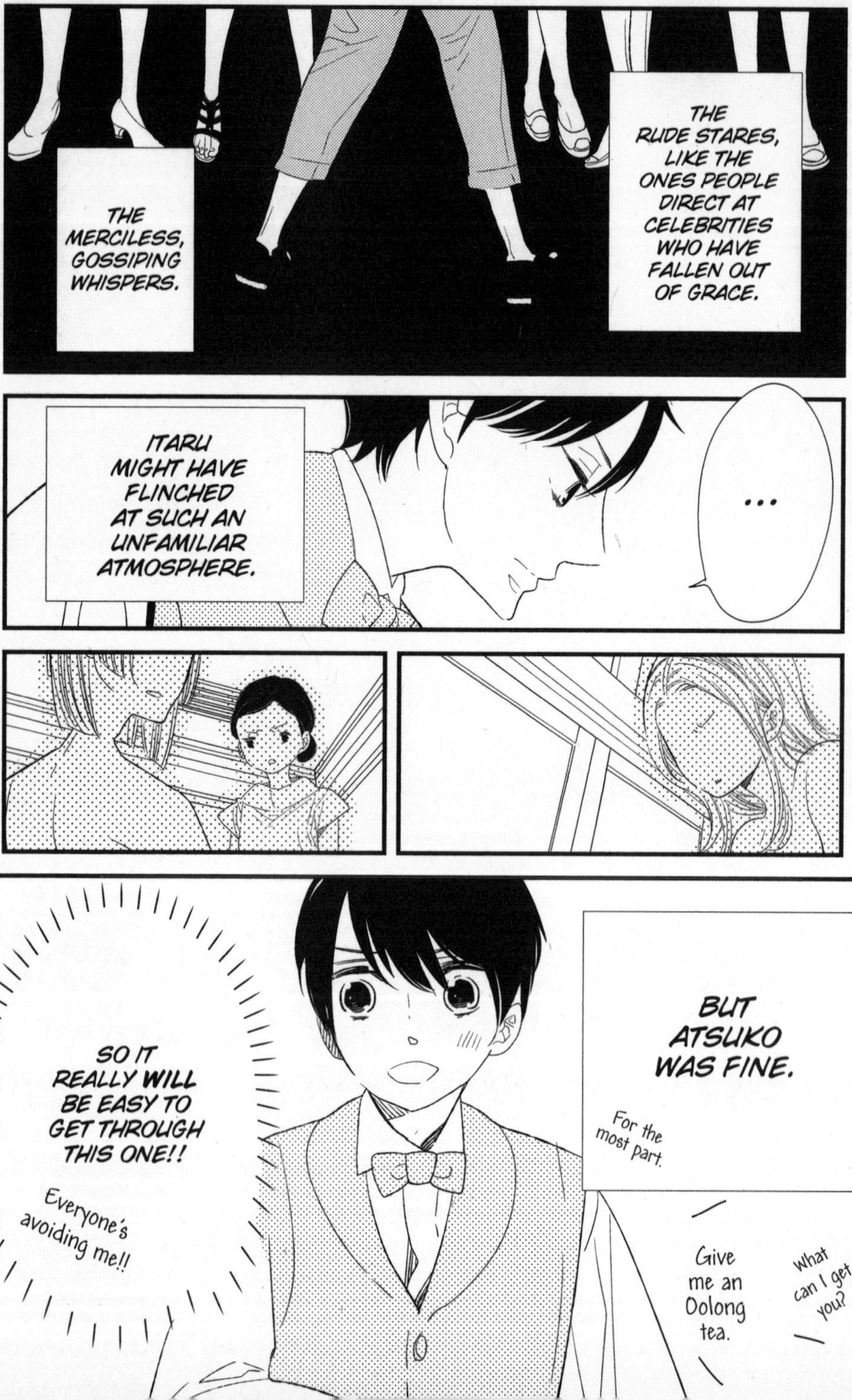
THE RUDE STARES, LIKE THE ONES PEOPLE DIRECT AT CELEBRITIES WHO HAVE FALLEN OUT OF GRACE.
THE MERCILESS, GOSSIPING WHISPERS.
...
ITARU MIGHT HAVE FLINCHED AT SUCH AN UNFAMILIAR ATMOSPHERE.
BUT ATSUKO WAS FINE.
For the most part.
What can I get you?
Give me an Oolong tea.
SO IT REALLY WILL BE EASY TO GET THROUGH THIS ONE!!
Everyone's avoiding me!!

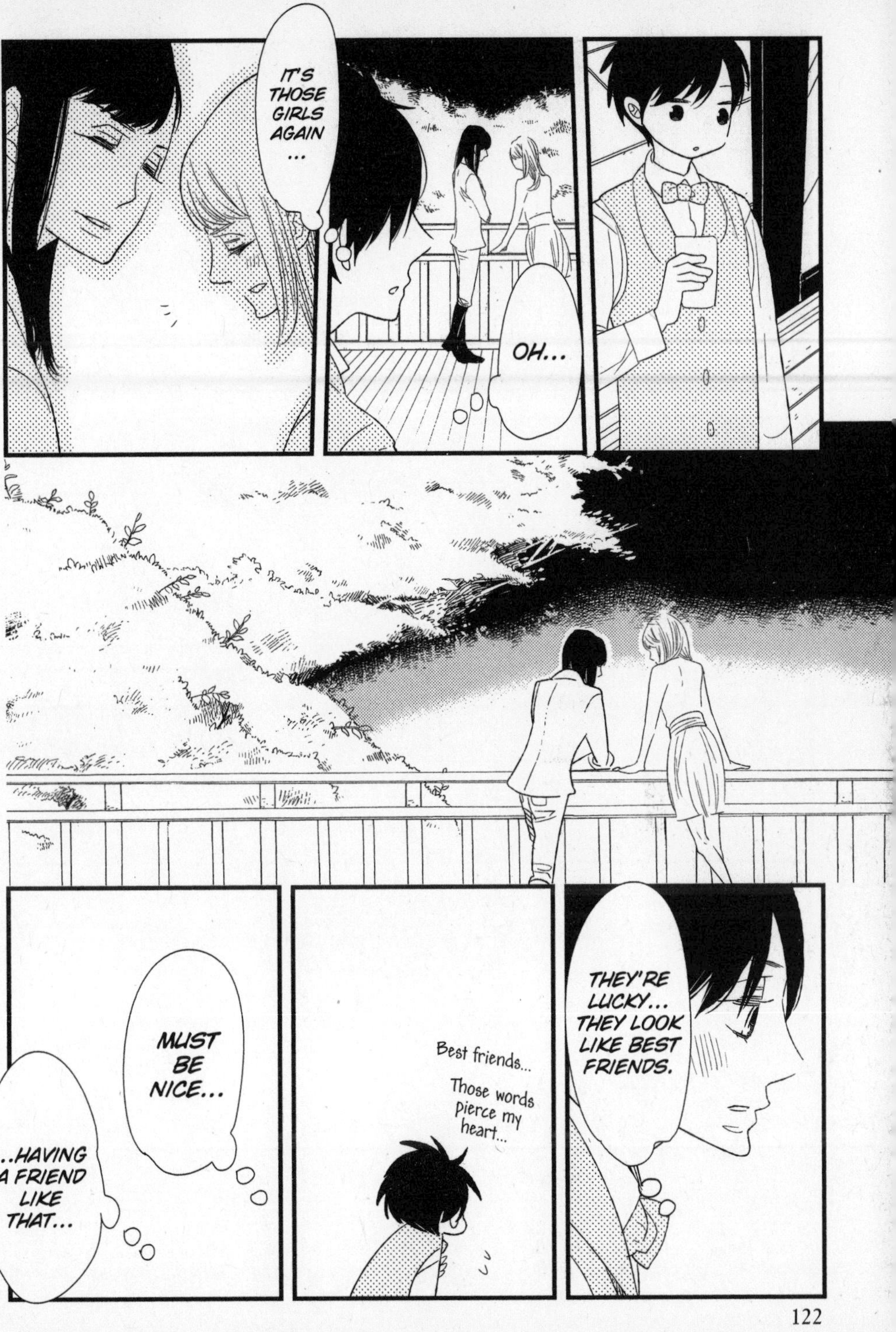
OH...
IT'S THOSE GIRLS AGAIN...
THEY'RE LUCKY... THEY LOOK LIKE BEST FRIENDS.
Best friends...
Those words pierce my heart...
MUST BE NICE...
...HAVING A FRIEND LIKE THAT...

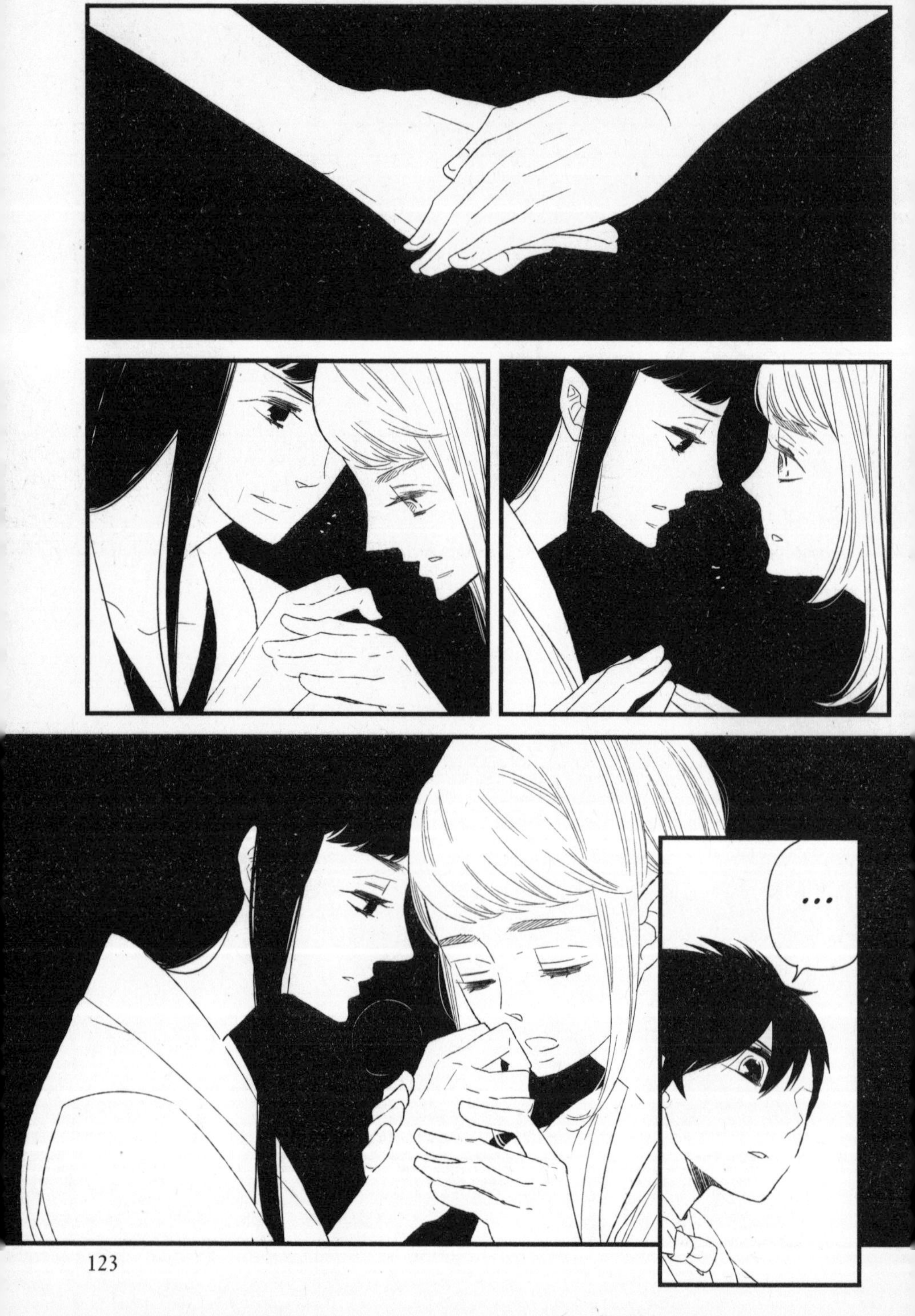
...

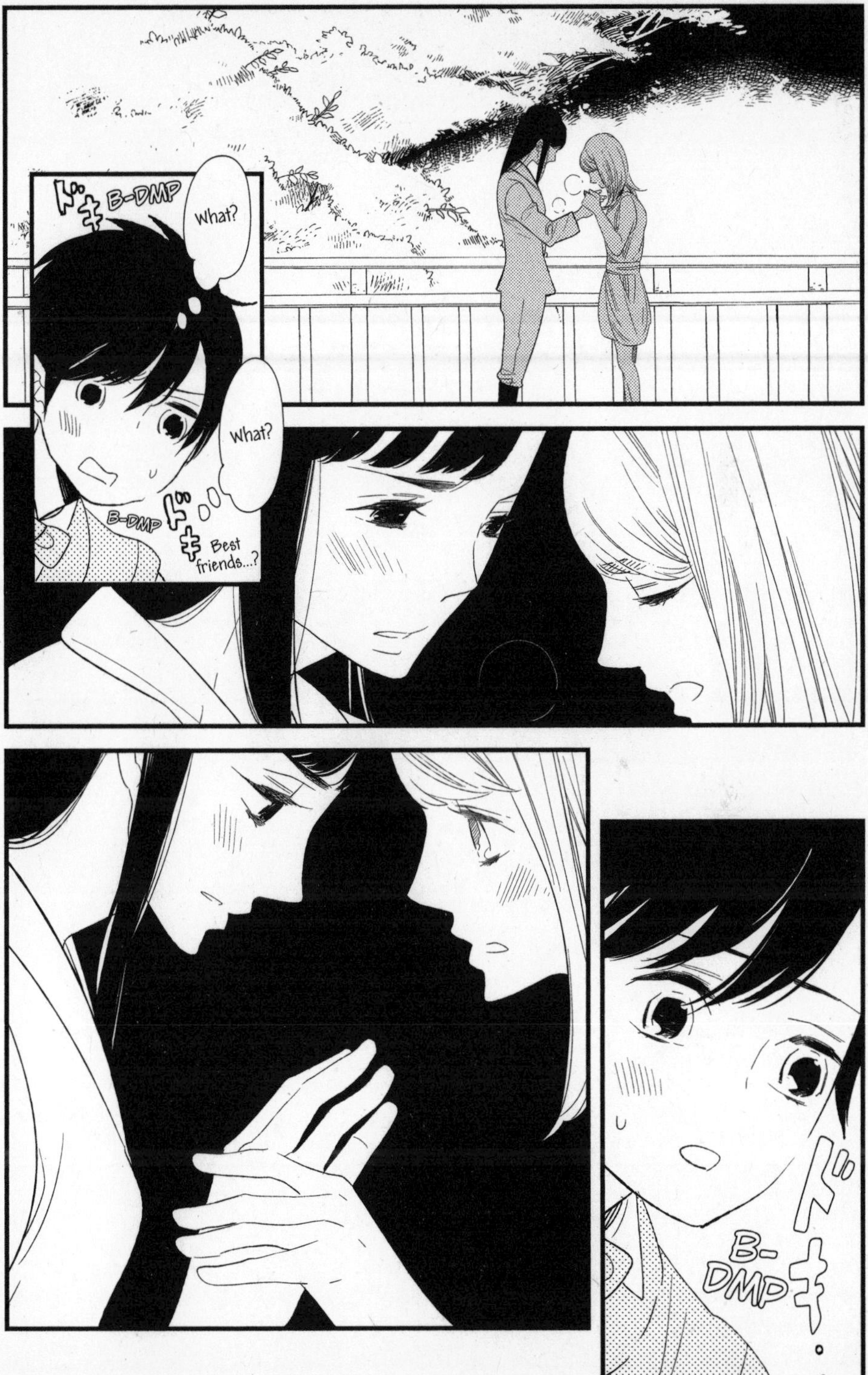
What?
ドキ B-DMP
What?
ドキ B-DMP
Best friends...?
ドキ B-DMP...

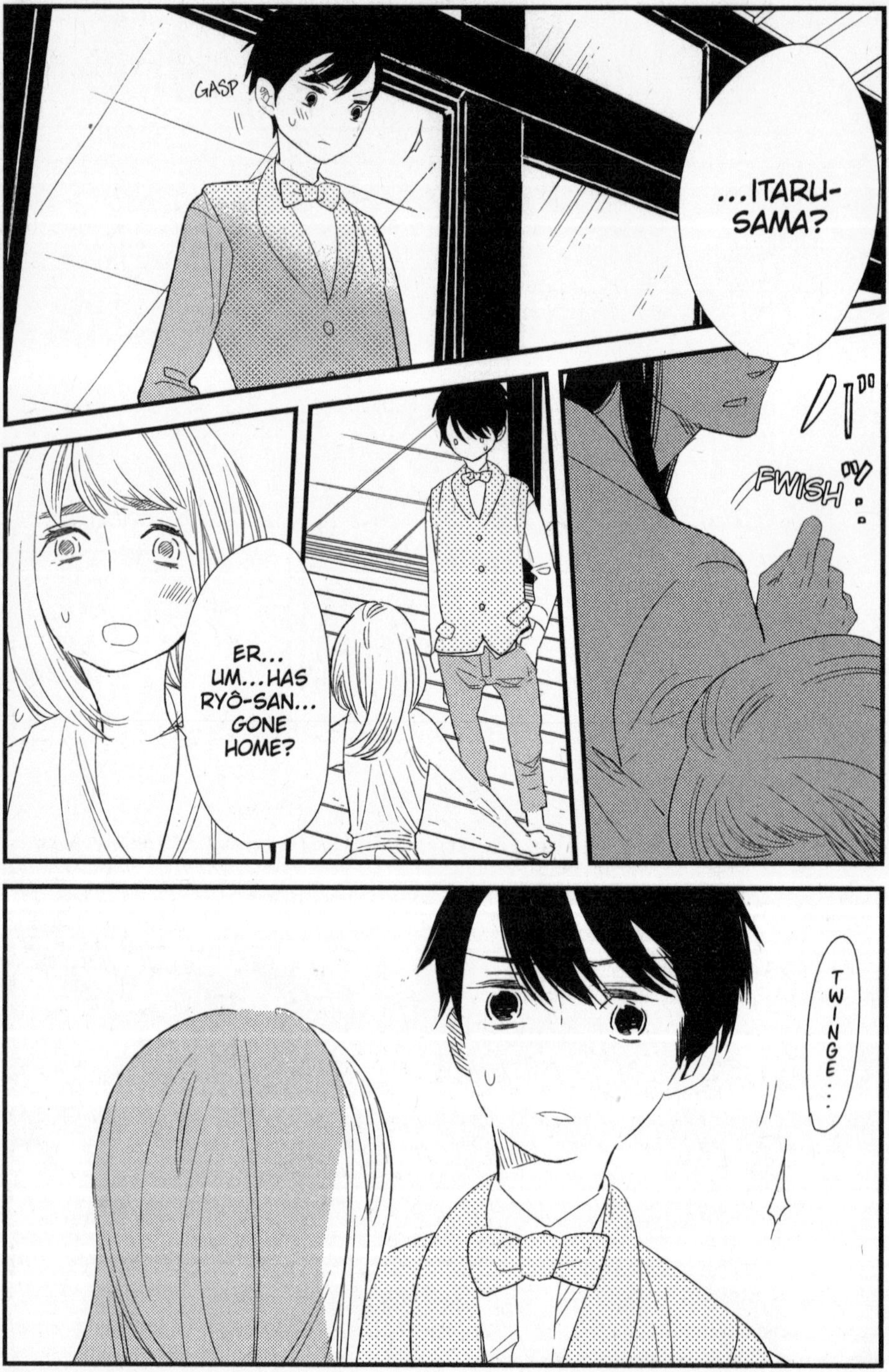
...ITARU-SAMA?
GASP
FWISH
ER... UM...HAS RYÔ-SAN... GONE HOME?
TWINGE...

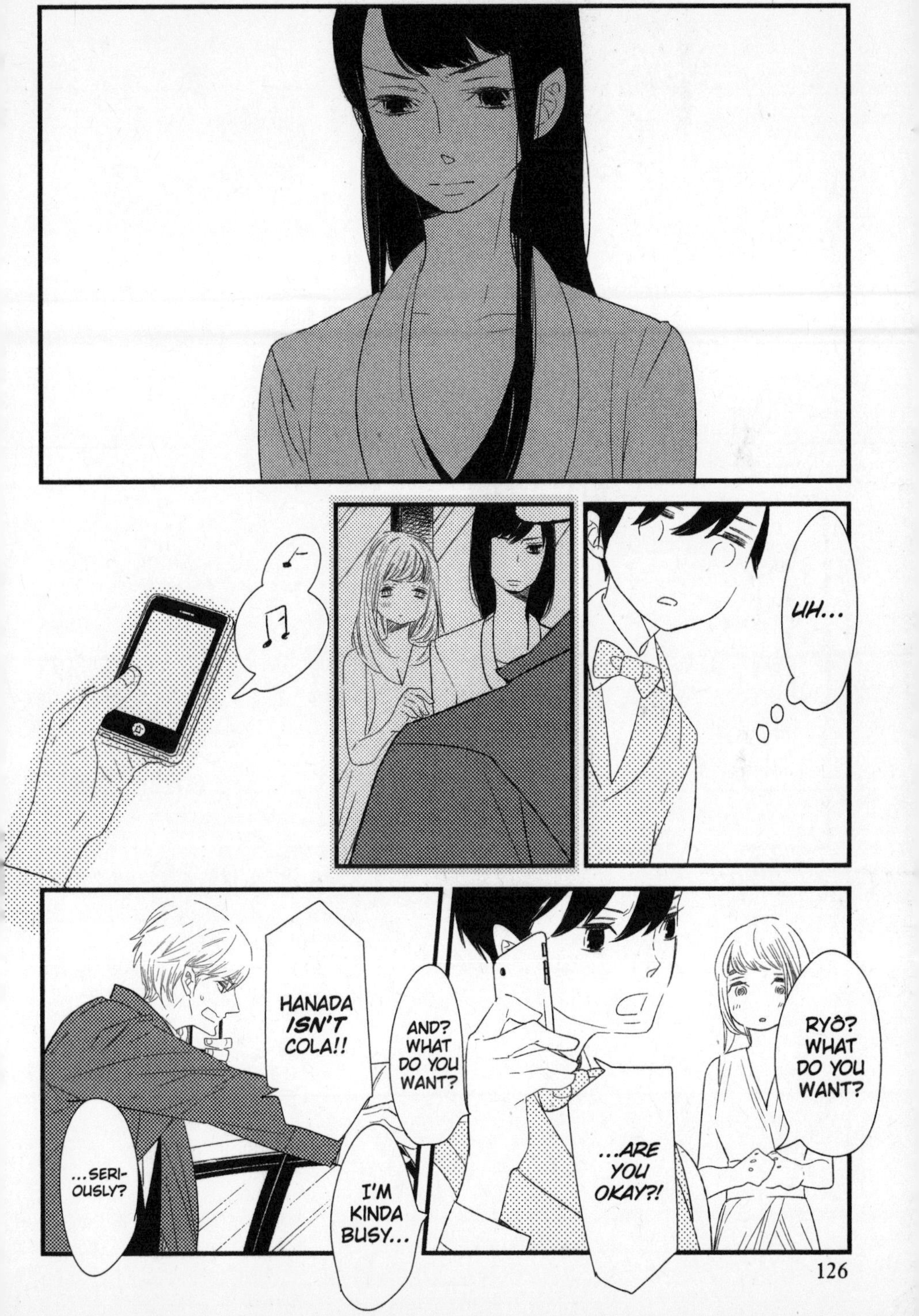
UH...
RYÔ? WHAT DO YOU WANT?
...ARE YOU OKAY?!
AND? WHAT DO YOU WANT?
I'M KINDA BUSY...
HANADA *ISN'T* COLA!!
...SERI-OUSLY?

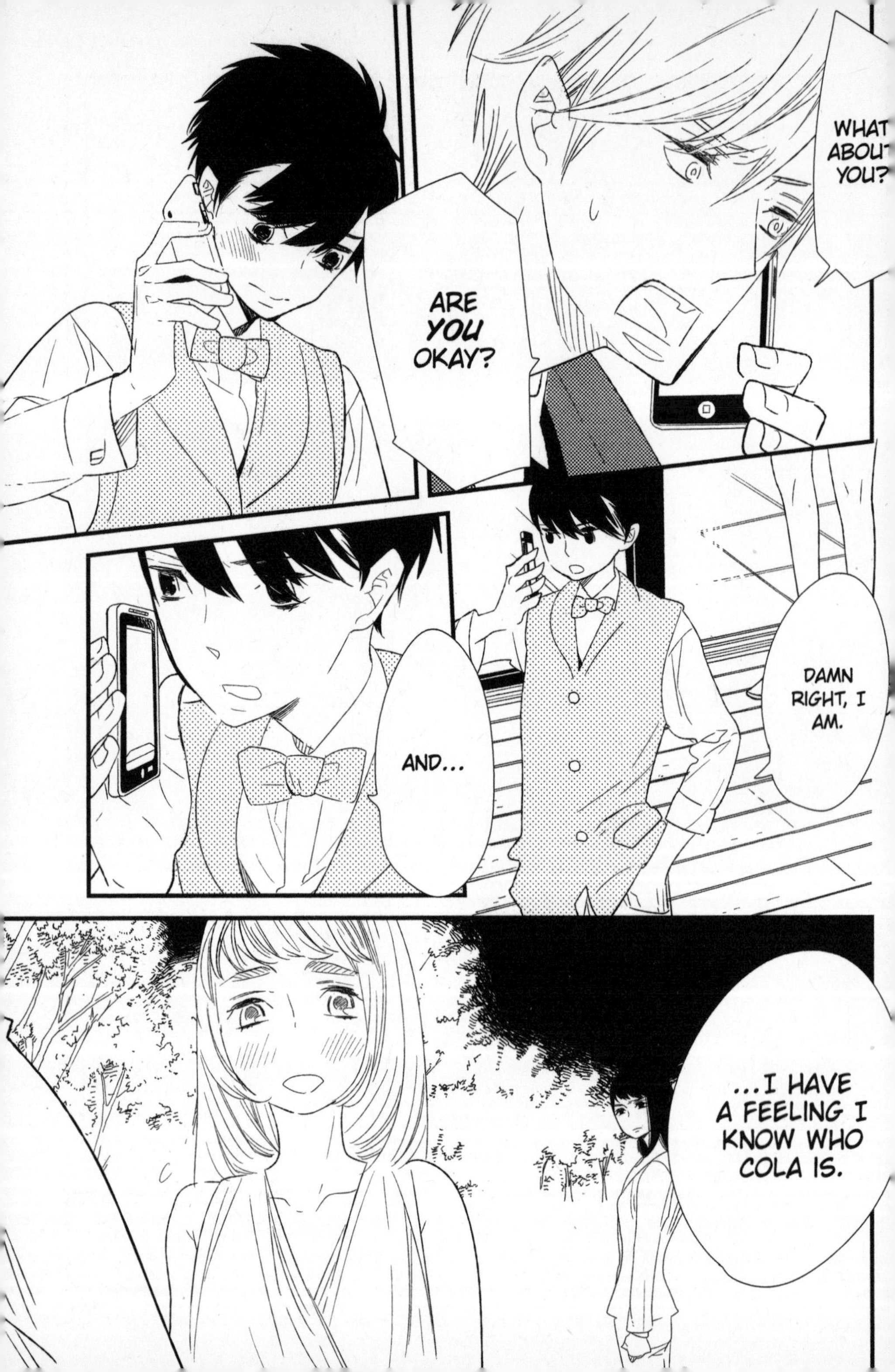
WHAT ABOUT YOU?
ARE YOU OKAY?
DAMN RIGHT, I AM.
AND...
...I HAVE A FEELING I KNOW WHO COLA IS.

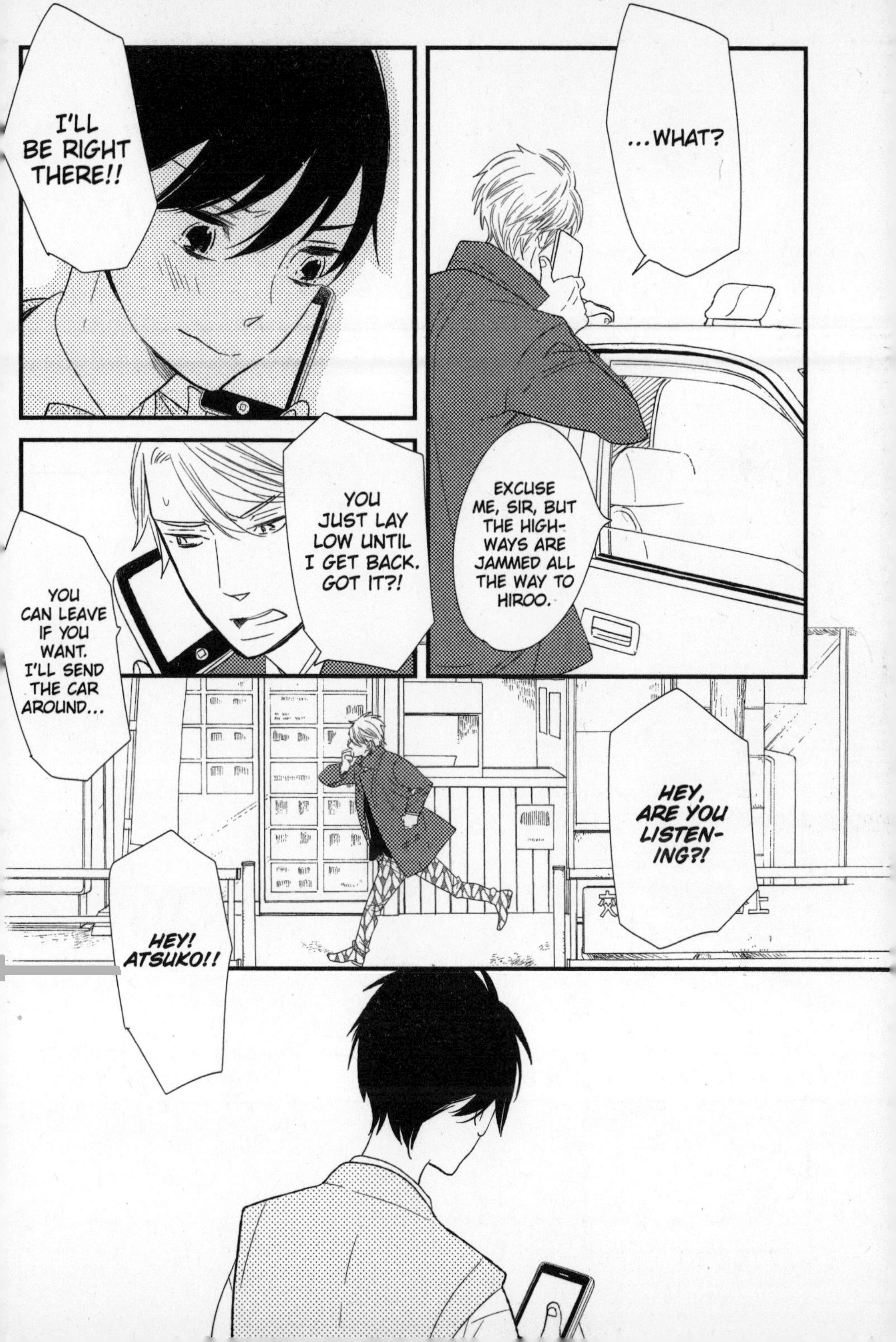
...WHAT?
EXCUSE ME, SIR, BUT THE HIGH-WAYS ARE JAMMED ALL THE WAY TO HIROO.
I'LL BE RIGHT THERE!!
YOU JUST LAY LOW UNTIL I GET BACK. GOT IT?!
YOU CAN LEAVE IF YOU WANT. I'LL SEND THE CAR AROUND...
HEY, ARE YOU LISTEN-ING?!
HEY! ATSUKO!!

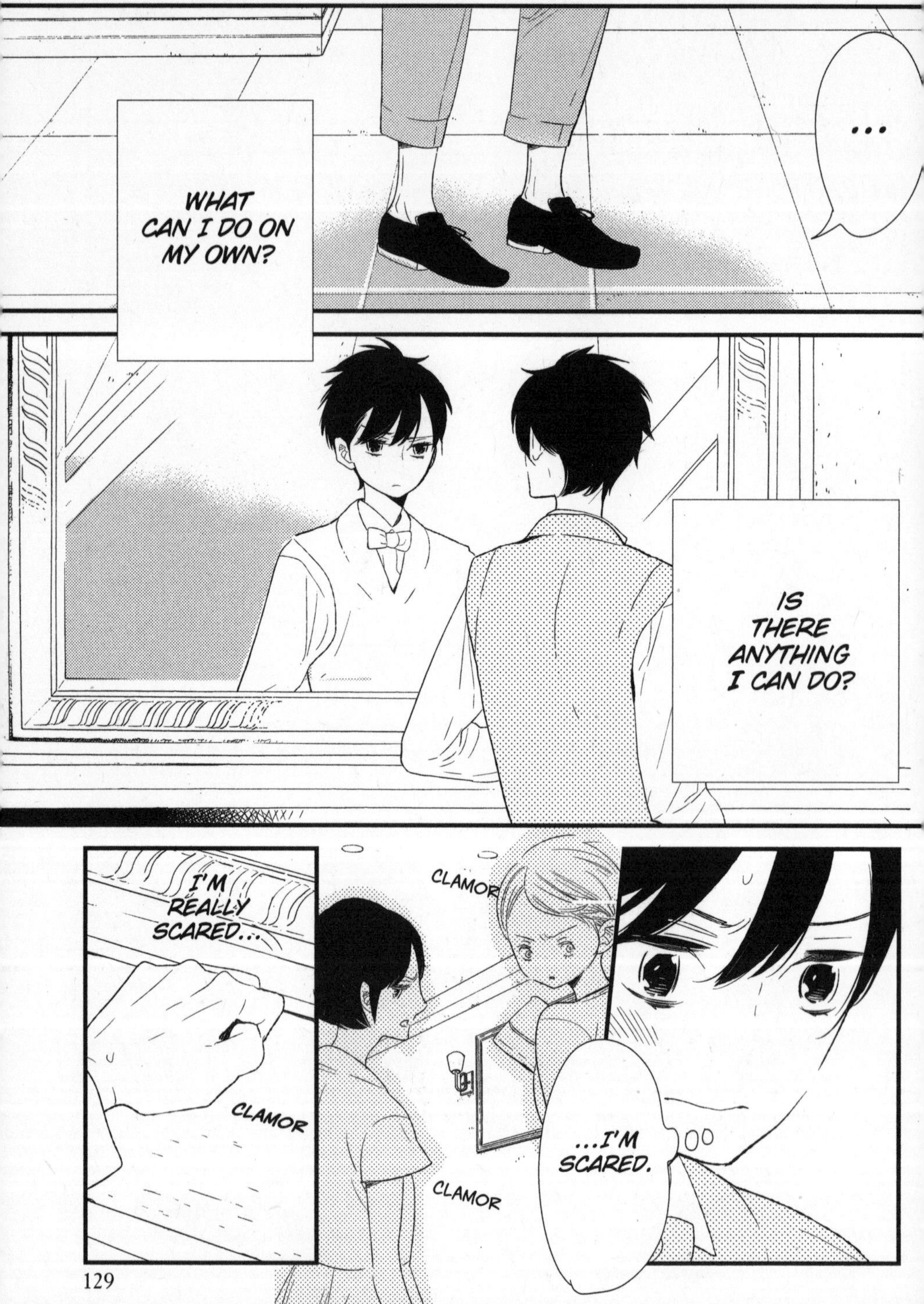
...
WHAT CAN I DO ON MY OWN?
IS THERE ANYTHING I CAN DO?
...I'M SCARED.
CLAMOR
CLAMOR
I'M REALLY SCARED...
CLAMOR

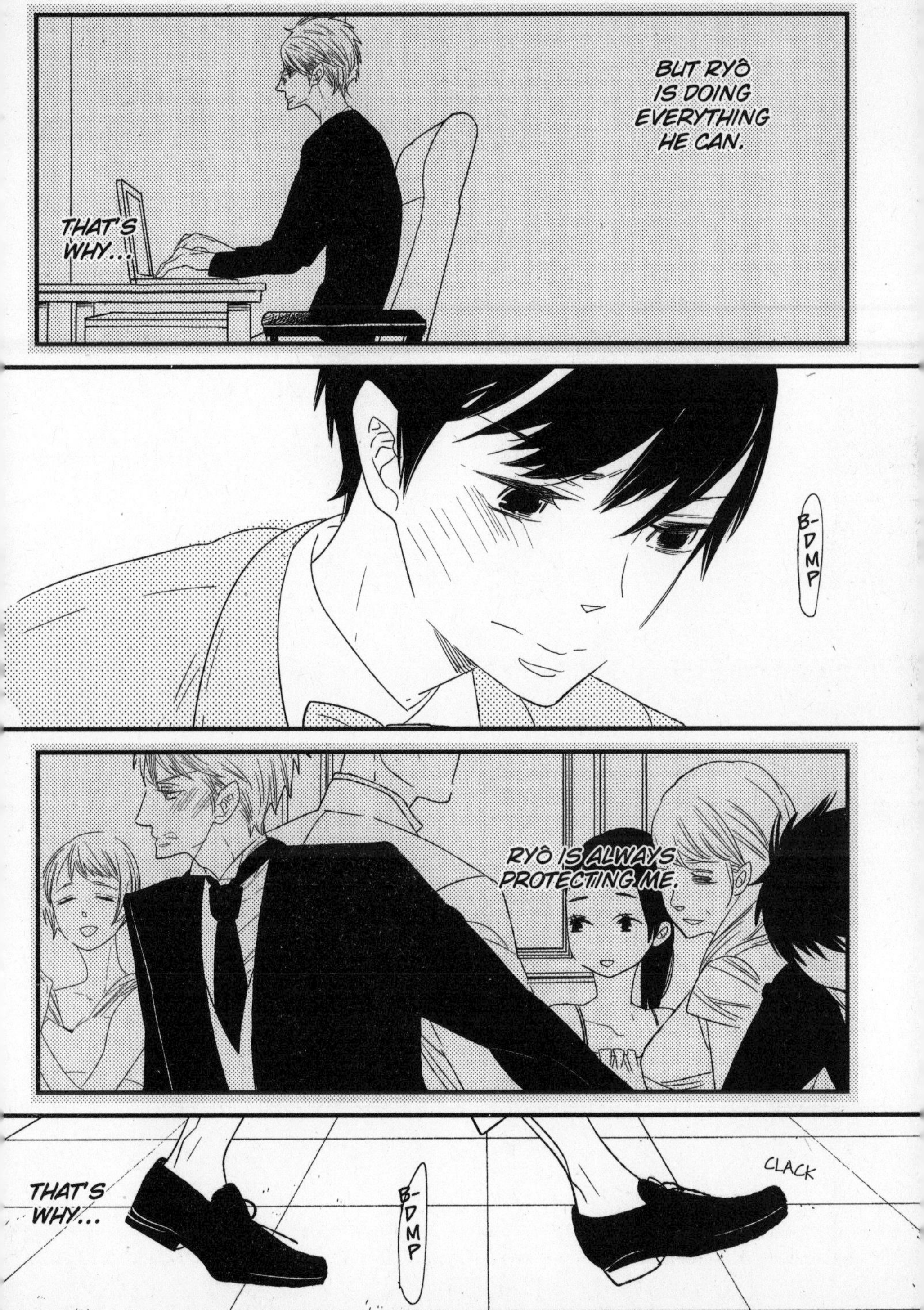
BUT RYÔ IS DOING EVERYTHING HE CAN.
THAT'S WHY...
B-DMP
RYÔ IS ALWAYS PROTECTING ME.
CLACK
B-DMP
THAT'S WHY...

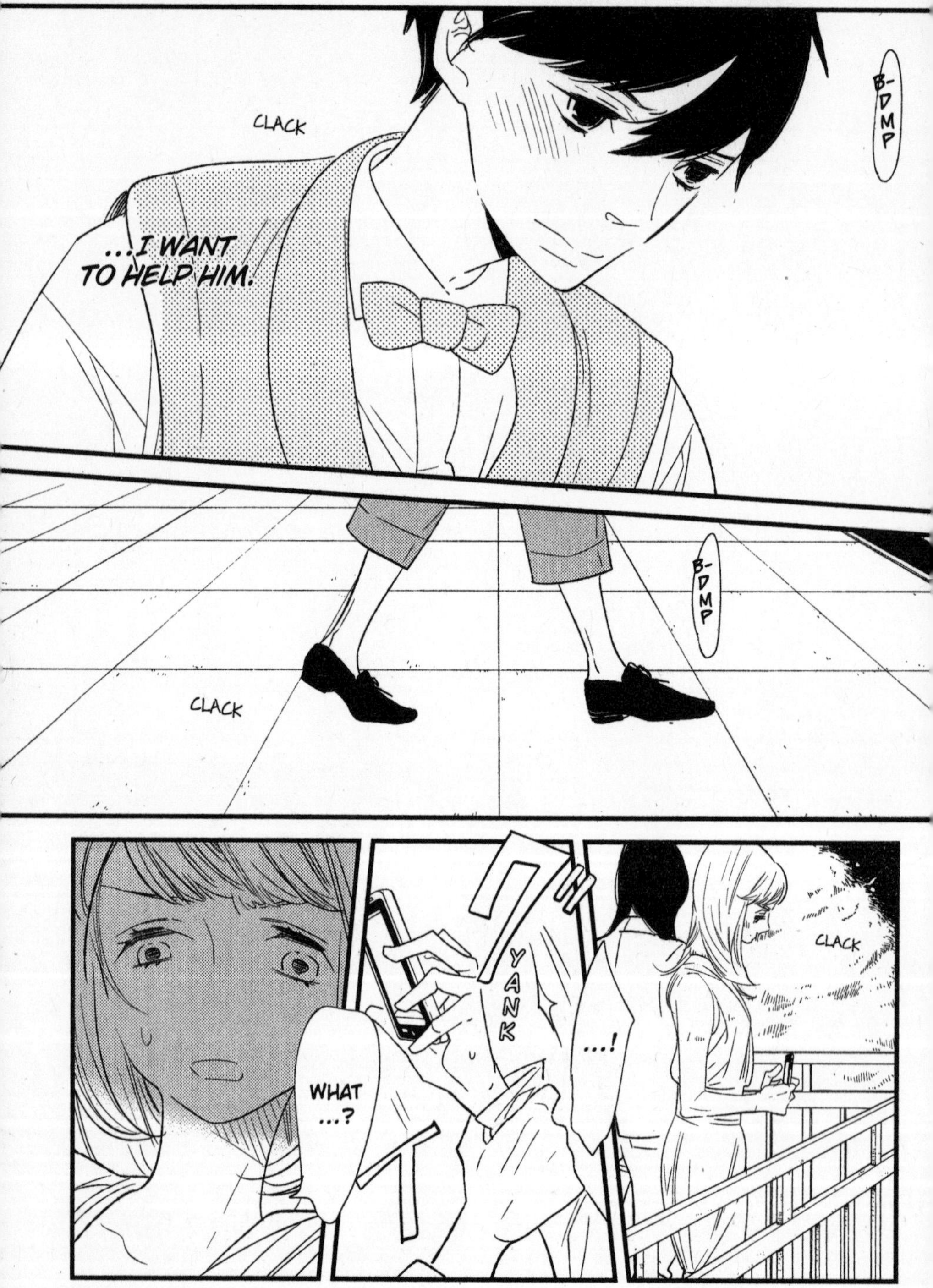
B-DMP
CLACK
...I WANT TO HELP HIM.
B-DMP
CLACK
CLACK
...!
YANK
WHAT ...?

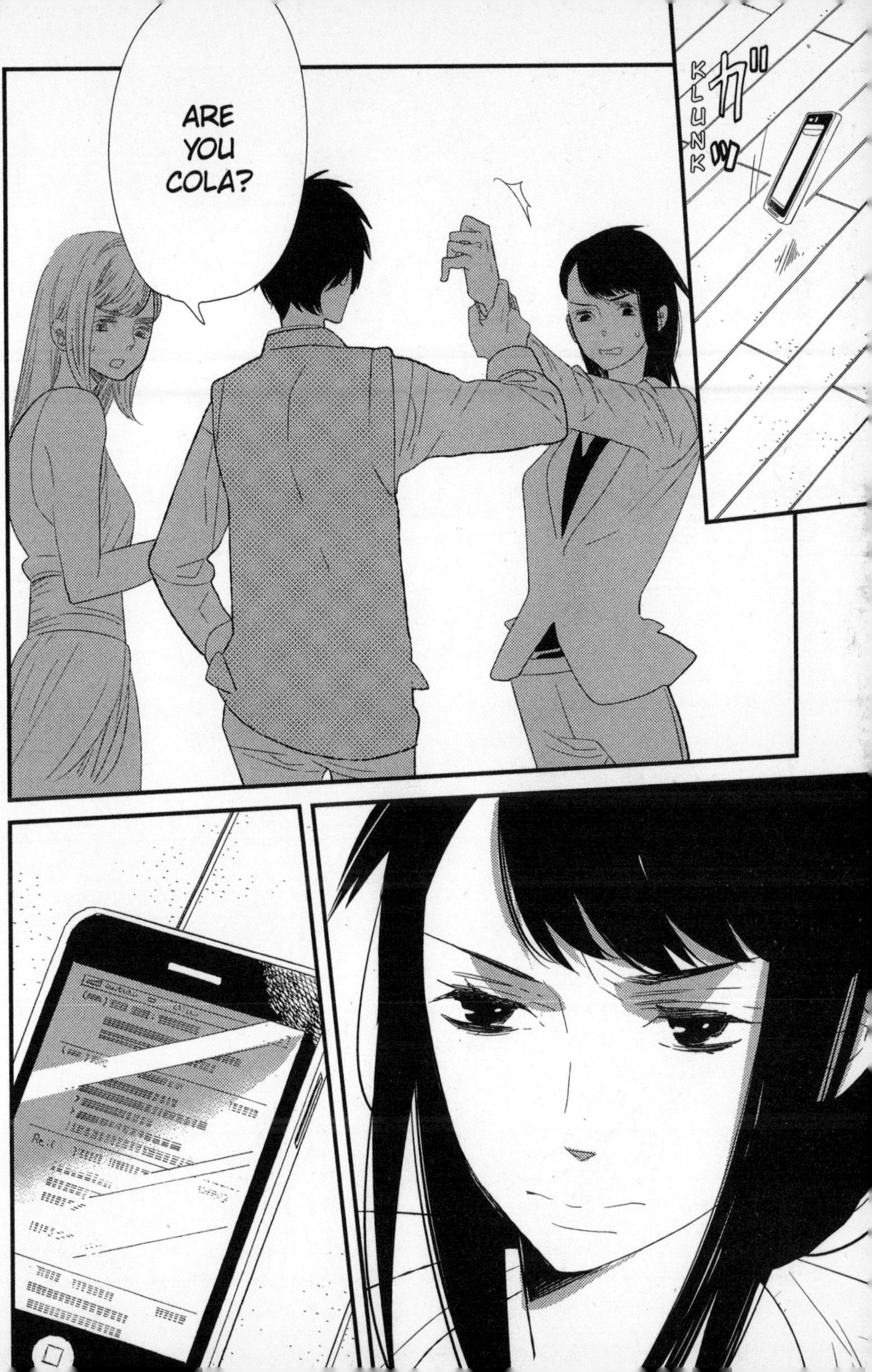
ガッ
KLUNK
ARE YOU COLA?

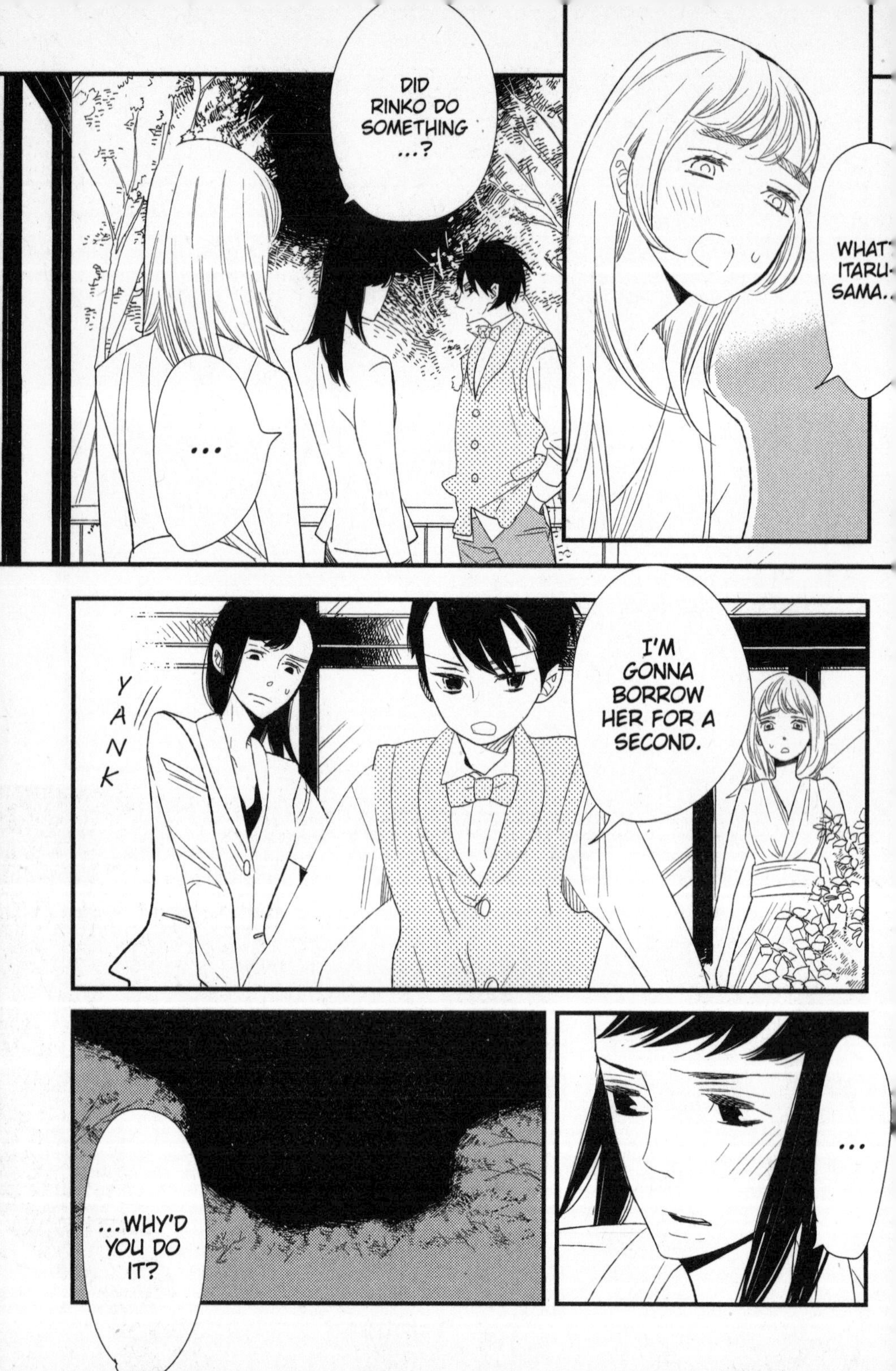
WHAT? ITARU-SAMA..
DID RINKO DO SOMETHING ...?
...
I'M GONNA BORROW HER FOR A SECOND.
YANK
...
...WHY'D YOU DO IT?

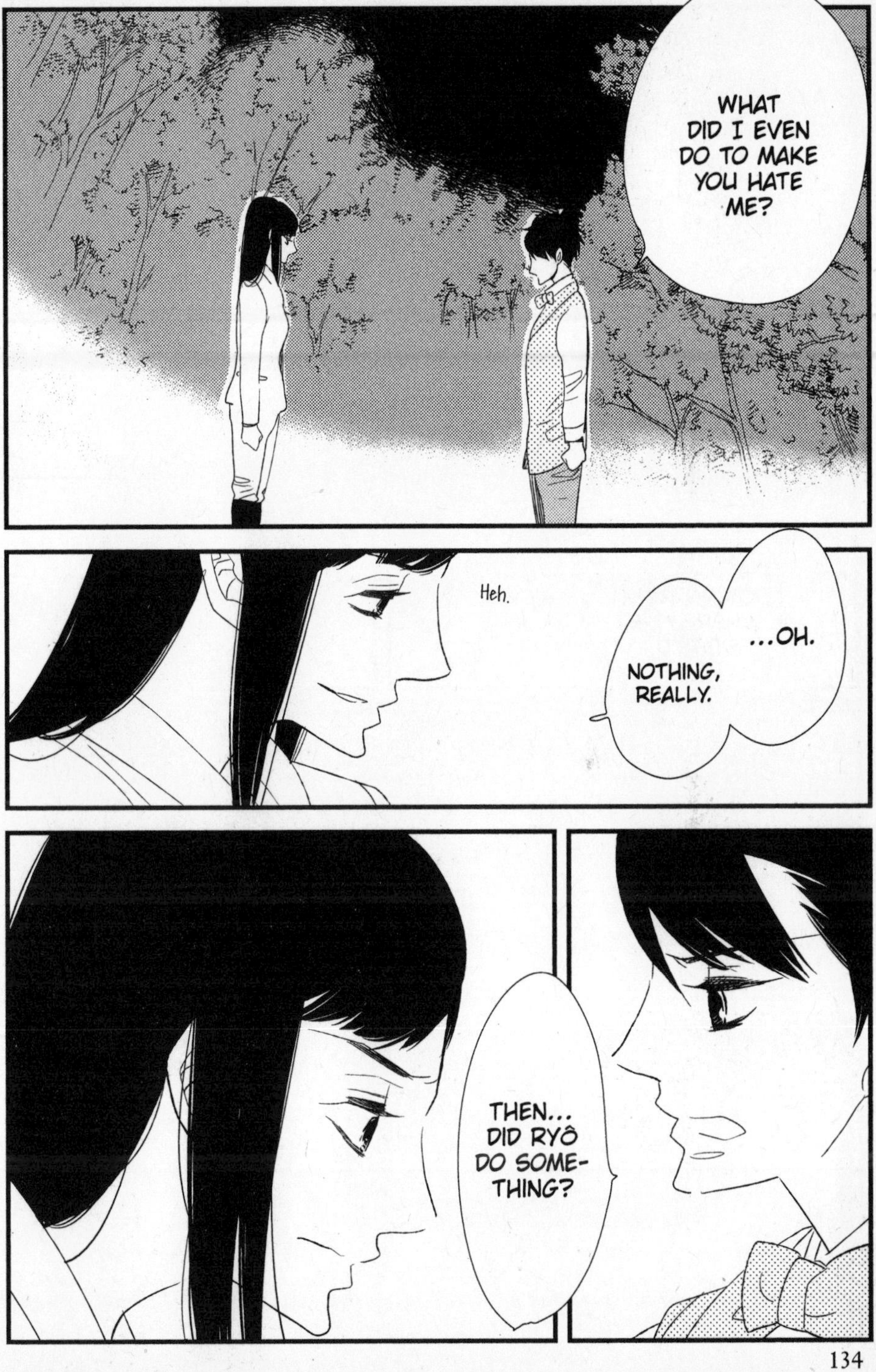
WHAT DID I EVEN DO TO MAKE YOU HATE ME?
...OH.
NOTHING, REALLY.
Heh.
THEN... DID RYÔ DO SOME-THING?

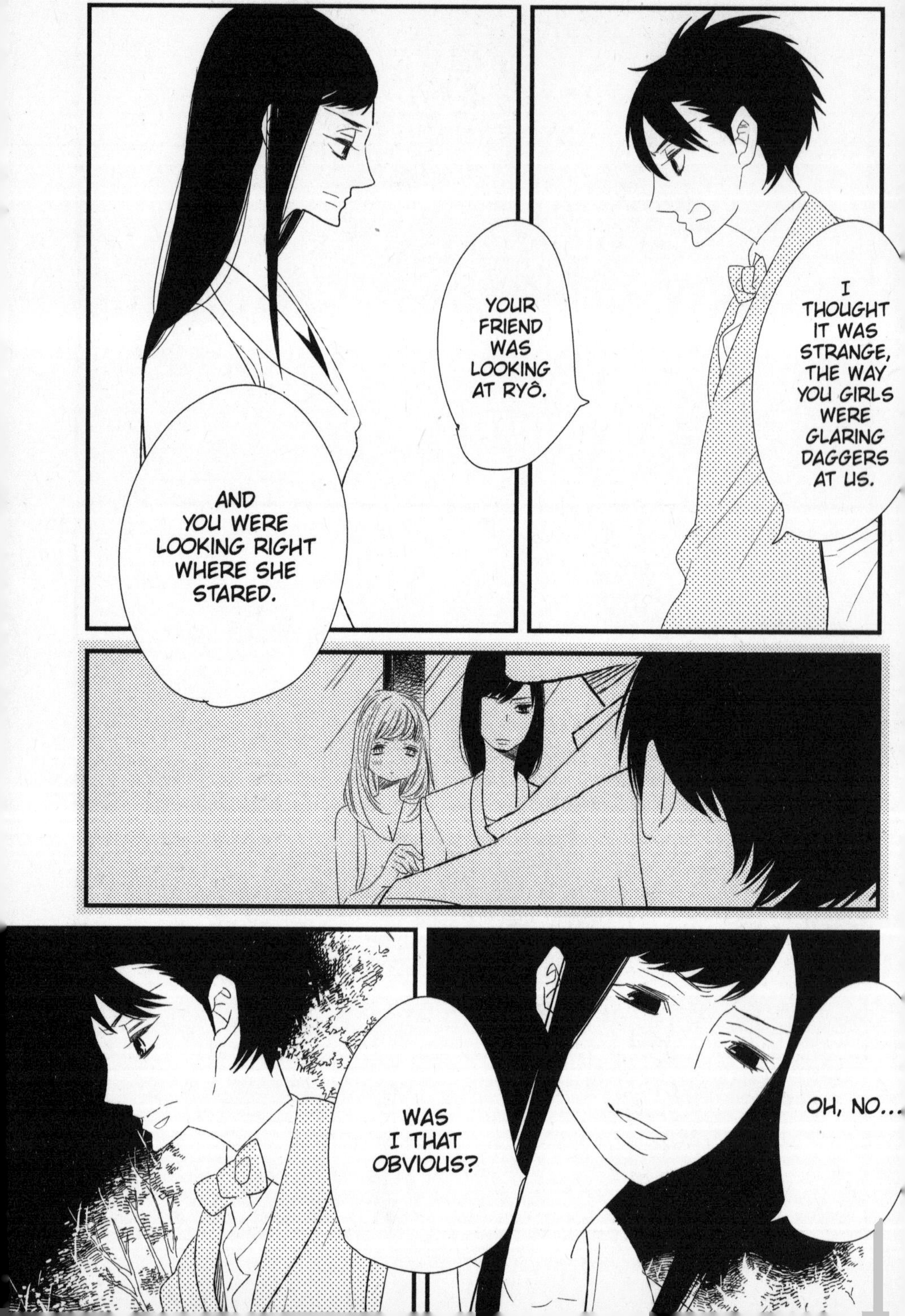
I THOUGHT IT WAS STRANGE, THE WAY YOU GIRLS WERE GLARING DAGGERS AT US.
YOUR FRIEND WAS LOOKING AT RYÔ.
AND YOU WERE LOOKING RIGHT WHERE SHE STARED.
OH, NO...
WAS I THAT OBVIOUS?

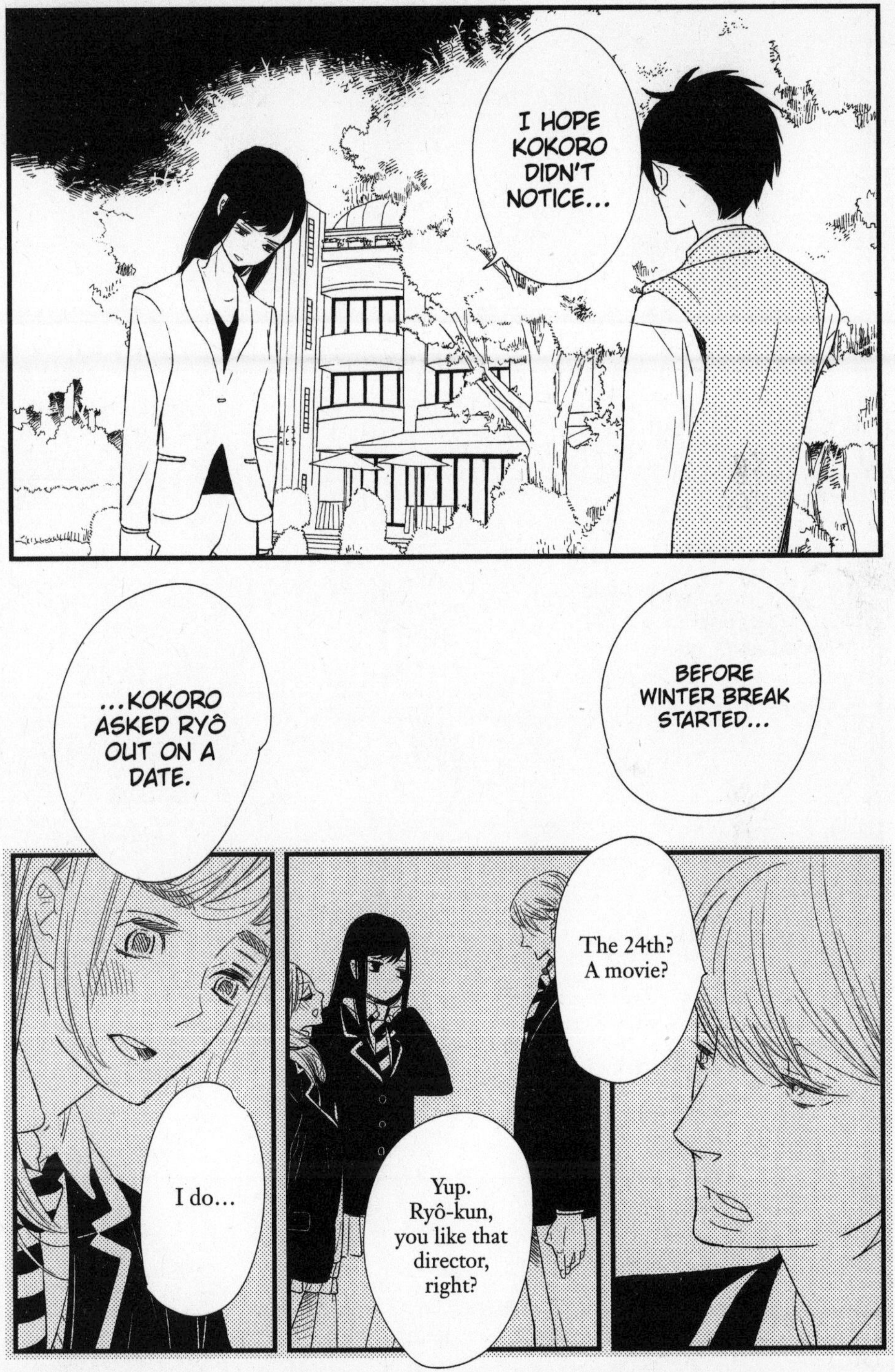
I HOPE KOKORO DIDN'T NOTICE...
BEFORE WINTER BREAK STARTED...
...KOKORO ASKED RYÔ OUT ON A DATE.
The 24th? A movie?
Yup. Ryô-kun, you like that director, right?
I do...

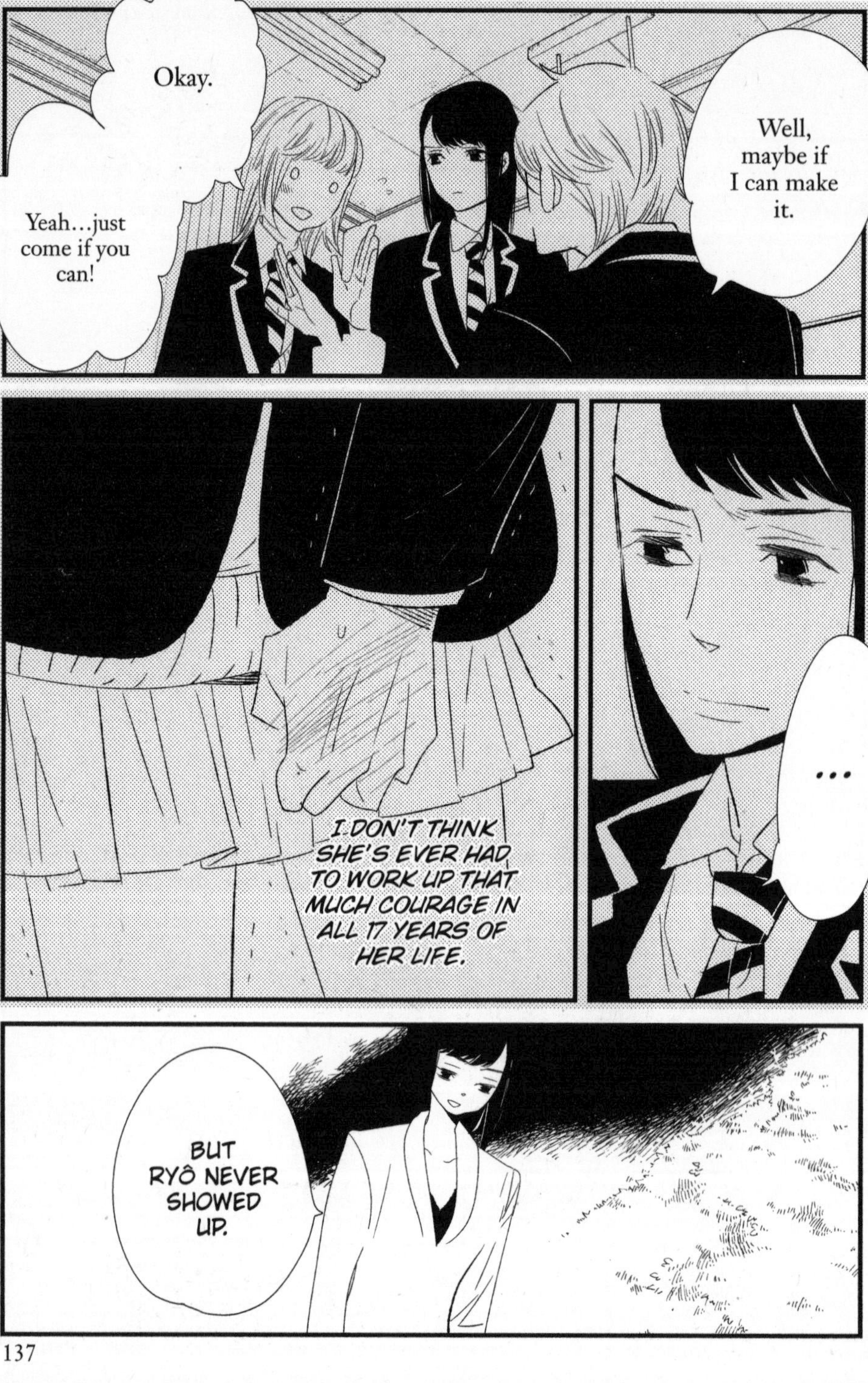
Well, maybe if I can make it.
Okay.
Yeah…just come if you can!
...
I DON'T THINK SHE'S EVER HAD TO WORK UP THAT MUCH COURAGE IN ALL 17 YEARS OF HER LIFE.
BUT RYÔ NEVER SHOWED UP.

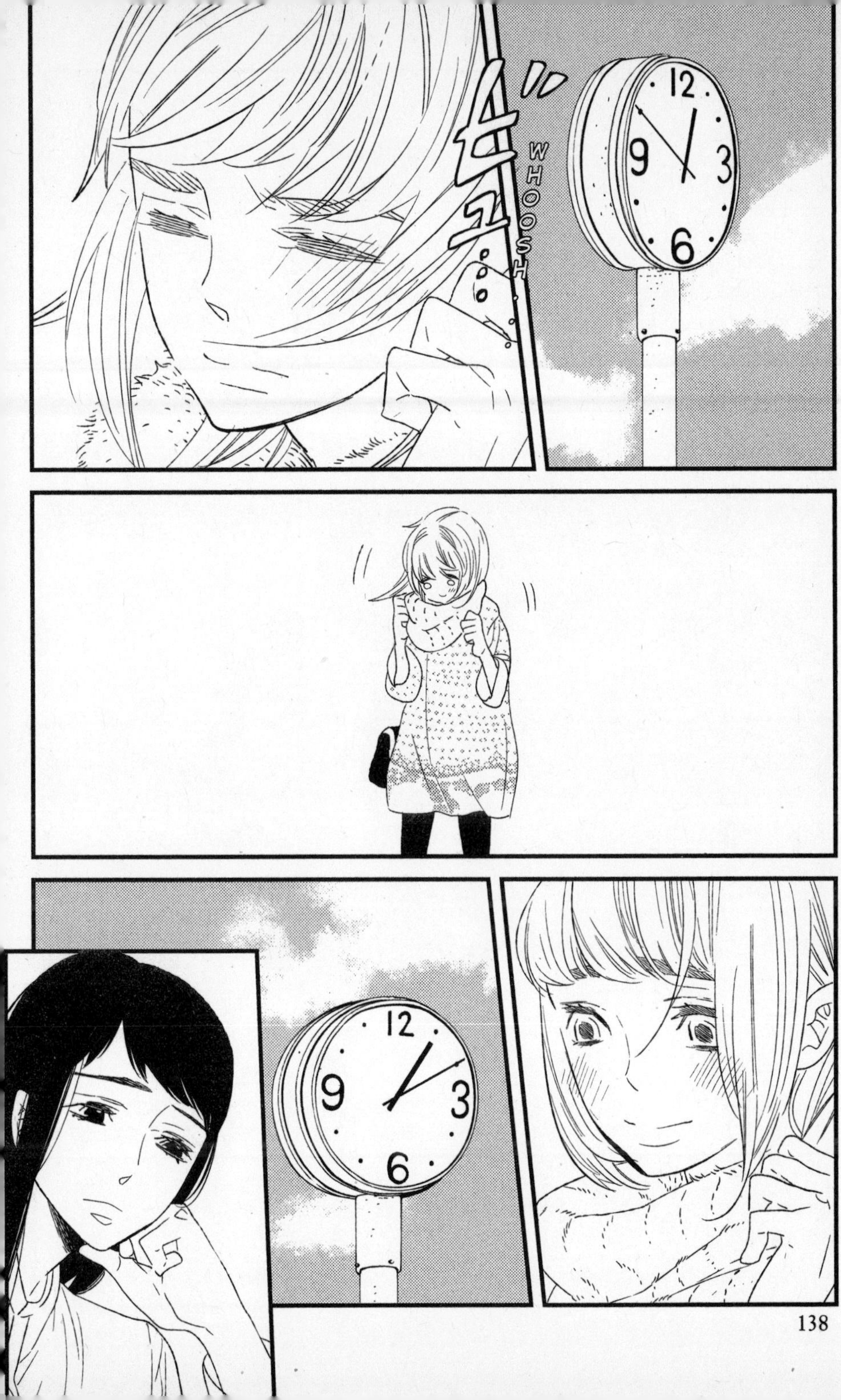

ヒュ
WHOOSH

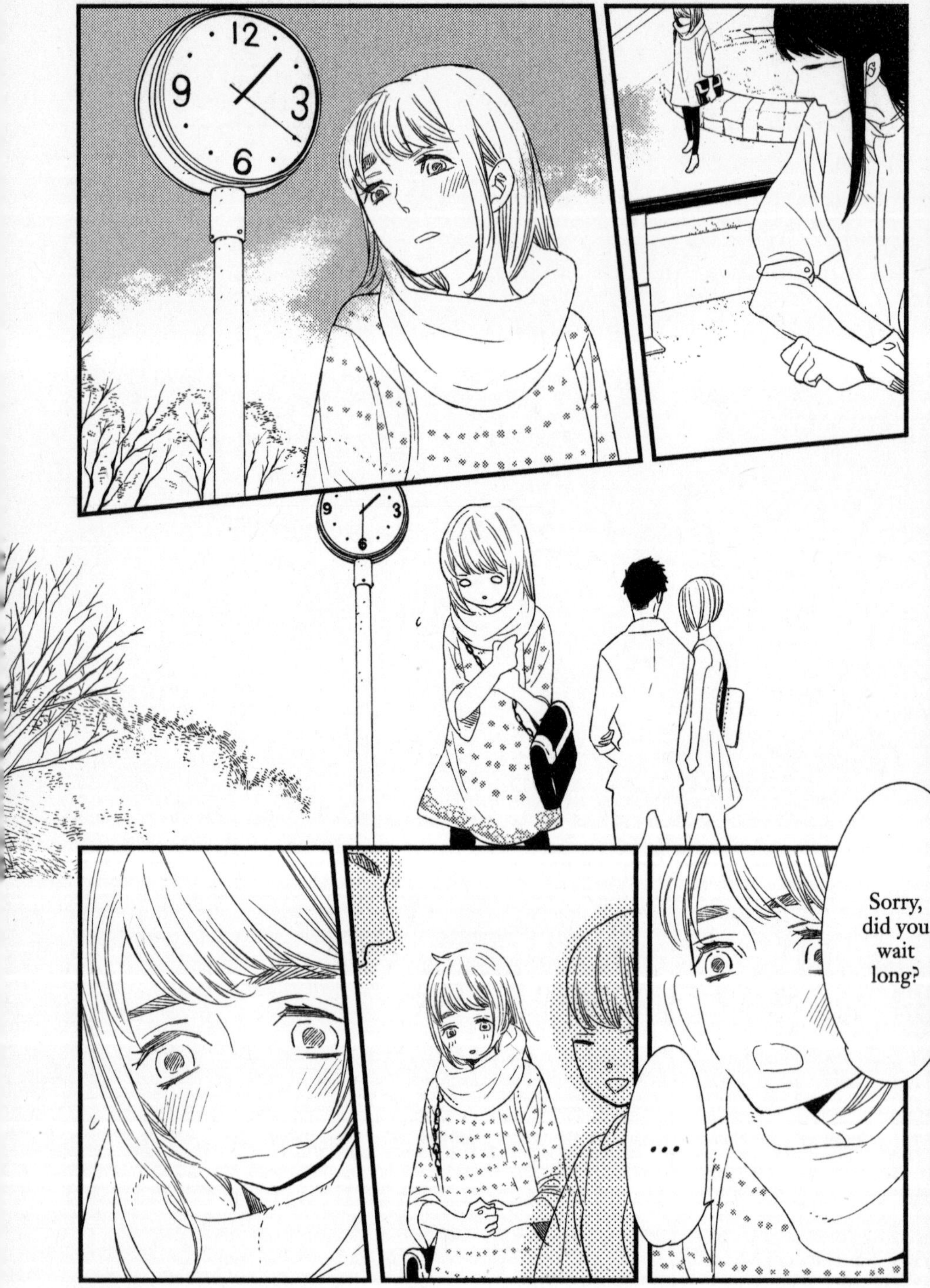
Sorry, did you wait long?
...

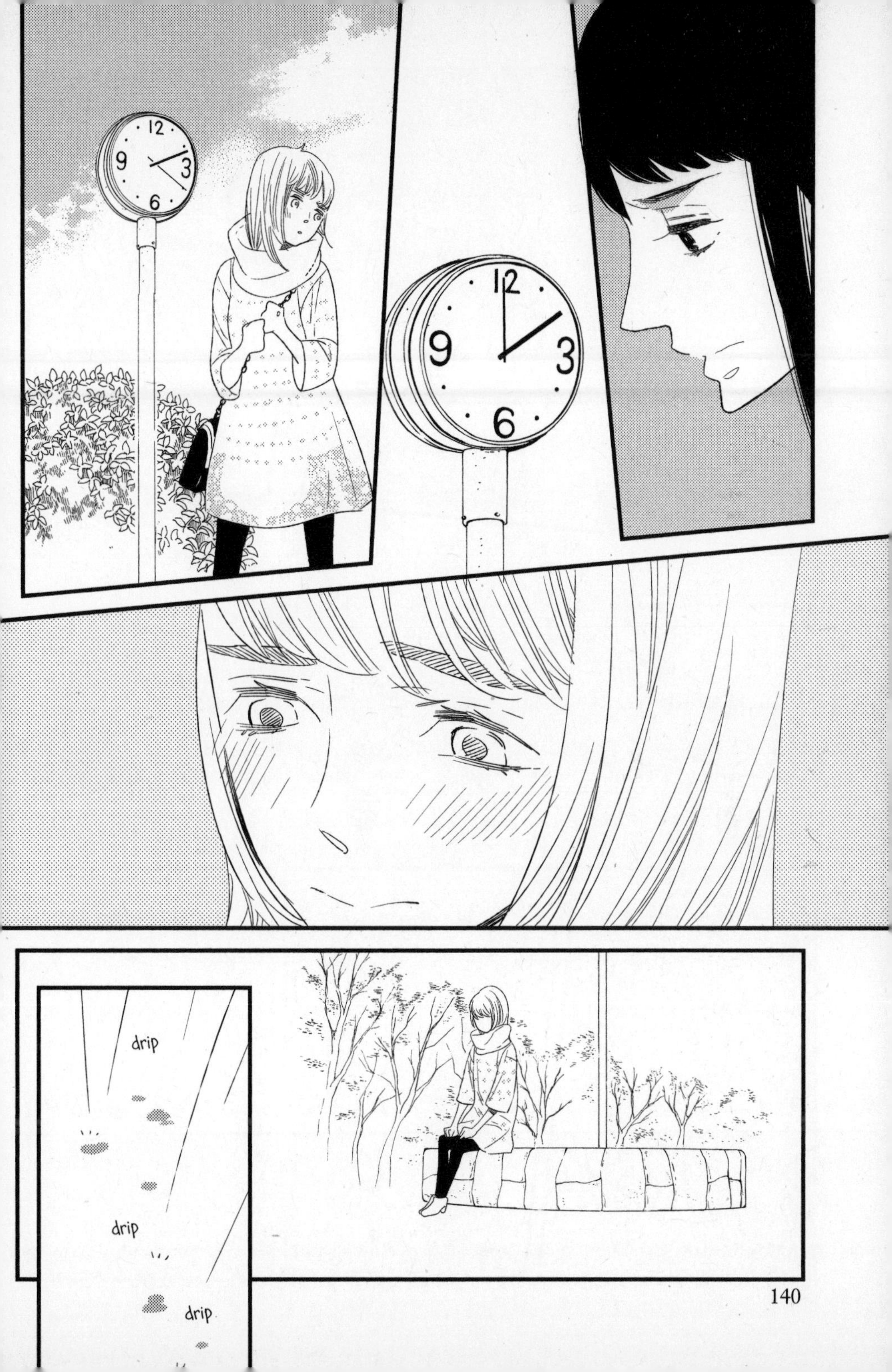
drip
drip
drip

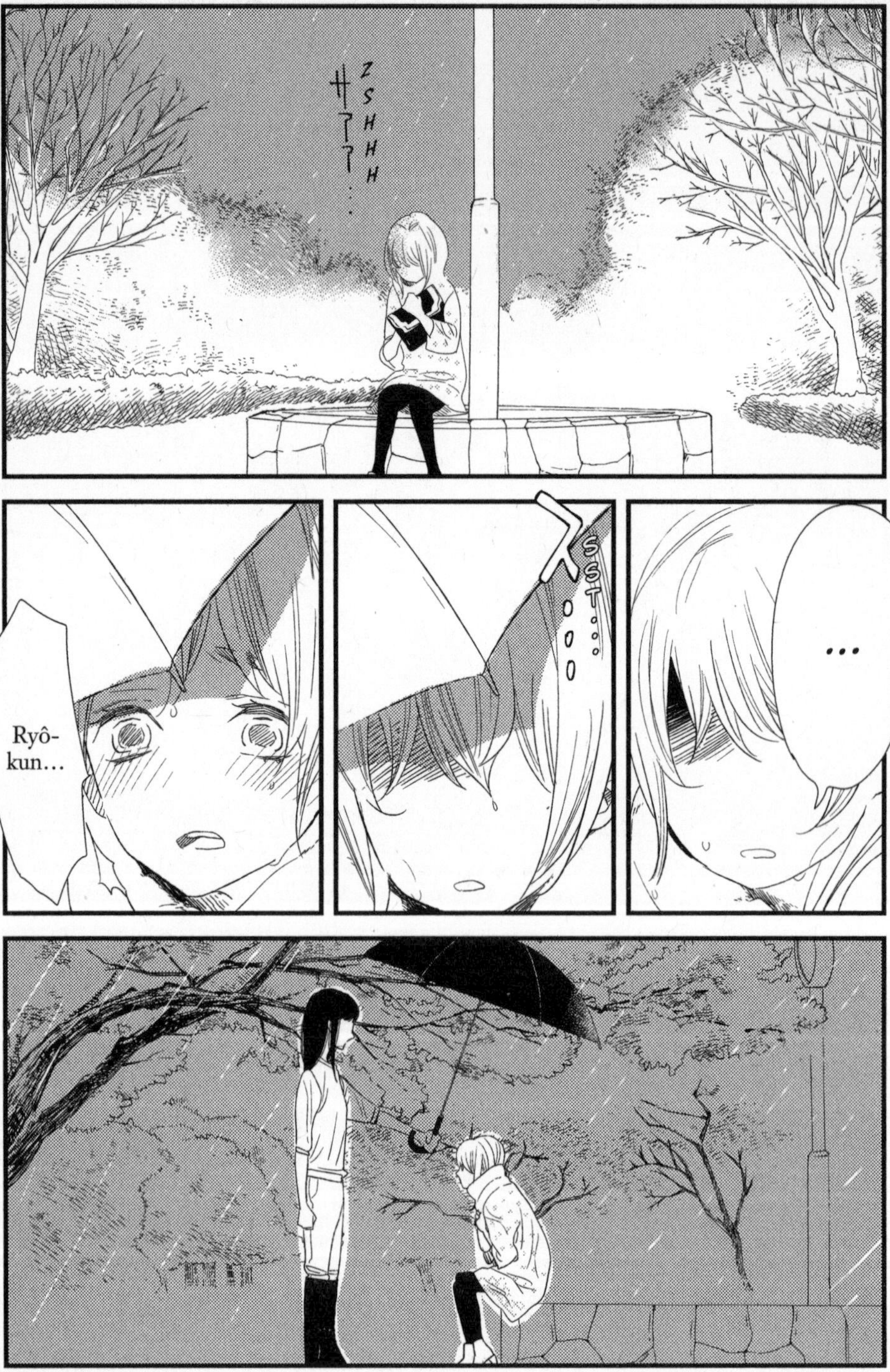
ザァァ…
ZSHHH
…
スッ
SST…
Ryô-kun…

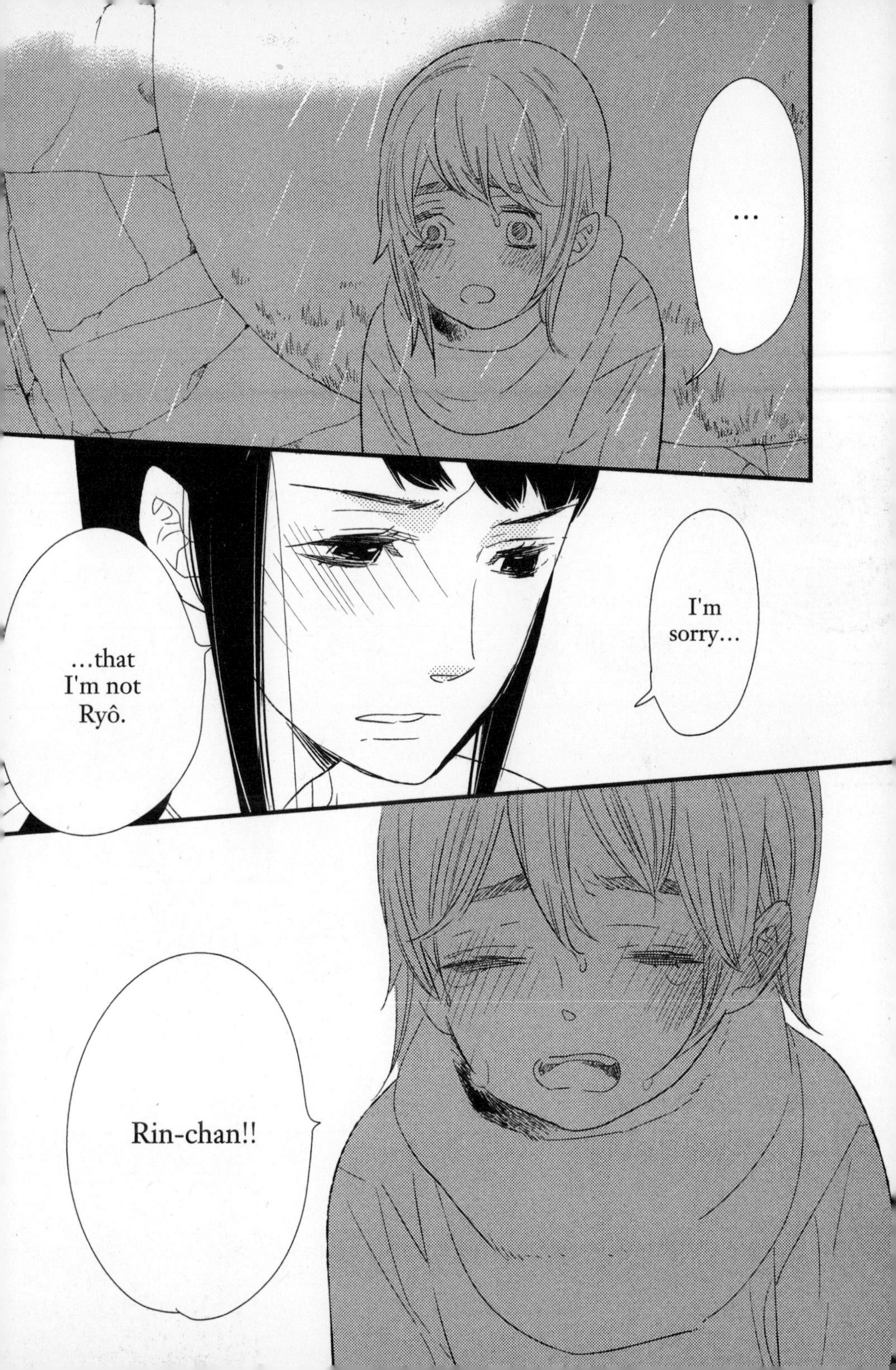
...
I'm sorry...
...that I'm not Ryô.
Rin-chan!!

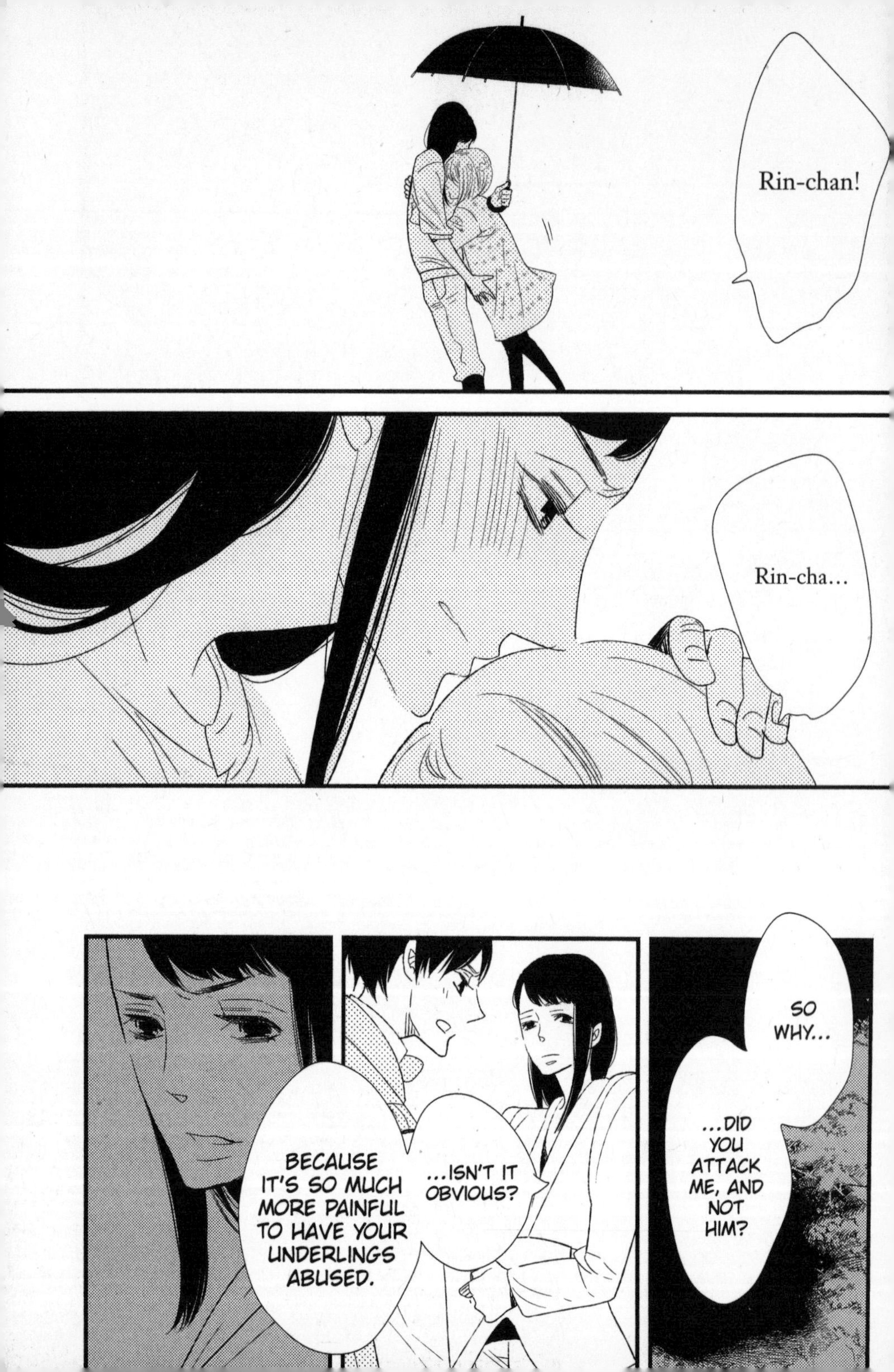
Rin-chan!
Rin-cha…
SO WHY…
…DID YOU ATTACK ME, AND NOT HIM?
…ISN'T IT OBVIOUS?
BECAUSE IT'S SO MUCH MORE PAINFUL TO HAVE YOUR UNDERLINGS ABUSED.

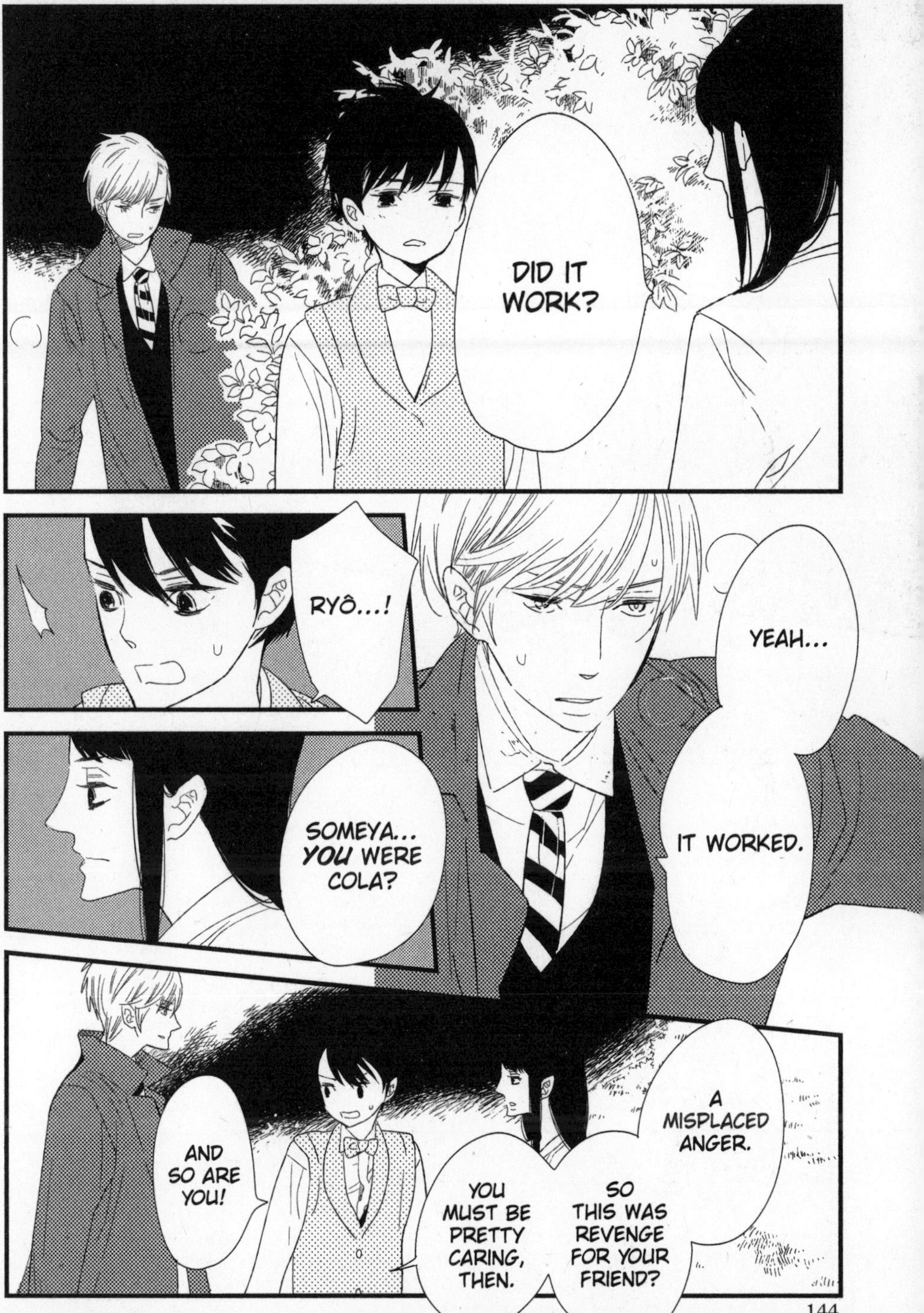
DID IT WORK?
YEAH...
IT WORKED.
RYÔ...!
SOMEYA... *YOU* WERE COLA?
A MISPLACED ANGER.
SO THIS WAS REVENGE FOR YOUR FRIEND?
YOU MUST BE PRETTY CARING, THEN.
AND SO ARE YOU!

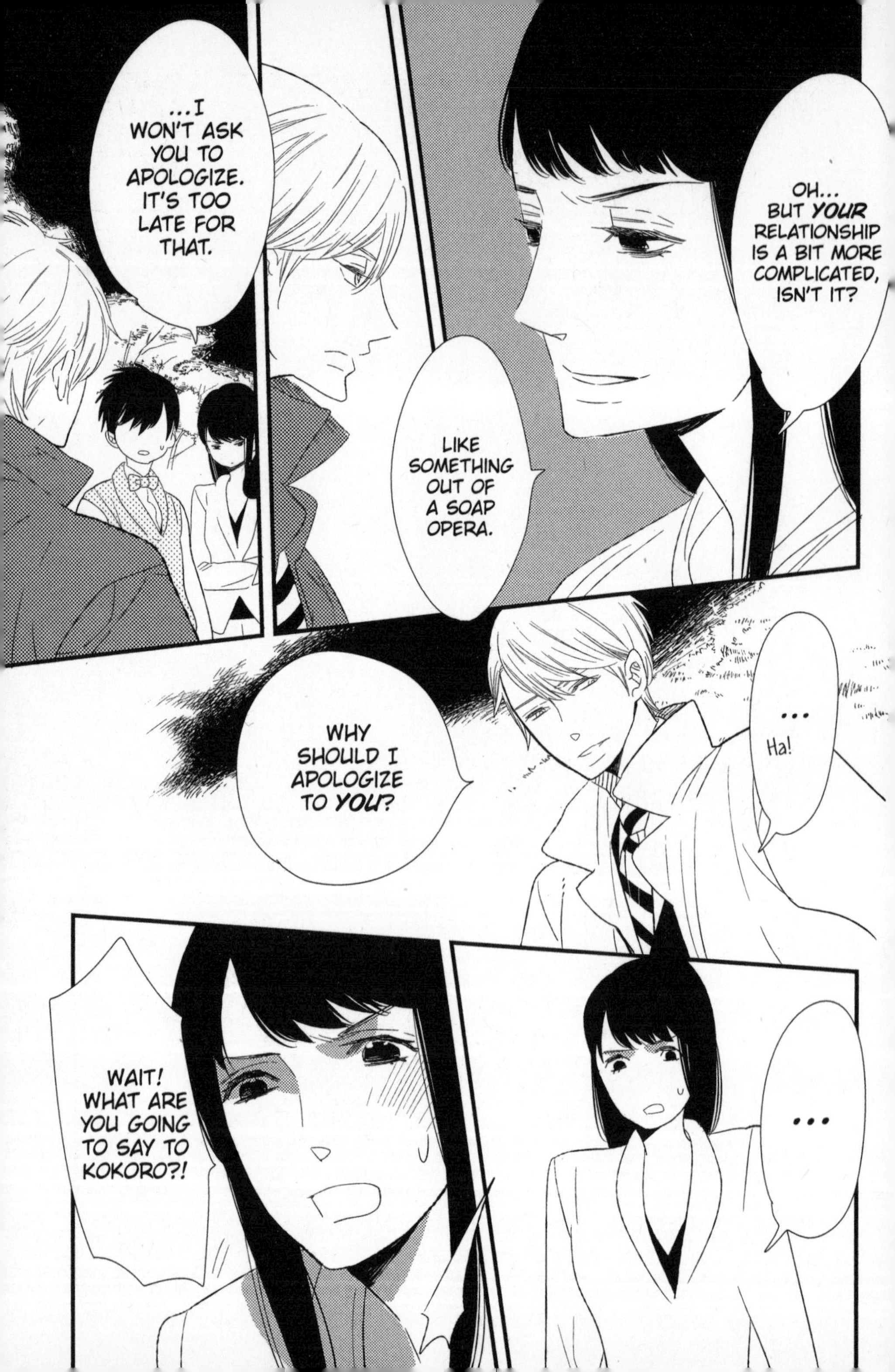
OH... BUT *YOUR* RELATIONSHIP IS A BIT MORE COMPLICATED, ISN'T IT?
LIKE SOMETHING OUT OF A SOAP OPERA.
...I WON'T ASK YOU TO APOLOGIZE. IT'S TOO LATE FOR THAT.
... Ha!
WHY SHOULD I APOLOGIZE TO *YOU*?
...
WAIT! WHAT ARE YOU GOING TO SAY TO KOKORO?!

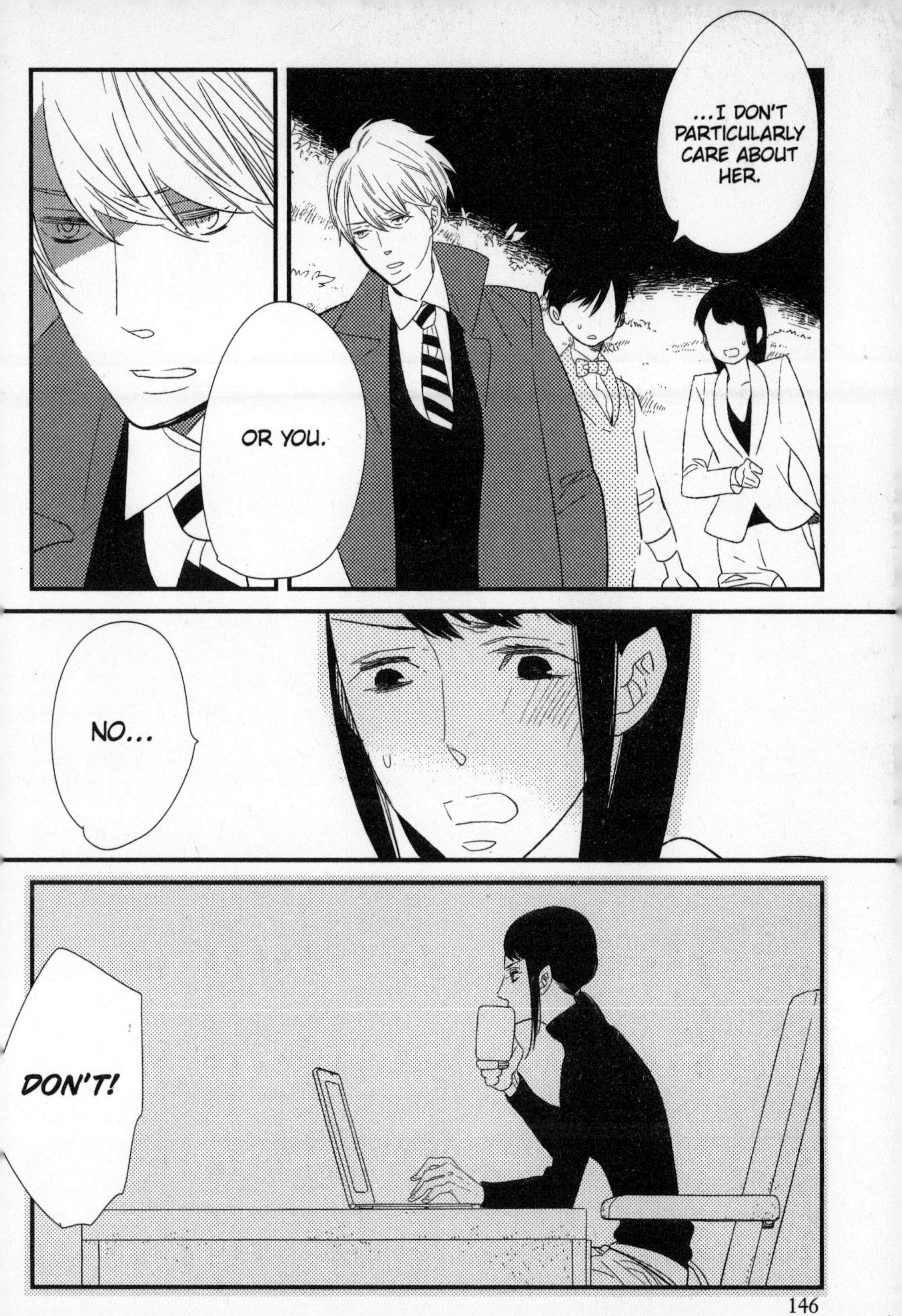
...I DON'T PARTICULARLY CARE ABOUT HER.
OR YOU.
NO...
DON'T!

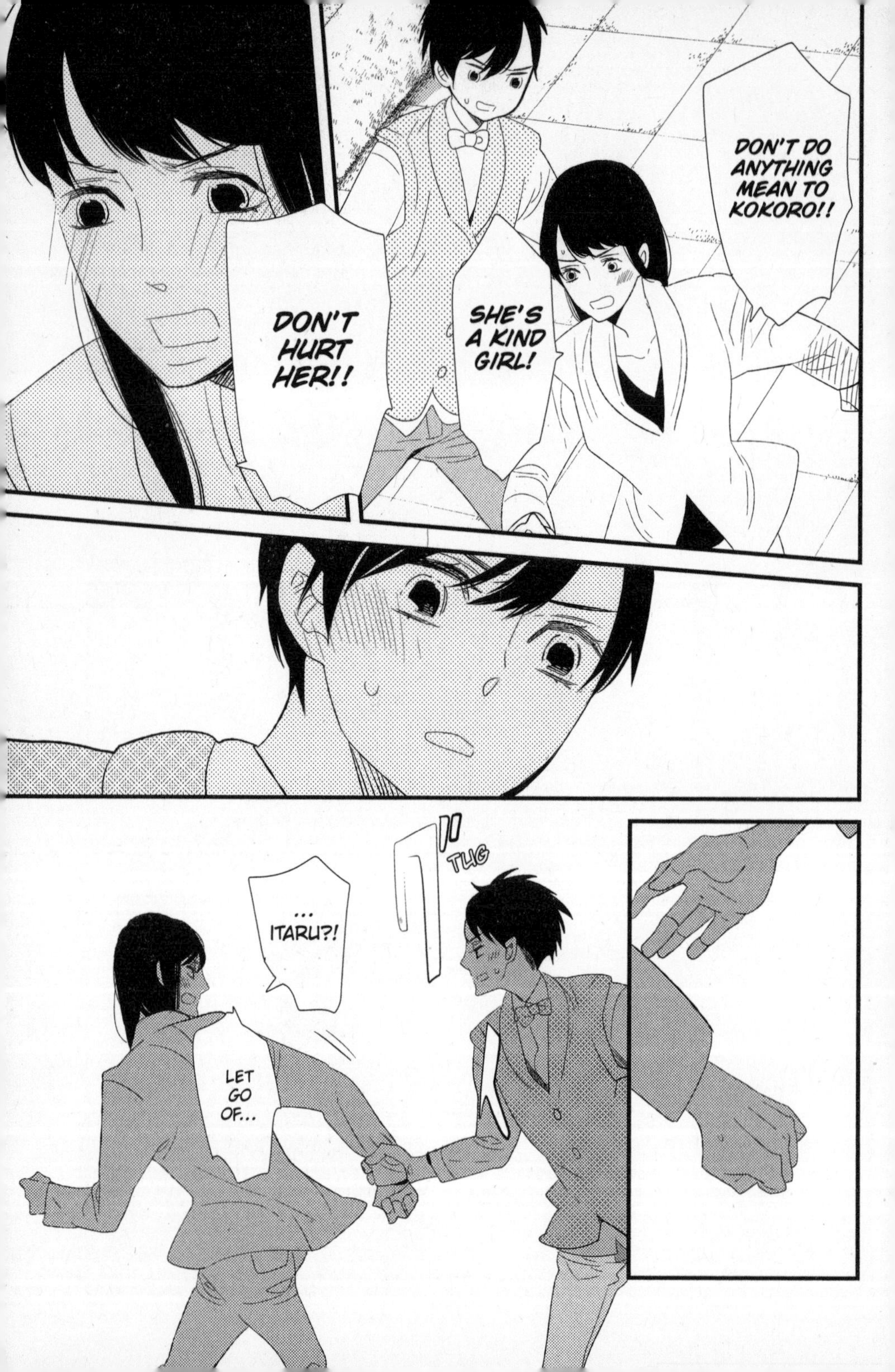
DON'T DO ANYTHING MEAN TO KOKORO!!
SHE'S A KIND GIRL!
DON'T HURT HER!!
TUG
... ITARU?!
LET GO OF...

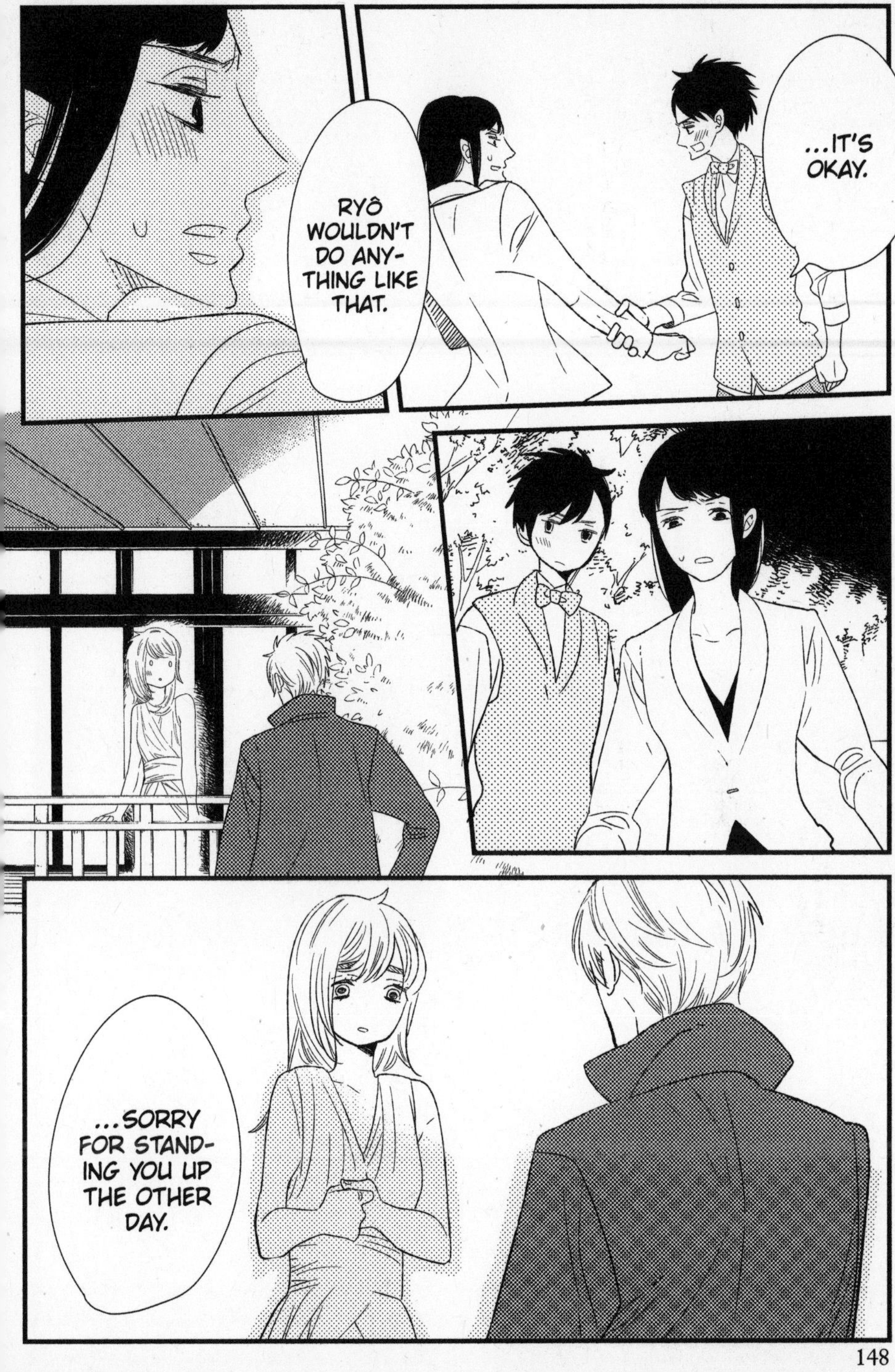
...IT'S OKAY.
RYÔ WOULDN'T DO ANY-THING LIKE THAT.
...SORRY FOR STAND-ING YOU UP THE OTHER DAY.

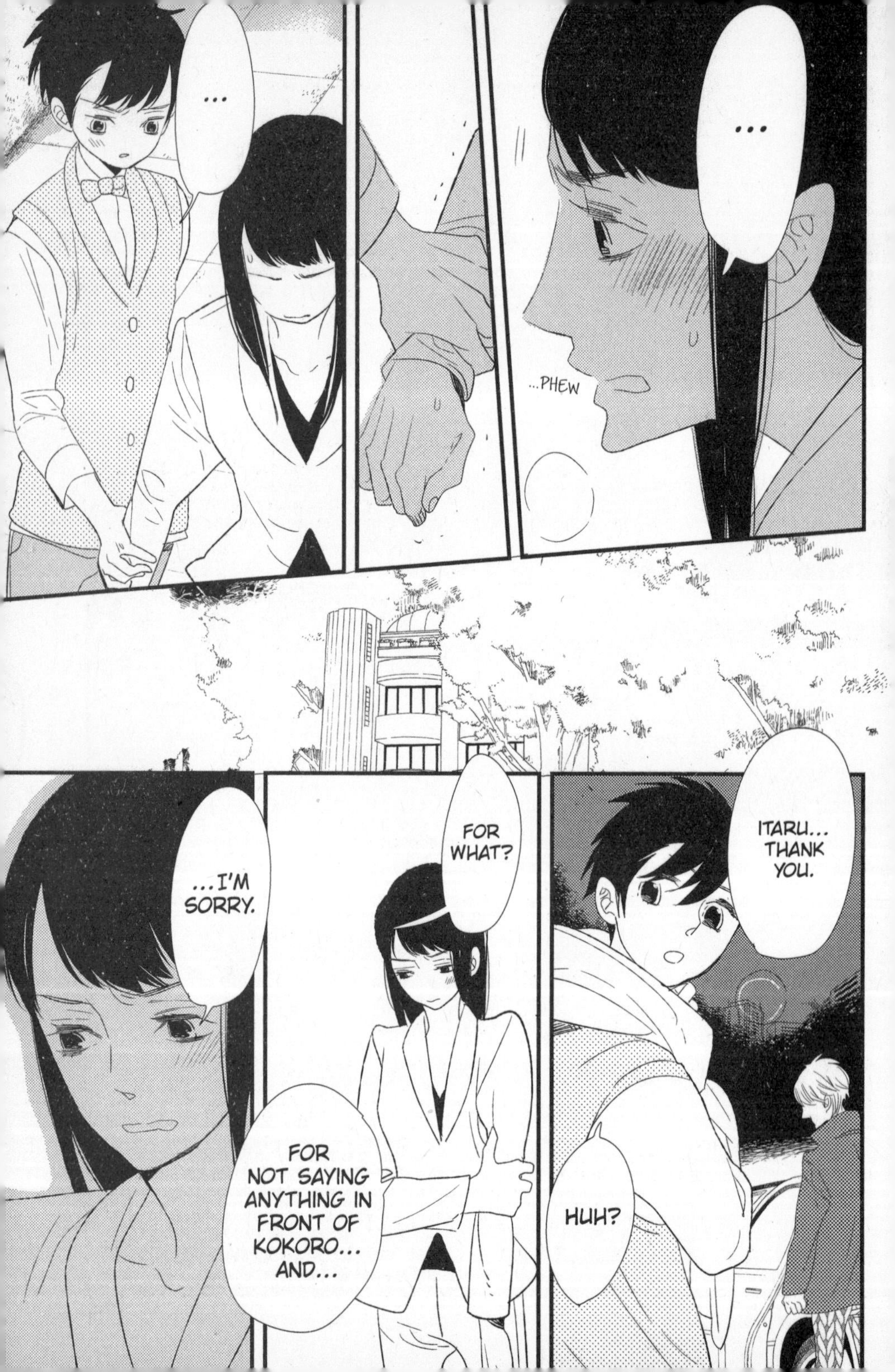
...
...PHEW
...
ITARU... THANK YOU.
HUH?
FOR WHAT?
FOR NOT SAYING ANYTHING IN FRONT OF KOKORO... AND...
...I'M SORRY.

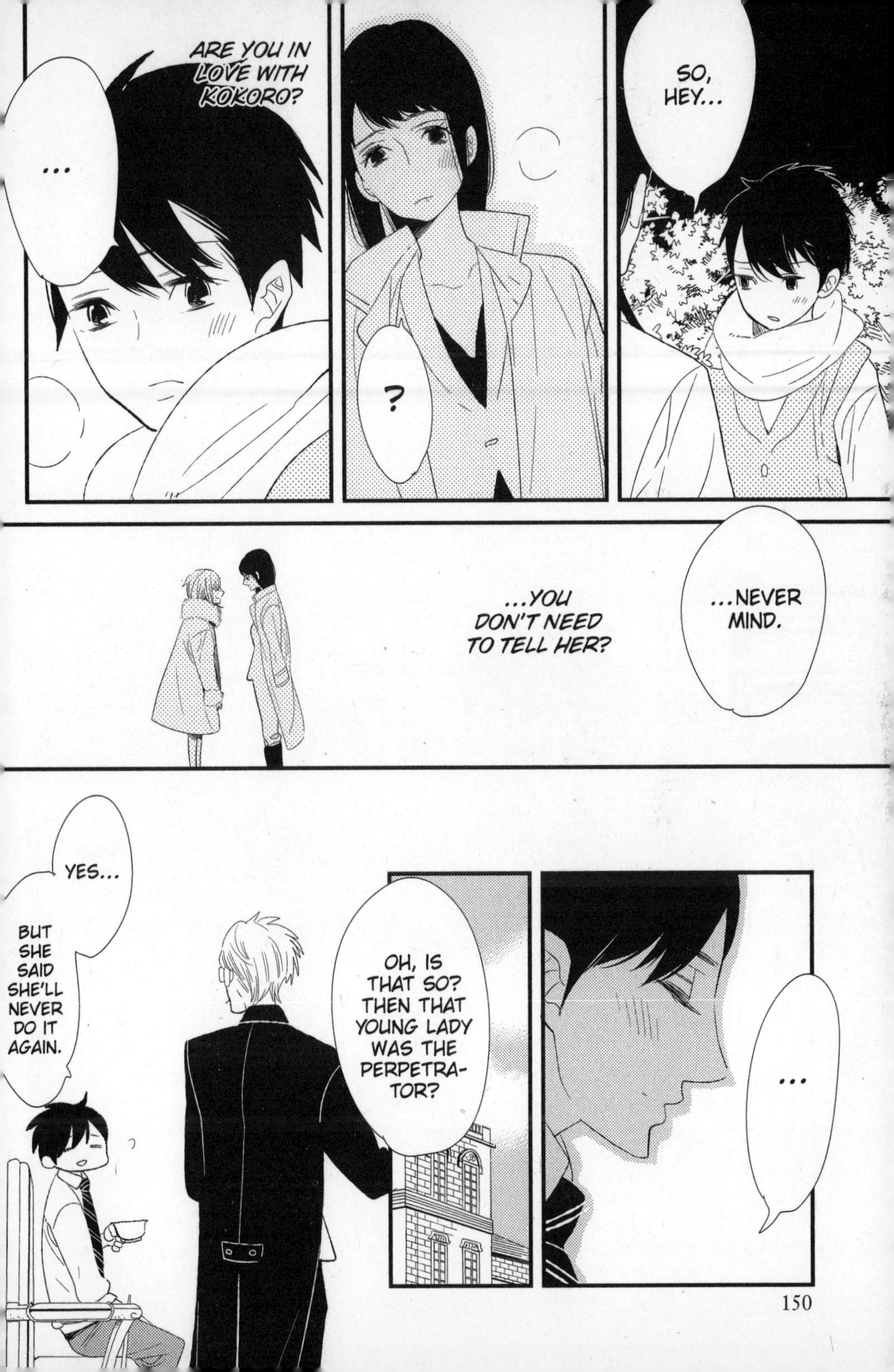
SO, HEY...
?
ARE YOU IN LOVE WITH KOKORO?
...
...NEVER MIND.
...YOU DON'T NEED TO TELL HER?
...
OH, IS THAT SO? THEN THAT YOUNG LADY WAS THE PERPETRATOR?
YES...
BUT SHE SAID SHE'LL NEVER DO IT AGAIN.

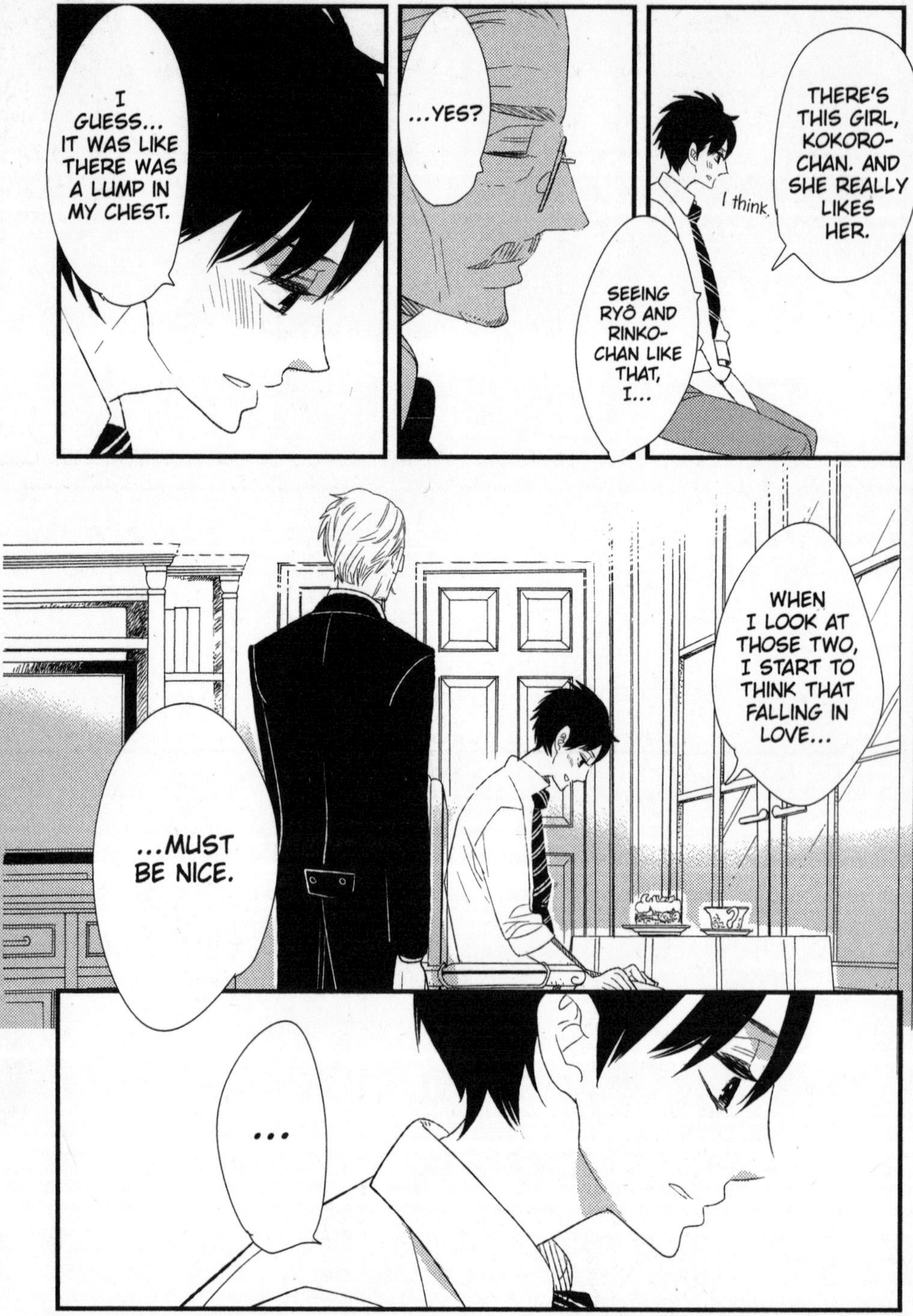
THERE'S THIS GIRL, KOKORO-CHAN. AND SHE REALLY LIKES HER.
I think.
SEEING RYÔ AND RINKO-CHAN LIKE THAT, I...
...YES?
I GUESS... IT WAS LIKE THERE WAS A LUMP IN MY CHEST.
WHEN I LOOK AT THOSE TWO, I START TO THINK THAT FALLING IN LOVE...
...MUST BE NICE.
...

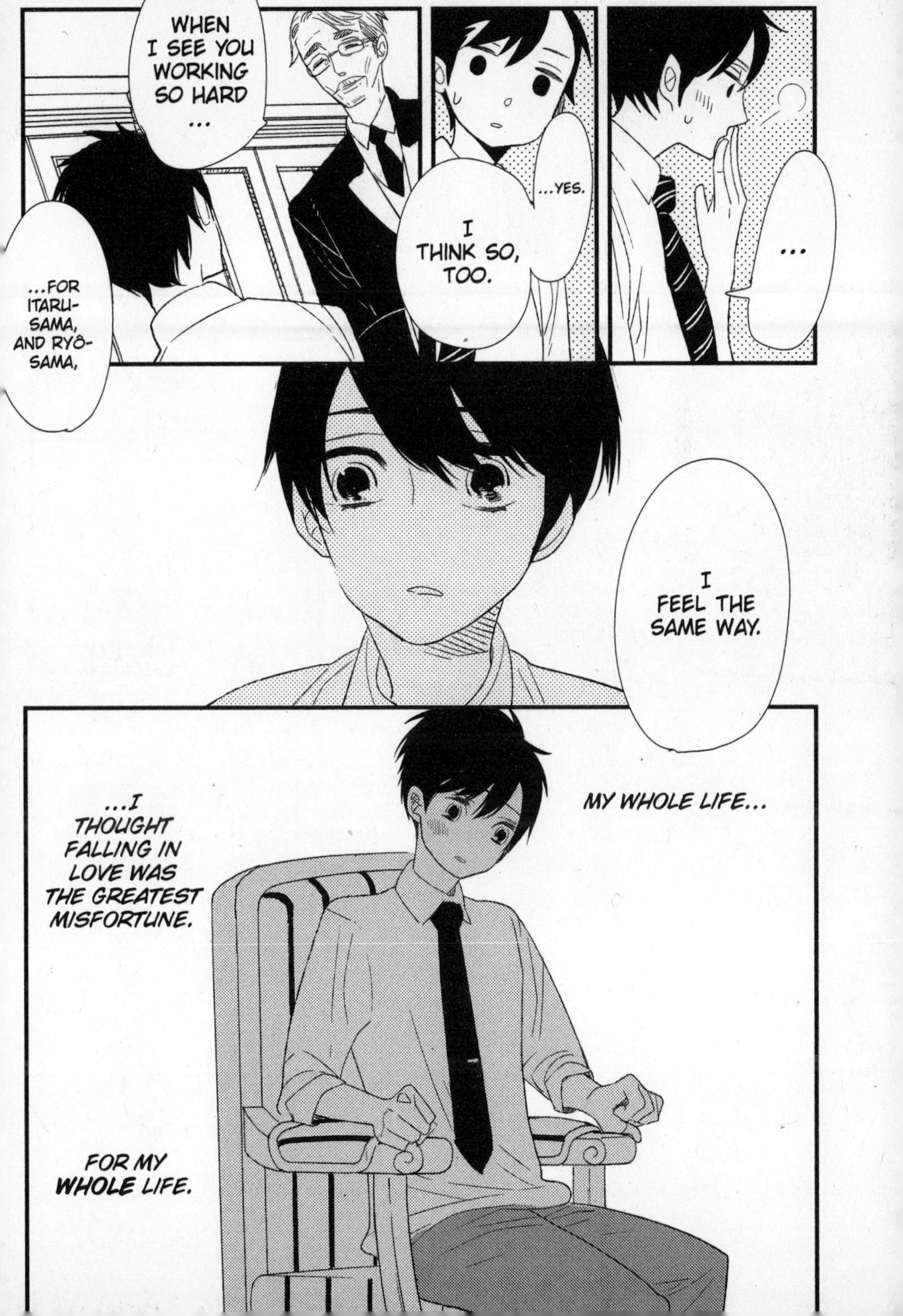
...
...YES.
I THINK SO, TOO.
WHEN I SEE YOU WORKING SO HARD ...
...FOR ITARU-SAMA, AND RYŌ-SAMA,
I FEEL THE SAME WAY.
MY WHOLE LIFE...
...I THOUGHT FALLING IN LOVE WAS THE GREATEST MISFORTUNE.
FOR MY WHOLE LIFE.

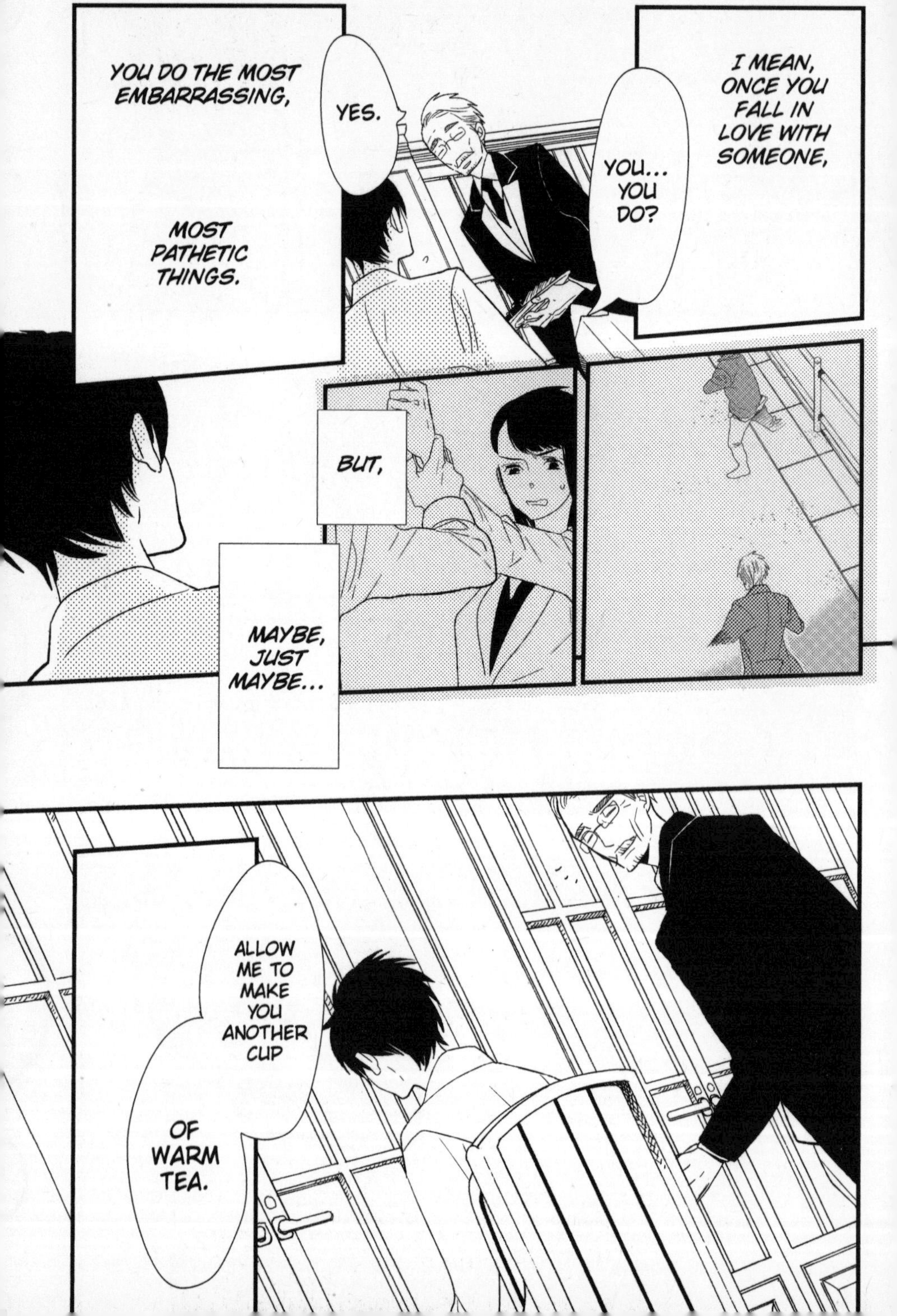
I MEAN, ONCE YOU FALL IN LOVE WITH SOMEONE,
YOU... YOU DO?
YES.
YOU DO THE MOST EMBARRASSING,
MOST PATHETIC THINGS.
BUT,
MAYBE, JUST MAYBE...
ALLOW ME TO MAKE YOU ANOTHER CUP
OF WARM TEA.

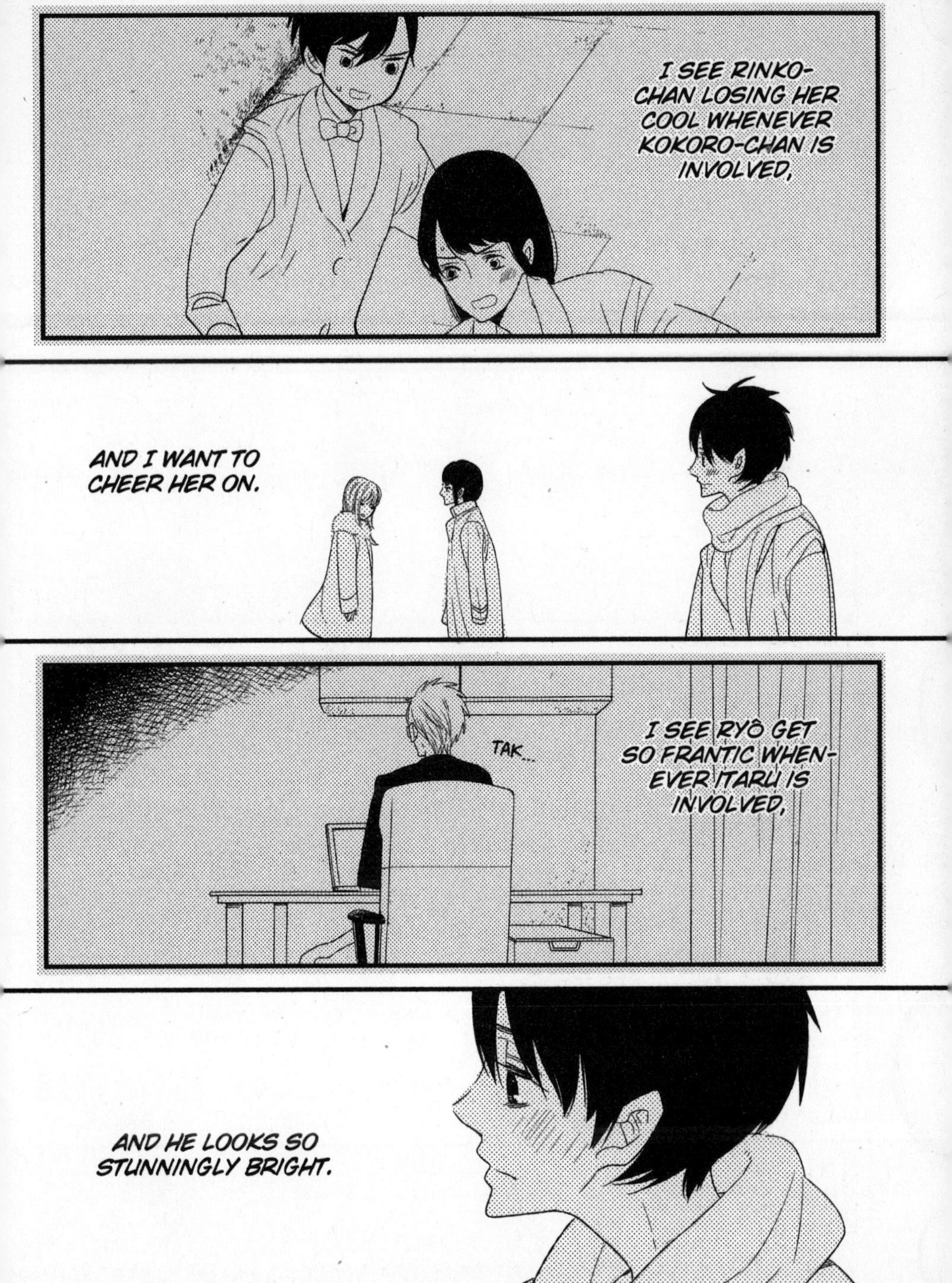
I SEE RINKO-CHAN LOSING HER COOL WHENEVER KOKORO-CHAN IS INVOLVED,
AND I WANT TO CHEER HER ON.
I SEE RYÔ GET SO FRANTIC WHEN-EVER ITARU IS INVOLVED,
TAK...
AND HE LOOKS SO STUNNINGLY BRIGHT.

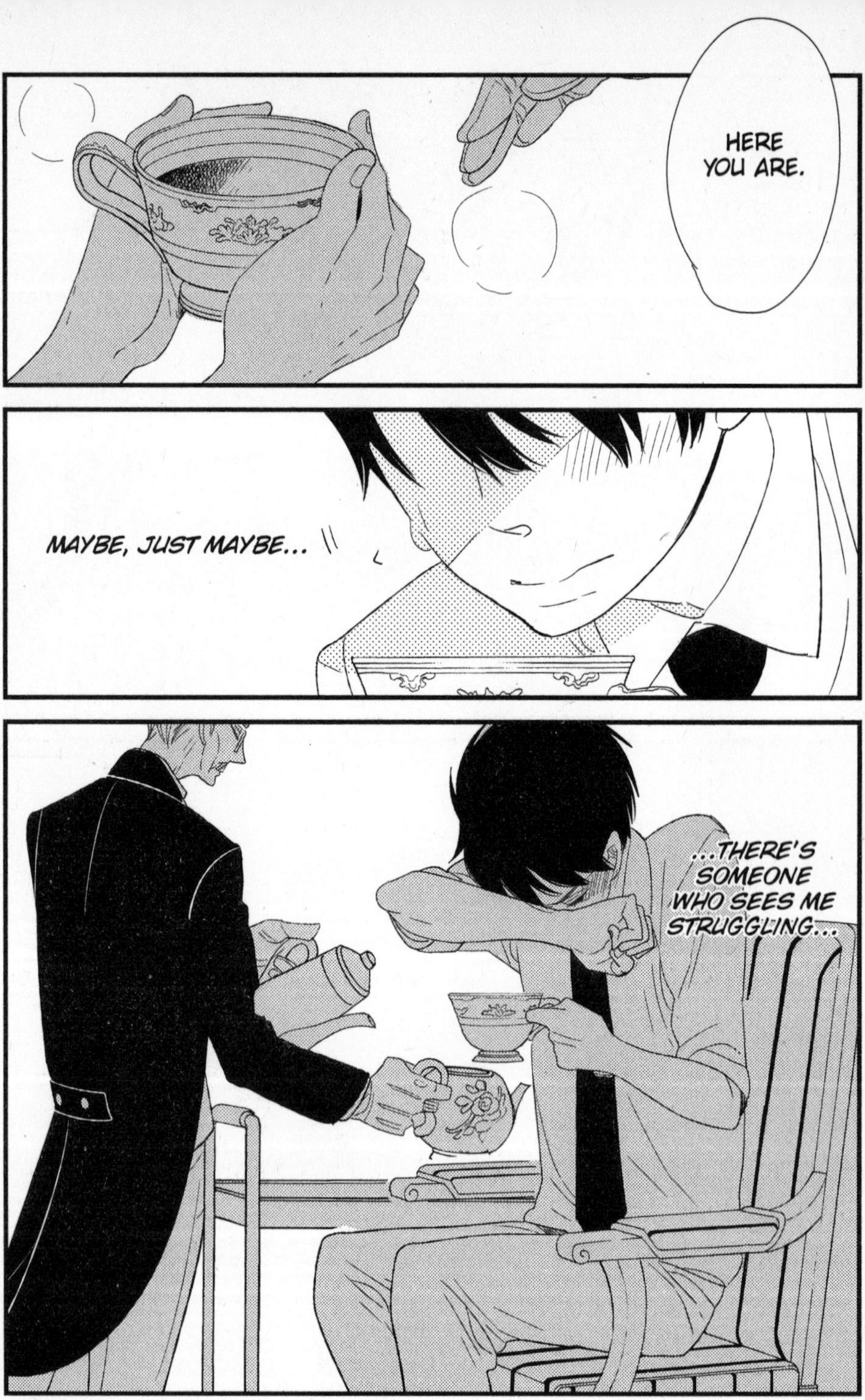
HERE YOU ARE.
MAYBE, JUST MAYBE...
...THERE'S SOMEONE WHO SEES ME STRUGGLING...

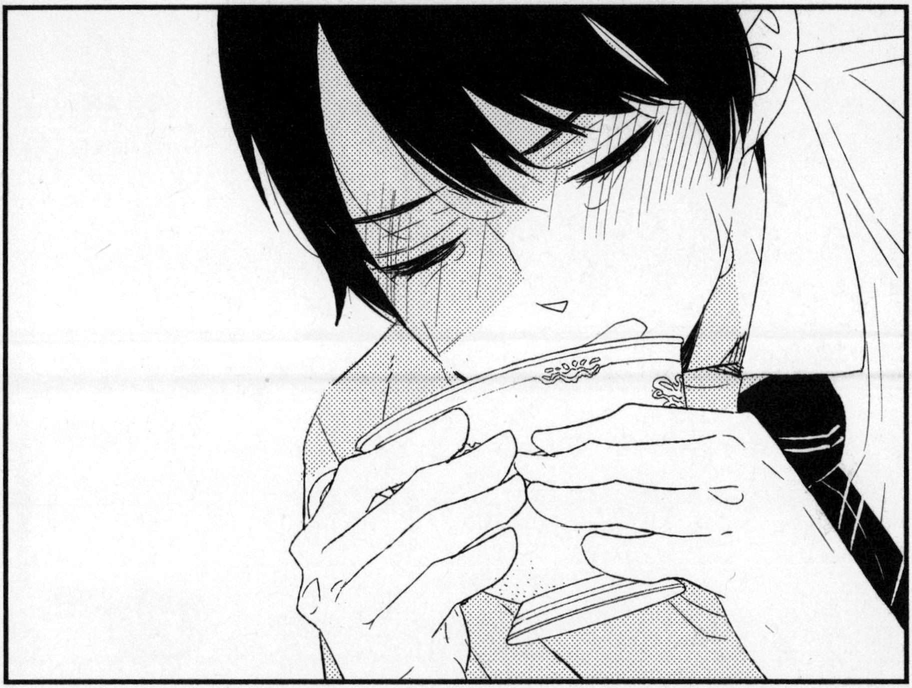

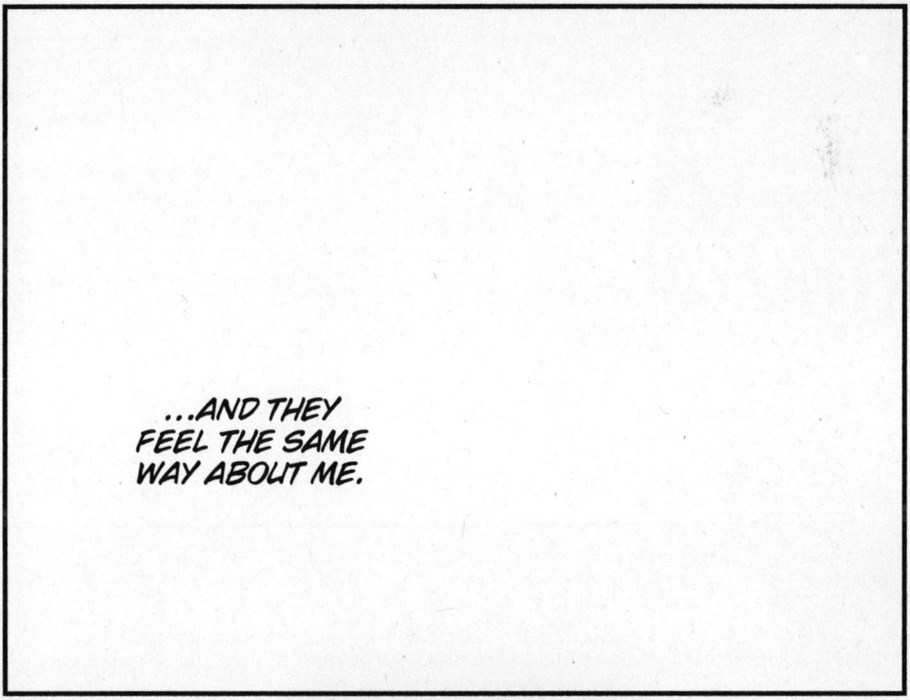
...AND THEY FEEL THE SAME WAY ABOUT ME.

to be continued in vol. 4

the prince in his dark days
hico yamanaka

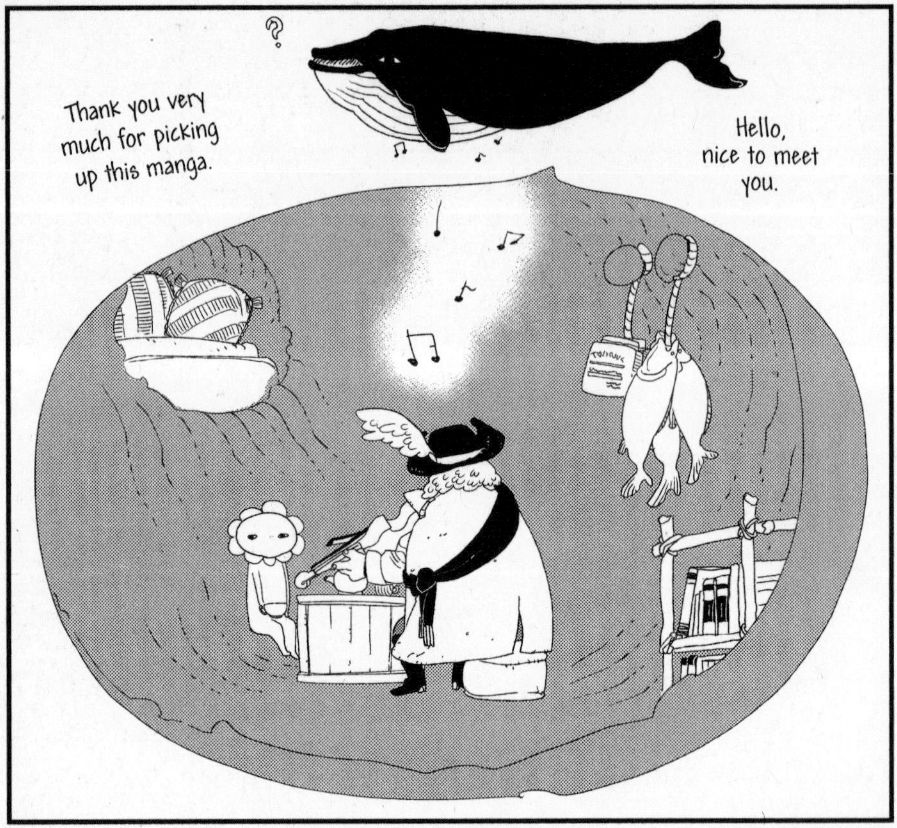
Hello, nice to meet you.
Thank you very much for picking up this manga.

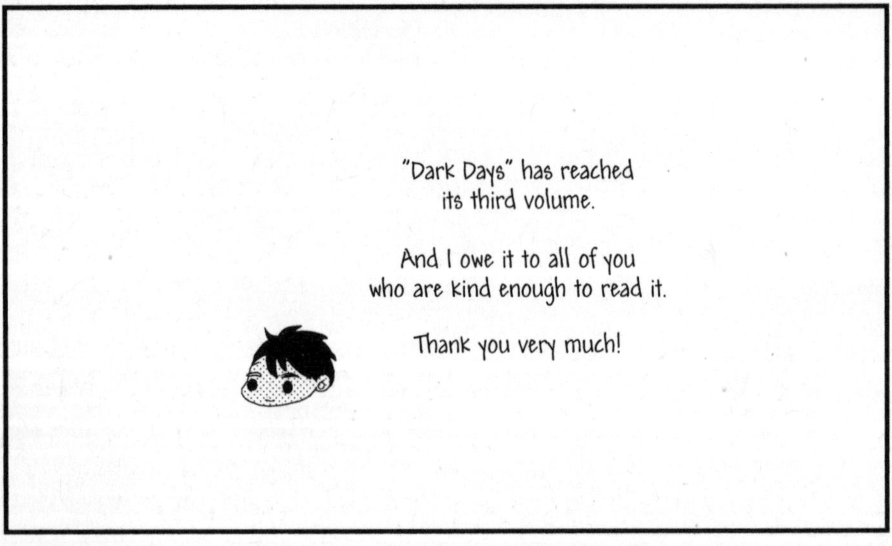
"Dark Days" has reached its third volume.
And I owe it to all of you who are kind enough to read it.
Thank you very much!

Translation Notes

'art-time school, page 19

\s the name suggests, a part-time school is one that doesn't have classes all day, every lay, like regular schools. Most of the time, classes for these schools are held at night to ccommodate students who work during the day. It's like night school, but for high school tudents. In Japan, compulsory education ends after junior high school.

ocial anxiety, page 44

o be specific, Daigo asks Atsuko if she is fflicted by a disorder known as TKS, or *aijin kyofusho*, which translates to "fear of interpersonal contact." In this specif- : form of social anxiety, the sufferer is fraid, not of embarrassing themselves, out of offending others or making them ncomfortable with his or her presence– vhether it is from body odor, accidental offensive behavior, or anything else.

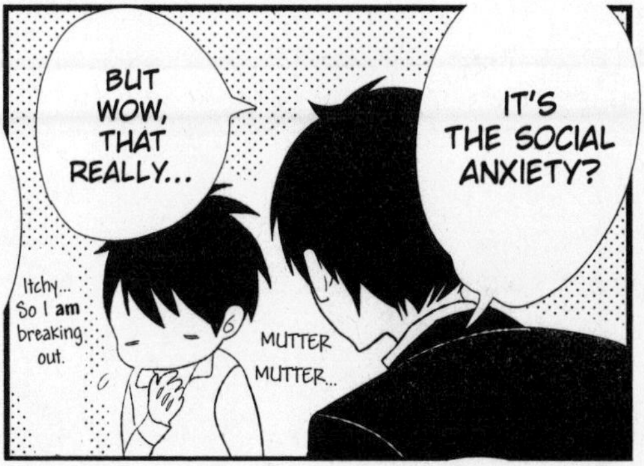
IT'S THE SOCIAL ANXIETY?
BUT WOW, THAT REALLY...
MUTTER MUTTER...
Itchy... So I **am** breaking out.

hinjuku Ni-chôme, page 70

hinjuku Ni-chôme is an area in Tokyo that was historically–and is currently–known as a gay eighborhood. It is the hub for Japan's same-sex and LGBT subculture, and houses many estaurants, bars, bookstores, parks, clubs, and more.

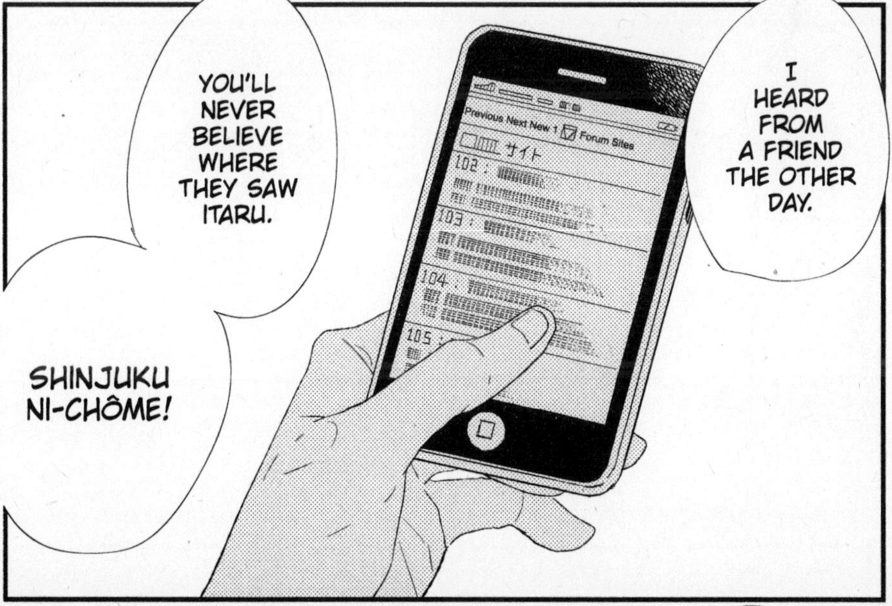
I HEARD FROM A FRIEND THE OTHER DAY.
YOU'LL NEVER BELIEVE WHERE THEY SAW ITARU.
Previous Next New 1 Forum Sites
サイト
102 :
103 :
104 :
105 :
SHINJUKU NI-CHÔME!

He's into some kinky stuff, page 71

A more literal translation of the Japanese phrase used here, *tokushu na seiteki shikô* is "a unique or peculiar sexual preference." *Seiteki shikô* can mean anything from being attracted to people with short hair, to having more specific fetishes and kinks. In this context specifically, because of the bullying tone of the rumor, *tokushu* (the word for unique or peculiar) implies that the sexual preferences in question are unnatural and deviate from the heteronormative standard in Japan.

N-gauge, page 87

This is a reference to the distance between the rails on the tracks of Kenya's model trains. The N-gauge has tracks 9mm wide, making it much smaller than the models the group was playing with earlier.

Center Gai, page 102

Roughly translated to "Center Street," Center Gai is a street in Shibuya, Tokyo. It is lined with popular stores, fast food restaurants, and nightclubs, making it a popular hangout for young people.

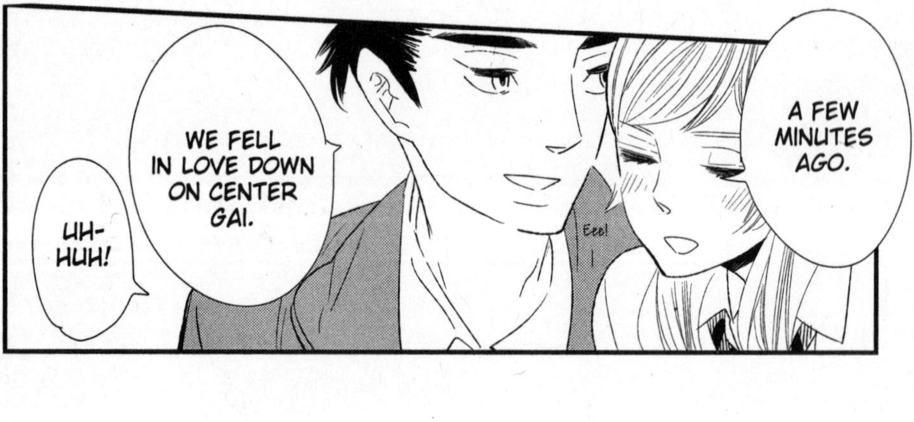
A FEW MINUTES AGO.
Eee!
WE FELL IN LOVE DOWN ON CENTER GAI.
UH-HUH!

The Prince in His Dark Days volume 3 is a work of fiction. Names, characters, places, and incidents are the products of the author's imagination or are used fictitiously. Any resemblance to actual events, locales, or persons, living or dead, is entirely coincidental.

A Kodansha Comics Trade Paperback Original
The Prince in His Dark Days volume 3 copyright © 2012 Hico Yamanaka
English translation copyright © 2017 Hico Yamanaka

Published in the United States by Kodansha Comics, an imprint of Kodansha USA Publishing, LLC, New York.

Publication rights for this English edition arranged through Kodansha Ltd, Tokyo.

ISBN 978-1-63236-398-5

Printed in the United States of America.

www.kodanshacomics.com

9 8 7 6 5 4 3 2 1
Translation: Alethea and Athena Nibley
Lettering: Maggie Vicknair
Editing: Haruko Hashimoto
Kodansha Comics edition cover design by Phil Balsman

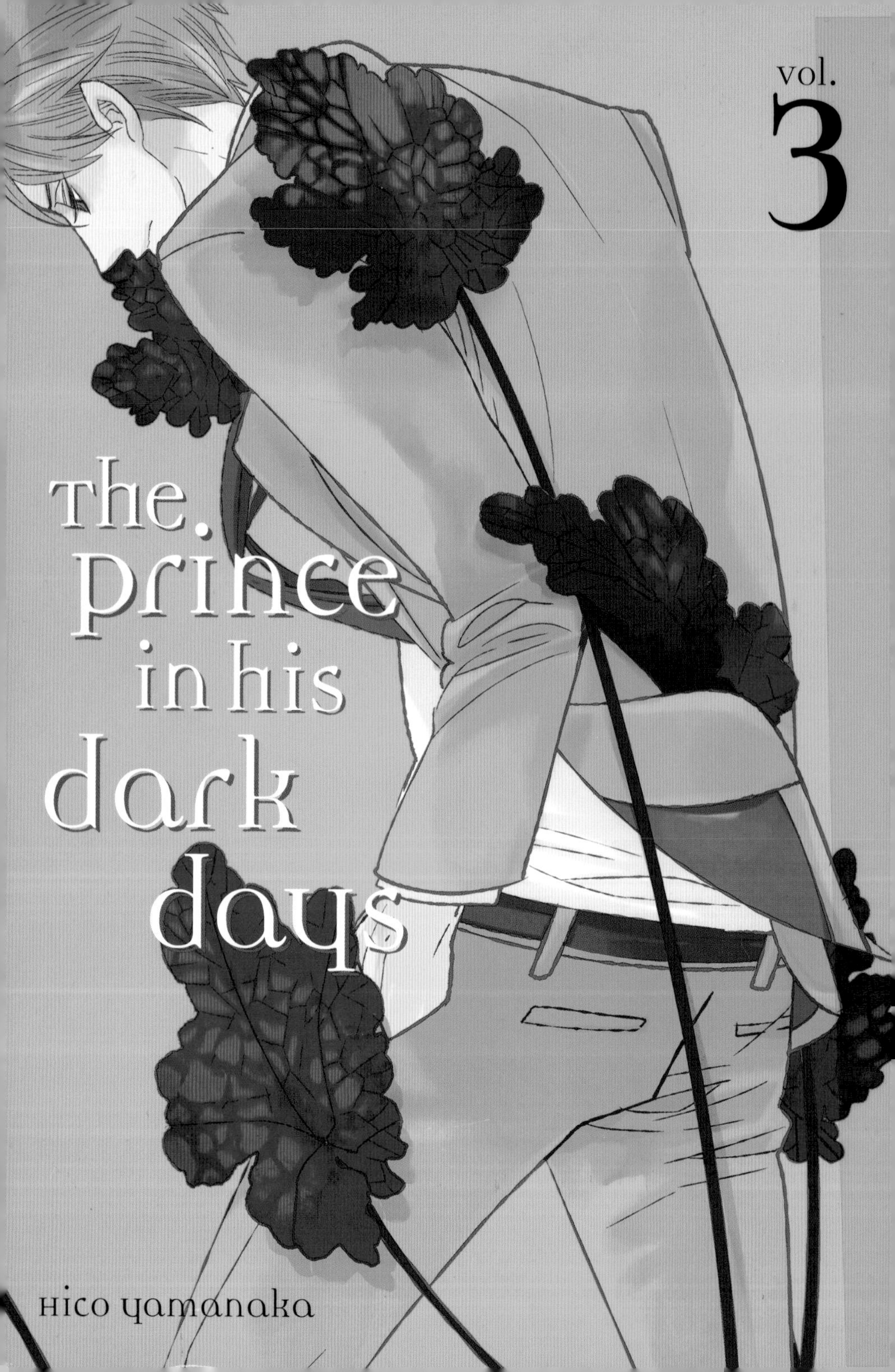
vol.
3
the prince in his dark days
Hico yamanaka